55

50¢

A Survey of
Religious Education

A Survey of
Religious Education

BY

J. M. PRICE

*Director of the School of Religious
Education, Southwestern Baptist
Theological Seminary*

JAMES H. CHAPMAN

*Professor of Religious Education
Howard College*

A. E. TIBBS

*Professor of Religious Education
Baptist Bible Institute*

L. L. CARPENTER

*Editor of Biblical Recorder;
formerly Chaplain and Professor of Bible,
University of South Carolina*

THE RONALD PRESS COMPANY

NEW YORK

43,888

FOREWORD

A Survey of Religious Education owes its inception to a project sponsored by the Association of Southern Baptist Teachers of Bible and Religious Education to develop a better technique in the teaching of religion. An Introduction to Religious Education was the first text prepared by this group for college and seminary use.

A Survey of Religious Education is not a revised edition of the first text, but an entirely new production. It offers a comprehensive survey of the findings now approved by scholars in the field, and is strictly in accord with present educational procedure. It is intended for use as an orientation text in religious education for both college and seminary use, as well as for private study.

Thanks are hereby expressed to the various authors and publishers who have given us permission to quote from their books and periodicals. Individual acknowledgments appear throughout the book as footnotes, giving the title of the book, the author, and the publisher.

THE AUTHORS

February 15, 1940

CONTENTS

Part I

BACKGROUNDS OF RELIGIOUS EDUCATION
J. M. Price

vii

Part II

PRINCIPLES OF RELIGIOUS EDUCATION
JAMES H. CHAPMAN

Part III

RELIGIOUS EDUCATION IN THE CHURCH
A. E. TIBBS

Part IV

RELIGIOUS EDUCATION BEYOND THE CHURCH
L. L. CARPENTER

A Survey of
Religious Education

Part I

Backgrounds of Religious Education

CHAPTER I

MEANING OF RELIGIOUS EDUCATION

In the very beginning of our study it is well to inquire as to what we mean by religious education. For though the term is commonly used, and in fact has been rather popular, it has different meanings and is not always clear. It is easy to take the meaning for granted, and never have a clear-cut understanding of the term, even though we use it glibly.

DEFINITION OF EDUCATION

Our first task is to inquire into the meaning of the word "education." Here again it is likely that we will find we have been using a word rather freely without a very clear idea as to just what we mean by it.

Based on Etymology.—Generally, the idea obtains that the word education comes from the Latin term *educere*, which is of the third conjugation, and means "to lead out." Education is thought of, therefore, in terms of drawing out the powers inherent in the person and developing them. In other words, it carries the idea of expression. The idea is good as applied to education, but unfortunately it is not involved in the word itself. For were the word derived from the third conjugation it would have to be "eduction" instead of "education."

Looking a little further, we find that the word is from the first conjugation and the form is *educare*. This term, however, has a very different meaning. Instead of signifying "to lead or draw out" it means "to nourish or nurture." This carries the idea of supplying food or sustenance rather than drawing out or exercising. It is the "impressional" rather than the "expressional" idea. From this viewpoint education consists in supplying ideas or inspiration more than securing responses.

13

A full conception of the educational process, however, requires both ideas. First there is an infilling process which includes the inculcation of ideas and the forming of ideals. Second there is a drawing out aspect which includes the activity side. In other words, a complete process of education includes both impression and expression— nourishing and exercising. We shall use it in this two-fold sense.

Based on Aims.[1]—When we turn to the definitions given we will find that some of them grow out of aims or objectives. What we consider to be the end in view determines the concept of education.

If we approach education from the viewpoint of the materials used in acquiring it, we may consider it as *familiarity with the cultural inheritance* of the race. In other words, education consists in the acquiring of a mass of materials. This is the older view that obtained when the material-centered and cultural emphasis held sway. It is the transmission idea in education. Recently this material-centered stress has been discounted.

Viewed from the standpoint of the individual and the maturing of innate potentialities, education has been defined as the *development of unfolding powers*. Instincts hold a prominent place in this definition, and the idea of mental discipline is involved in part. This is a subjective approach and is rather individualistic in nature. The objective is the growing of a well-rounded and symmetrical personality.

Looked at from the angle of society, education may be considered as *preparation for efficient living*. From this point of view the purpose of the school is to fit the individual to take his place in the life of the world. It is an objective approach to education, and stresses the utilitarian emphasis in which social studies and practical arts play a prominent part.

Based on Procedures.—Definitions of education also grow out of our concept of the process or method employed as well as out of the aim or objective to be attained in the life of the individual.

One emphasis based on method is that education is the *guidance of growth*. This definition proceeds from the point of view of the person rather than the materials, and also from the viewpoint of the unfolding life. Hence, education is a continuous process rather than a completed one. The emphasis is on guidance rather than the instillation of ideas or the determination of a course of conduct. This view gives more emphasis to the creative aspect.

---

[1] For definitions by prominent men see Coe, Geo. A., *Education in Religion and Morals*, p. 18 (Fleming H. Revell Co., New York, 1904).

Another definition growing out of method is that education is the *introduction of control into conduct*. From this point of view the thought is not so much the intellectual or emotional aspect of life as the volitional. Conduct is the goal. This is to be determined by our ideal, and this ideal is stimulated by education. Properly facing and solving life's problems is the emphasis here. This theory looks toward a life controlled and directed by dominant ideals.

Other definitions shading off from these might be given, but these are adequate. The whole truth does not lie in any one of them, but rather in the combined elements of all, together with other features involving emotions, attitudes and desires. Education is a process involving life and a lifetime.

Nature of Religious Education

Having considered the nature of education in general the questions naturally arise: What is its relation to religion? How far can religion be taught? What is religious education? How is it differentiated from general and Christian education?

Relation of Education to Religion.—Education involves religion. Since religion has to do with man's thoughts, feelings and actions in relation to the supernatural, it is very evident that it has a place in education. In fact any system of education that ignores the spiritual aspect of man's nature is incomplete. Training the intellect without relating it to God makes a cynic or atheist. Training in skills without stressing the spiritual makes a materialist. Since man has moral and spiritual inclinations, education to be complete must develop these. Religion, therefore, is involved in a complete process of education.

But religion also involves education. There are some extremists who think that religion is a matter of feeling and so does not require any education. There are others who over-emphasize the divine aspect and think no education is needed. But any common-sense point of view makes it clear that if the religious life is to be balanced and complete, education is necessary. Information is needed for an enlightened experience. Without such it tends toward bigotry and mere emotionalism and gets practically nowhere in the life of the individual.

Education and religion, then, are vitally inter-related. Each is incomplete without the other. President H. C. King says, "The relation is here so intimate that we can not separate either at its best from the essential spirit of the other."[2] He thinks they are essentially the same in aims, spirit, means, methods and results. No system of education is complete that does not include the religious element, and no system of religion is adequate that does not involve education. It is inaccurate to call anyone fully educated who is not religious, and just as inaccurate to think that religion can reach its climax without education. They are like the Siamese Twins.

How Far Can Religion Be Taught?—The conclusion that education is involved in religious experience does not fully clarify the matter. How much of religious experience is communicable from one person to another?

Negatively it is evident that the supernatural element in the experience cannot be humanly imparted. As T. H. Fickes has said: "It is not within the province of education to control or to supplant the operation of the Divine Spirit in the heart and mind of the individual."[3] There is that divine element in the new birth and Christian growth which teaching can stress but cannot impart. It has been the fear of leaving God out of the process that has made many fearful of education.

Nor can the crisis in Christian experience be determined by education. The teacher may give information about, and lead the pupil to, the entrance into the kingdom of God, but the final step in that experience must be taken by the individual. Neither God nor man can over-ride the human will. There is a personal, private element in the experience that no one can have for another.

Positively considered there are a number of things that teaching may do for the individual. It may help him to understand his natural condition, what God has done for him, and what he must do for himself. It is through instruction that the plan of salvation is made clear. Moreover, it is through education that attitudes, conducive to entering the Christian life, are built up. In this way a sub-conscious basis is laid for the conversion experience, and to this extent the will is influenced.

Nor is this all, for after one has entered the Christian life there is much that teaching and training may do for him. The responsibilities of church membership, the obligation of stewardship, and the applications of Christianity to current life, are matters that require a great deal of instruction and guidance. Dr. J. B. Gambrell spoke wisely

[2] *Personal and Ideal Elements in Education*, p. 72 (The Macmillan Company, New York, 1904).

[3] *Principles of Religious Education*, p. 78 (Fleming H. Revell Co., New York, 1938).

Dr. N. Weener – Religious Education is a serious attempt to discover divine process by which individuals grow toward christlikeness and to grow toward that process.

when he said: "We have evangelized and we have baptized, but we have not taught, and out of that have come the most of our troubles." No one is born full-fledged into the kingdom of God. Character must be grown. And education plays a large part in furnishing the information and inspiration to that end.

What Is Religious Education?—Something of the nature of religious education must now be evident. Viewed from the standpoint of content we may think of it as acquiring *religious culture*. The Bible, which gives us that background, is taught. Religious ideals are built up and a foundation is laid for the Christian life. A doctrinal understanding is acquired. The least that religious education can hope to do is to give such an understanding of the Bible and the Christian way of life.

Considered as an unfolding process, we may think of religious education as the *harmonious development of innate powers*. This means that it should help the individual to develop his instinctive tendencies in the direction intended by Divine Providence, and in the proper relation to one another. It involves nothing less than a well-rounded, Christian personality. Religious teaching and training will give both the ideal and dynamic needed.

From the angle of Christian citizenship and its obligations, religious education seeks to lead the individual into the *right relation to God and humanity*. This involves, of course, the expressional side of religion. It is an effort to realize the kingdom of God on earth, and touches every phase of domestic, recreational, business and civic life. Much instruction and guidance are necessary for right living, especially in this complex and conflicting age.

Considered from the standpoint of problems and procedure, religious education seeks the *religious control of conduct*. Walter S. Athearn has said: "Religious education is the introduction of control into experience in terms of religious ideas and ideals."[4] In other words, it seeks a God-controlled life, with its problems solved according to the Christian ideal and spirit. This involves much teaching and personal guidance.

Differentiation from Other Education.—As distinguished from *public education*, one can readily see that religious education differs greatly. The former is under the direction of the state and is therefore secular in nature, while the latter is under the control of the church and other religious agencies and is religious and moral. Public education deals largely with knowledge and skills, while

---

[4] *The Minister and The Teacher*, p. 17 (The Century Co., New York, 1932).

religious education is more concerned about motives and attitudes. Religious education is not something tacked on to general education, but rather supplies a part not provided. And, too, it seeks to provide the spirit and dynamic which will motivate all education. It is therefore at the very heart and center of the whole educational process.

Differentiated from *Christian education*, as the term is most commonly used, religious education is broader in scope and different in its point of view. The term "Christian education" for the most part has been used to designate the work of the denominational college, and deals, therefore, with college subjects from a Christian point of view. The term "religious education," on the other hand, is used to cover religious and moral instruction in the home, the church, the academy, the college, and the press. It is definitely from the Christian point of view as evangelicals use it today.

FACTORS IN THE EDUCATIONAL PROCESS

A number of factors are involved in the process of religious education. Each is important and has its part to play. Without any one of them the activity would be incomplete. With them, we can go a long way toward building a Christian civilization.

The Pupil.—The first and most important factor in religious education is the pupil. All else exists for, and centers around, him. For him buildings are erected, teachers employed, teaching materials provided, and the whole activity carried on. He is, therefore, the most significant factor in the educational task. Religious education today, like Christ of old, puts the child or pupil in the center. The development of this immature being is the first consideration. Martin Luther believed that adults exist to nurture the young. And in varying degrees all of the students of all ages are immature and in need of development.

The Teacher.—The second most important factor in the religious-educational process is the teacher. All remaining factors are secondary to him. This idea is dominant in the statement of President James A. Garfield that his idea of a college was a log with Mark Hopkins on one end and himself on the other. The teacher is supposed to be more mature than the pupil, at least so far as the immediate thing being taught is concerned. It is his business to serve as instructor, inspirer and guide in the process of religious training. He works on the soul and fashions life. No wonder the Jews considered him the true guardian of the city, and a recent appraisal designates him as "the keeper of the gates of tomorrow!"

The Aim.—Probably next in importance is the aim or objective. This is the goal toward which the teacher leads and the pupil strives. It is determined in part by the definition one gives to religious education. The stage of development already attained helps also to fashion it. This goal is a moving rather than a fixed one. It includes Christian conversion, character development, and kingdom service. Since objectives will be discussed in detail in another chapter, they will not be discussed here. It may be said, however, that one of the greatest weaknesses in the average teacher is his lack of clear-cut aims. Nothing helps more to give definiteness, furnish incentives, and provide a measuring rod, than worthy objectives.

The Curriculum.—The fourth factor in the process of religious education is the curriculum. This includes all of the materials to be used in the teaching and training activities. In a large measure what comes out in the final product is dependent on what is put into the process. On the whole, not enough attention has been given to this phase of our activity, especially in the Sunday school and particularly with regard to the Uniform Lessons. Much of the effectiveness of grading, equipment, and improved methods may be lost through inadequate materials. These materials are determined in a large measure by the objectives and naturally vary according to the age group. More will be said about the curriculum in another chapter.

The Equipment.—Although equipment is not as important a factor as the others mentioned, it is very significant. As an evidence of this fact one needs only to stand near the center of a one-room church while eight or ten classes are being conducted, particularly without curtains. Under such conditions one almost comes to feel that the equipment is the most important factor in efficiency. By equipment we mean not only a building but also departmental assembly rooms and class-rooms, and in additional suitable chairs, tables, blackboards, maps, record systems, and such provision for the library and recreational life as will enable a church school to carry on to the best possible advantage. In a sense the equipment is a part of the materials.

The Time Element.—Probably there is some question as to whether or not the time element should be considered in discussing the factors in religious education. It is, however, a very important element in the religious-educational process. Education, whether in the field of religion and morals or elsewhere, cannot be forced. It takes time to grow a mind and a character. Mushrooms may be developed over night, but it takes decades to grow a tree. Maltbie D. Babcock well says: "Good habits are not made on birthdays, nor

Christian character at the new year. The vision may dawn . . . the heart may leap with new inspiration on some mountain-top, but the test, the triumph is at the foot of the mountain on the level plain." Education requires time.

RELIGIOUS-EDUCATIONAL ACTIVITIES

Though discussed more fully in a later chapter, a brief statement of the activities in religious education will be given here in order to understand more clearly the meaning of the term.

Instruction.—Teaching is foundational. By whatever method employed the inculcation of ideas and the building up of ideals is the first responsibility in the activity of religious education. "Fruitful knowledge" is essential to right living. W. S. Athearn was right in saying: "Ideals are the pulleys over which we lift original nature to higher levels." Whatever stress may be given to habit formation, instruction must not be minimized. The transmission of truth from teacher to pupil is necessary. Involved in it, also, is the development of right attitudes. Satisfaction must accompany information for it to be effective.

Evangelism.—Evangelism may be defined as the effort to lead the individual to a personal acceptance of Christ and his way of life. This, evangelical Christians regard as the activity next after instruction and the most important until accomplished. It may be done privately, in a class, a department, or a school assembly either during a revival meeting or apart from one. Some religious educators think this activity is out of harmony with the educational method. Betts devotes four pages to contrasting the educational and evangelistic points of view.[5] He thinks they are antagonistic and mutually exclusive, but such is not the case. If education includes response to truth taught, then it involves evangelism, for it is leading the pupil to respond to the truth taught about Christ.

Worship.—More and more we are coming to see the importance of worship in order to keep us in vital touch with God, to give us a true perspective of life, and to help us keep a grip on ourselves in this materialistic, nerve-strained, pleasure-loving age. Increasingly, we recognize that to be most effective, worship must be adapted to the age and experience of the individual. It should, therefore, be graded and made a part of the educational program of the church. This is

[5] *The New Program of Religious Education,* pp. 28-31 (The Abingdon Press, New York, 1921).

being done in an increasing measure with suitable songs, scriptures, and other materials provided in our various departmental programs.

Giving.—In recent years it has become increasingly evident that occasional, spasmodic collections based largely on emotion, are not an adequate means of developing a generation of givers. It is more and more felt that the giving of one's money should grow out of an enlightened conscience and be a regular, systematic affair, based on one's income. In other words, training in giving should tie up with teaching about it and become a regular activity of our educational program. The Sunday school is especially suitable since it reaches most people and is best adapted to this procedure. Consequently, development in giving is being made a regular activity with excellent results both in the development of character and in the securing of funds.

Service.—Since religious-educational activity includes the development of habits and skills as well as the imparting of proper information and the forming of right attitudes, it is natural that service activities should be included in our religious-educational procedures. Increasingly this is being done through the enlistment work of Sunday school organizations, the personal service phase of missionary agencies, and the expressional activities of the Training Union. Through this means people are led to grow in Christian graces since they express them as well as hear about them. In other words, we follow the principle of learning to do by doing which is the highest type of education.

Recreation.—Recently we have come to recognize that developing the social instinct, and giving relaxation to jaded nerves are vital elements in personality development. Also we have come to realize that what people do during hours of leisure enters as vitally into character as what they do during the time of work. Since recreation has come to be recognized as an important activity in religious education, emphasis has been given to the various social-recreational organizations as well as to the graded social activities in church life. New results in character education are emerging as a result of the positive emphasis along this line.

AGENCIES FOR RELIGIOUS EDUCATION

Since a somewhat detailed discussion of the agencies involved in carrying out the program of religious education will be found in Parts III and IV of this book, only brief attention will be given to them here—merely enough to explain something of the scope of religious education.

The Home.—Naturally, education in religion as in all other matters begins in the home. It was first in the history of the race, is first in the life of each individual, and should be first in emphasis. Because the home has the child before any other institution, at the most impressionable period in life, for the longest period of time, when external control is greatest, and under the most impressionable circumstances, it has possibilities beyond any other agency. No one ever gets away from the good of the positive religious influences of the home or the harm of the non-religious or anti-religious elements. This is true whether the method is the unconscious influence of the life and activity of the parents, or their conscious and deliberate efforts. Folsom well says: "The probabilities are that the early home influence will outlast all others and prevail in the end."[6]

The Church.—Next to the home comes the church. With the modern emphasis on the Cradle Roll and the Nursery class the child is under the influence of the church very early in life. Several organizations function in religious education!

The *Sunday School*, designated as the teaching agency, is set for the task of teaching the Bible to all ages through graded classes and by means of adapted materials and methods. It utilizes more workers, reaches more people, has them for a longer period of time, covers a wider range of activity, and probably accomplishes more than any other educational agency in the church. It is still primary.

Along with the teaching agency comes the *Training Union*, whose primary task is to train immature Christians into full-fledged church members. Its emphasis, therefore, is on the expressional side of education. Through the discussion of topics, discharging official responsibilities, and various kinds of service activities, young Christians are developed as kingdom servants. It has helped greatly in creating Christian morale.

The *Woman's Missionary Union* has developed as the particular agency for training in the field of missions. While primarily for women, boys through the Intermediate age are included. Through weekly meetings, training courses and personal service, including giving, they have accomplished much. In fact, they have led the way in missions.

While the *Brotherhood* for men is not so thoroughly organized,

[6] *Religious Education in the Home*, p. 15 (The Methodist Book Concern, New York, 1912).

generally promoted, or definitely educational, it is seeking more and more to enlist the men and develop them in fellowship, stewardship and general church responsibility. It, also, has helped to stimulate morale.

Within recent years the *Vacation Bible School* has come to fill a unique and large place in the educational work of the church. Coming during the vacation period when boys and girls are idle and subjected to temptation, it meets daily with emphasis on recreation, hand-work, and moral and patriotic topics as well as definitely religious ones. It is attracting many and rendering a distinct service.

Growing in recognition is the *week-day school* or class for religious instruction. Ordinarily, for the high-school ages, it meets once a week during the school year, and is correlated with, if not credited by, the public school. Since it has the possibility of reaching more people and giving more thorough instruction than the other agencies it is exceptionally valuable. The future will see more of it.

The College.—The Christian college carries on beyond the range of the home and the church. The period covered is a critical one in the life of the individual because of the varied subjects studied, and also because the student is away from the influence of the home and the home church. The denominational college has an advantage over the state school in having Christian teachers, chapel exercises, the Christian point of view, and an atmosphere of religious influence. It has not only trained Christian leaders, but has also been a leavening influence in the educational world.

In recent years more attention has been given to work in the state schools. This is due in part to the increased realization of the need within the school, but more particularly because so many more students are now attending state institutions than denominational schools. Student secretaries and teachers have been employed, Bible courses for credit instituted in many places, B. S. U. organizations to head up religious life started, and in some cases dormitories under Christian influences provided. These schools constitute one of the ripest and most vital fields for service.

Other Agencies.—Prominent among character-building organizations are the *recreational* agencies such as Boy Scouts and Camp Fire Girls. While ordinarily sponsored by local churches, they are independent in their control and have national leadership. Hence, they are not definitely denominational. However, by virtue of the appeal that they make to the interests of youth, and the emphasis they give to character, they are very effective agencies for religious education. Fewer Scouts than Sunday school pupils have been convicted of crime.

The *religious press* is another outstanding agency. The religious paper published by the local church, the state denominational paper, and the various south-wide magazines have tremendous opportunities in shaping the thinking and living of people. In addition, good books and tracts circulated in homes and churches may accomplish much. And while somewhat different, we may well mention in this connection the possibilities for religious education in the use of the radio.

In this introductory chapter we have discussed briefly the nature of religious education, the activities involved, the factors included, and the agencies for promotion. This has given us some idea of the meaning and scope of the work. It has been seen as a major rather than a minor task. In fact it is central in the work of the kingdom of God. It is the true science of power as Benjamin Kidd has shown. Further study will carry us into an historical survey, an outline of principles, and a more detailed study of the institutions involved.

CHAPTER II

EDUCATIONAL ACTIVITIES IN THE OLD TESTAMENT

The Jewish people have always placed a great emphasis on education as a means of promoting religion. In fact, preaching and revivals have been secondary to it. Lehman says: "Among the Jews, that which has always been regarded as first in importance is religion; that which has been regarded as second in importance is education. The path leading to religion was education."[1]

Another prominent scholar has stated the Jewish emphasis on education in these strong words: "Judaism has always been in the truest sense a teaching religion. It has depended primarily for its perpetuation and extension, not upon preaching or upon creeds, or upon the new forms of worship, but upon the personal touch of the teacher and those taught. . . . Education was developed as among no other ancient peoples except possibly the Greeks."[2]

It is important, then, that we begin these historical background studies with an investigation of what the Jews have done. In this one chapter it is impossible of course to give a thorough treatment of educational activities in the Old Testament. Only a general survey from an institutional angle will be given.

THE HOME

The home was the first agency for religious training in the history of the race, as it is in the life of each individual now. Everything considered, it has always been the most powerful one.

Commands.—The Lord selected *Abraham* as national leader and put upon him the responsibility to "command his children and his household after him that they may keep the way of Jehovah to do righteousness and justice; to the end that Jehovah may bring upon Abraham that which he hath spoken of him" (Gen. 18:19). James

[1] *Encyclopedia of Sunday Schools and Religious Education,* Vol. 2, p. 587 (Thomas Nelson & Sons, New York, 1915).
[2] Kent, Charles F., *The Great Teachers of Judaism and Christianity,* pp. 7-9 (Eaton and Mains, New York, 1911).

says: "God's immediate purpose in calling Abraham unto a separated life was that he might engage in a process of domestic education."[3]

Moses commanded the Israelites to educate in the home, saying: "Thou shalt teach them (these words) diligently unto they children, and shalt talk of them when thou sittest in thy house and when thou walkest by the way, and when thou liest down, and when thou risest up. And thou shalt bind them for a sign upon thy hand, and they shall be for frontlets between thine eyes. And thou shalt write them upon the door-posts of thy house and upon thy gates" (Deut. 6:7-9).

The oft-quoted exhortation in *Proverbs*, "Train up a child in the way he should go, and even when he is old he will not depart from it" (22:6), was primarily an emphasis to parents. All along the importance of parental instruction was stressed.

Other Old Testament scriptures emphasize home training, some implying the training of servants and retainers as well as children in the immediate family, by the patriarchal head, as in the case of Abraham and his 318 trained men (Gen. 14:14).

Teachers.—The *parents* were of course the chief teachers in the home, both emphasizing morals and religion with the father instructing the son in industrial arts, and the mother the daughter in domestic arts. Children were urged to "hear the instruction of thy father and forsake not the teaching of thy mother" (Prov. 1:8).

It also seems that the *patriarch* was expected to teach the children of all of the families under his leadership. In Genesis 14:14, we are told that Abraham "led forth his trained men, born in his house, three hundred and eighteen." Trumbull says this reference "would presuppose a process of school instruction under Abraham's oversight."[4]

In addition to parents and patriarchs there were various *private* teachers, often professional or semi-professional in nature. Nursing fathers and nursing mothers who were guardians or governesses, carried on nurturing or teaching activity (Num. 11:12, Isa. 49:33), Naomi served as such to Ruth's child (Ruth 4:16), and the great men of Samaria to Ahab's son (2 Kings 10:5). It is possible that other private, professional teachers were employed from time to time (Prov. 5:13, Ps. 119:99). There are also specific instances of indi-

---

[3] *Reasons for Christian Education*, p. 24 (Baptist General Convention of Texas, 1915).

[4] *Yale Lectures on the Sunday School*, p. 6, footnote (John D. Wattles, Philadelphia, 1893).

vidual instruction such as Melchizedek teaching Abraham with regard to the tithe (Gen. 14:18f).

Teaching.—The elements of *culture* were included in the instruction. This involved the rudiments of learning such as reading, writing, and calculation. The history of the chosen people was inculcated in various ways. Manners relative to eating and to right relationships to parents and others were instilled.

Much attention was given to *practical arts*. The child learned of suitable and forbidden foods and other matters relative to health. The boys were skilled in agricultural and mechanical activities. Girls were taught domestic arts. Some attention was probably given to music, athletics, and military tactics.

Morals received particular emphasis. This covered the whole range of ethical virtues such as temperance, purity, honesty, obedience, and industry. Right relationships to others were stressed. In fact the Book of Proverbs is a rather comprehensive manual of practical ethics.

Religion was of course stressed. In various ways, ideas relative to the true God, providential dealings, stewardship of money, the Sabbath, worship, and other matters pertaining to religion were emphasized. The religious attitude permeated all of the other instruction given.

Characteristics.—One feature was *informality*. A formal system of instruction as we conceive it today, had not been thought of. Conversation, imitation, and example played a large part then as they do in rural life today. Often this is the most effective kind of instruction.

The instruction was *vital*, centering around the problems and needs in every-day living. This is the element that educators have been striving recently to get into modern education. Life-centered activities and problems are prominent in all educational discussions these days. Jewish education centuries ago was similar.

Participation played a large part. While stories, questions, and memorizing entered in, they were not the dominant methods. Rites as in circumcision, festivals such as the Passover, garbs worn during prayer and at meals and other activities gave ample opportunity for participation. While the project method as such has never been heard of, its principles were being carried out.

Achievements.—The training in the home in the patriarchal as well as in later periods of Hebrew life, resulted in high *ideals* in religion and morals. The concepts of God, the Sabbath, holiness and obligation to man and God were far above those of surrounding peoples. One of Judaism's distinctive contributions has been the loftiness of its ideals.

Outstanding characters developed as another result. Joseph was so instructed as to withstand Egypt's temptations and become a ruler; Moses became the outstanding leader and author of his day; Samuel developed into a great judge and ruler; and David, Solomon, Daniel and others made preeminent contributions to the life of their times.

National greatness was another outcome. Surrounded by peoples with civilizations of long standing the Hebrew nation came to a place of preeminent influence. This was due to the character of its people which, in turn, was largely the result of its home life.

THE FEASTS

The various feasts or festivals may very well be viewed as educational activities, since they did much to impress certain significant facts as well as provide occasions for social fellowship.

Number.—Apart from the ceremonials accompanying birth, marriage, and other such occasions, and those connected with the weekly, monthly, and other fast days, there gradually developed a number of outstanding feasts.

Prominent among these were the Passover commemorating the death angel's passing over the first born in Egypt and the exodus from that country; Pentecost celebrating the giving of the Law, and Tabernacles recalling the period of wandering in the wilderness.

As time went on and significant events happened others were added, such as Atonement, Dedication, and Purim, commemorating outstanding occasions. During later Judaism, the number had so grown that approximately a month during the year was given to such celebrations. Sometimes one day emphasized several events.

Nature.—These occasions were of the nature of festivals, sometimes involving feasts and sometimes fasts. Social as well as commemorative features were usually connected with them. The length of time they lasted varied from a day to a week or more.

Passover is a good illustration of a feast. It was observed annually at night in imitation of the eating of the last meal before leaving Egypt while the death angel passed over the Hebrew homes and slew the first-born of the Egyptians. One or more families dressed in the garb of travelers and with staff in hand stood around a table and ate hurriedly the roasted paschal lamb or kid served with bitter herbs and unleavened bread. At a certain time during the procedure the youngest child asked what it all meant and the head of the household explained the occasion. Following this, all left-overs were burned and the family remained in the house until morning.

Characteristics.—A number of features distinctively educational characterize these various festival occasions.

For one thing, they were *objective.* They made distinct appeals to the eye and other senses. This made them much more effective than speeches and books, especially for little children. Modern education is putting much stress on the use of pictures and objects in teaching.

They involved *activity.* Since the people themselves participated in the occasion rather than merely listened to some one read or tell the story, it was more powerful educationally. This principle of activity is emphasized today as being essential to the most effective educational procedure.

These feasts were also *dramatic.* The participants re-enacted the scenes in an appropriate garb and in the natural setting, as far as was practicable. Acting added greatly to the didactic effectiveness. It added movement and costume and appealed to the eye.

Intensiveness was another very effective feature. Some lasted for a week or more. All of the attention during this time was centered on this festival. By such means, attention was focussed and continued, and the impression deepened as in a Daily Vacation Bible School or continued revival meeting.

Results.—These feasts helped to fix in mind significant *historical* events in the life of the chosen nation as they could not have been done by merely reading about them or hearing them described. It was a wise piece of educational strategy and accomplishment.

Interest in things Jewish was stimulated by these periodic gatherings with their social, patriotic and religious emphasis. They were to the Hebrews what the Fourth of July or Lincoln's birthday are to us. Zeal for things Jewish was naturally stimulated.

National and religious *solidarity* was the final result. There was gradually built up a sense of divine leadership and unity that has persisted through the centuries, for even now it is difficult for a Jew to desert his religion or to marry a Gentile.

TABERNACLE AND TEMPLE

At first thought it would not seem that the activities of the Tabernacle and Temple were in any particular sense educational. But on more careful consideration it is evident that they were in many ways very much so. Since the Temple was largely just an enlargement and amplification of the Tabernacle, the main treatment will be given to the latter.

Construction.—Surrounding the Tabernacle was a wall made of colored, embroidered curtains fastened on silver-tipped posts. Within the enclosure was an altar overlaid with gold. The Tabernacle proper was a tent, two-thirds of which was the Holy Place and one-third the Holy of Holies, containing the Ark of the Covenant, which enclosed the Ten Commandments. The Temple was much more elaborate and substantial in its construction than the Tabernacle.

This striking construction had educational significance because it impressed upon these Hebrew people fresh from the darkness of Egypt and later in the wilderness, the grandeur of God and the beauty of religion as against the animal worship of heathenism. It raised their sense of values and appreciation of religion even as a beautiful structure today is more impressive than a crude tabernacle. A new sense of the worth of religion naturally emerged.

Arrangement.—As previously indicated, a curtained wall surrounded the Tabernacle and the enclosure, thus keeping the masses on the outside. They could bring their offering only to the entrance. Within the general enclosure and the Holy Place only the priests were allowed. But within the Holy of Holies only the High Priest went and then only once a year on the Day of Atonement. The Temple had more extensive arrangements including provisions for singers, and a court each for the women and for the Gentiles.

This separation and gradation had the effect of impressing on the minds of the people the sacredness of Jehovah and the fact that he could not be approached with the freedom with which one approaches idols or animals, as in Egyptian religions. Here was the education in awe and reverence so greatly needed at the time and, as a matter of fact, even now.

Priesthood.—The formation of the priesthood was an interesting part of the system. The priests were the guardians of the sacred shrines, directors of the sacrifice, and instructors of the people. Their garb was particularly striking. The priest wore an ephod of linen with threads of gold, purple, blue, and scarlet intertwined; a shoulder piece of gold set with onyx stones; a breastplate similar to the ephod set with twelve precious stones representing the twelve tribes; a blue robe with golden bells and pomegranates on the skirt, and a headdress mingled with gold, purple, and other colors.

This separated group, ministering at the altar, dressed in such elaborate and striking garb had the effect of impressing on the people the importance of the work of Jehovah in a new and significant way as contrasted with the crude gods of the Egyptians and others. It helped also to prepare the way for the idea of the priesthood of Christ.

Sacrifices.—The system of sacrifice was, educationally, particularly significant. It included a variety of offerings and quite a bit of ceremony connected with them. There were peace offerings indicative of right relations with God; sin offerings to atone for unwitting sins or errors, and also guilt offerings to make expiation to God for more serious sins. There were qualifications connected with the offering such as being without blemish and of a specified age. Certain conditions were required of the one making the offering such as cleansing and purifying, and the priest must offer it under certain conditions as to procedure and disposition of the various parts.

All of these things had tremendous value in objectively and effectively teaching a nation of people fresh from the environment of heathenism. Thus, the people learned about the nature, seriousness and consequences of sin, God's requirements of those who sin, and what was necessary to be right before God. They helped also to prepare their minds for the climax of the sacrifice of Christ in atoning for the sins of all humanity, particularly as the High Priest made the blood offering in the Holy of Holies once each year.

In addition to all of these things, there was in the Temple the reciting of scriptures, praying, various types of singing, and discussion and explanation of the Scriptures that had great value in helping the people to understand the way of the Lord more perfectly.

THE SYNAGOGUE

The outstanding educational agency in the Bible is the synagogue, especially when we consider the elementary school attached to it. It was primarily for instruction and training as the Tabernacle and Temple were dominantly ritualistic and worshipful.

The term "synagogue" literally means a leading or gathering together, and therefore an assembly. While the building where the people gathered came to be used as a public hall and place of worship, originally, "it was meant only for the exposition of the Law."[5]

Development.—The synagogue seems to have had its *origin* during the Babylonian captivity when the Temple was gone and the

[5] Levertoff, Paul, in *The International Standard Bible Encyclopedia*, Vol. V, p. 2878 (The Howard-Severance Co., Chicago, 1915).

people were in a foreign land. There a new generation was growing up without the benefits of religious instruction, and it was not feasible to have a central temple as in the home land. To preserve their religious heritage they developed the synagogue. It spread rapidly after the return from captivity, gradually coming to be found in most of the towns of Judea, and sometimes in Gentile communities. One writer says that by the time of Christ there were at least 460 in Jerusalem—as many as there were Sunday Schools in New York City two generations ago.

Provisions.—Generally a *separate building* was provided for the purpose. This was the expectation. The poor, however, were permitted to use a room in another building. The structure was rectangular in shape somewhat as our church buildings today. Probably they were on high ground facing toward the East. A chest containing the scrolls of Scripture was kept back of the pulpit.

There were several *officers* including a ruler for the organization whose duty it was to select from the congregation a leader for reading and preaching who might also direct the discussion. Christ seems to have served as a reader and preacher. An interpreter was also provided to translate the Law and the Prophets from Hebrew into Aramaic, the language of the hearers.

Activities.—The *services* of the synagogue were held on the Sabbath, on Monday, and on Thursday, when the country people came to market, and on feast and fast days. There were two services during the day, one mainly instructional and the other mainly devotional. This probably helps to explain the statement about Christ "teaching in their synagogues and preaching the gospel of the kingdom" (Matt. 4:23).

The *teaching* element in the services included the general recitation of selected Scriptures; the reading and translating of the Law, a verse at a time, covering it in three years; and the reading and translating in a similar fashion of the Prophets with three verses as a unit. This reminds us somewhat of the study of our Uniform Lessons in the Sunday School today. Following this minute study came a general, expository address applying the lesson to the life of the day. So the synagogue services were definitely educational.

Results.—Since synagogues were available to practically all, there was provided virtually *universal religious training* in the Law and the Prophets for those of both sexes. This was a distinct advance over the more limited and less educational activities of the Tabernacle and Temple, as well as the home. Hebrew children gradually acquired a considerable knowledge of the Old Testament.

Not only was religious training made practically universal through the synagogue, but this activity *led to the elementary schools* which came to be the outstanding school system of the time in any land. Indirectly, also, it led to the professional schools for the scribes.

THE ELEMENTARY SCHOOL

The elementary school is the only exclusively educational institution in the Bible. It was attached to the synagogue somewhat like the parochial schools of different denominations today are attached to churches. The idea may have come from the Babylonians who had schools connected with their temples. By the time of Christ, the elementary school was practically as general as the synagogue, the latter pre-supposing a school very much as a church today pre-supposes a Sunday school.

Pupils.—Constituency was limited to the elementary grades. It was of course for boys only, since the formal education of girls had not yet begun. The pupils started at about six years of age and attended until about sixteen. Apparently they went every week day. Ultimately, attendance was compulsory and even as important a matter as the re-building of the Temple was not sufficient to detain the children. They were graded into separate groups.

Teachers.—These were men only and must be married, since the mothers might come to visit the school. For the most part, the scribes were the teachers and they were God-fearing and conscientious men. A teacher was not to have more than twenty-five pupils, an assistant being employed if there were more, and two teachers if above fifty. They served without pay and made their living by other means. The Talmud said, "The true guardians of the city are the teachers."

Curriculum.—Foundational studies including reading, writing, and arithmetic were taught. These, of course, were means to ends. For history they studied the life of the Hebrew people. For ethics they had the morals and manners of Proverbs. As social science they had the civil, criminal, and ceremonial law of the Jews. The Psalms constituted the basis of study both in music and poetry. Scrolls were used as text-books, and the material was adapted to the age and ability of the pupil. The course of study was a thoroughly religious one.

Methods.—The methods were not quite like those of the present day. They were more formal. Memorization was prominent in the system with special emphasis on catechizing, drill and review. Even the young children memorized portions of Leviticus and knew important scriptures by heart.

Discipline also occupied a prominent place. Punishment was freely resorted to. The leaders believed in the depravity of human nature, and did not spare the rod for fear of spoiling the child. They included training as well as teaching.

The *material-centered* emphasis was prominent, more regard probably being paid to the text than to the pupil. Yet, with all of its weaknesses, it seems to have been the first compulsory system of public education and the most effective of the day.

OTHER EDUCATIONAL ACTIVITIES

There were a number of other educational activities carried on in the Old Testament period besides those of the agencies already discussed. For the most part they were individual and informal efforts, usually rather temporary in nature, and varying in importance. Some of these follow.

Work of Moses.—During the period involved in the journey from Egypt to Palestine, Moses carried on an extensive educational activity with the Israelites. This was necessary in order to counteract the heathen influences in Egypt and prepare for citizenship and leadership in the new land. For the most part, the activity was group instruction on such matters as the Ten Commandments, idolatry and worship; didactic discourse, memorizing the civil and ceremonial law as in Deuteronomy; judging disputes and explaining right conduct in connection therewith; and putting into writing the important teachings of Jehovah. These instructions touched almost every problem in personal, domestic, civic and religious relationships. They prepared the people for right living with God and man. Moses left instructions for periodic and systematic instruction for the years ahead.

Joshua's Services.—Following the example of Moses, Joshua, his successor, sought to carry on definite instruction. A particular instance was that of gathering the people into two groups facing each other in front of Mount Ebal and Mount Gerizin, and rehearsing in antiphonal fashion the blessings and the curses (Josh. 8:32f). Previously, the people had made a heap of stones gathered from the Jordan river to serve as a permanent memorial for emphasizing the entrance into the land of promise. Special studies of the entire Law were made every seventh year during the time of rest, and also each fiftieth or jubilee year. By these means, the people were informed as to what Jehovah required at their hands.

Jehoshaphat's Procedure.—Another specific effort of considerable interest and effect was the teaching activity fostered by the good king, Jehoshaphat, as a means of social and moral reform. The life of the people had reached a rather sinful state and preparatory to a reform movement he instituted a plan of popular religious instruction somewhat on the order of the Bible institutes. Sixteen priests and Levites were sent out in pairs to go from city to city throughout the land and carry on a brief course in religious teaching (2 Chr. 17:7f). The result was far-reaching. Civic leaders today might well profit by that example.

Schools of the Prophets.—Much has been said from time to time about the Schools of the Prophets carried on by Samuel, Elijah and Elisha. The emphasis has been overdone as they were not schools in the sense in which we think of schools today. Rather, they were more in the nature of training institutes. They were theological institutes only in embryo, whose purpose was to prepare the young prophets for their tasks. The locations were at Bethel, Gilgal, Jericho, and the Jordan. The prophets visited these places and instructed the young men in the elements of learning, religious history and literature and prophetic activities.

Teaching by the Prophets.—It has been well said that the prophet was a "forth-teller" quite as much as a "foreteller." Much of his task was to interpret the moral and religious significance of current events. He was, therefore, a teacher. This teaching work was done in various ways. One was by giving didactic names to children suggestive of problems facing the people as when Hosea named a daughter "unpitied," and Isaiah named his son "a remnant shall return." Sometimes they used dramatic illustrations to impress future events as when Jeremiah wore a wooden yoke about his neck, and Ezekiel scattered his hair to the wind. They also spoke and wrote vigorously, using some of the most effective literary forms. They were powerful portrayers of truth.

Efforts of the Wise Men.—Another character about whom very little is said is the wise man, or sage. These men were informal, self-appointed teachers of truth. They were usually advanced in years and were sometimes called "elders." They often sat near the gates of the city and discoursed to those who came in. Besides public discussion they gave private counsel and also trained a group of disciples, or pupils. In contrast to the prophets, who placed the emphasis on civic affairs, they dealt more with the personal graces that go to make a good citizen, home maker or business man. The statements in Proverbs are rather typical of their teachings, and show interesting literary forms as well as ethical instruction. They were the forerunner of the teaching class. Job, Solomon and others belong to this group.

Scribal Activities.—The most distinctively *teaching* person in the Old Testament was the Scribe. The word means "man of books" and carries the idea of copyist, interpreter or editor. They were journalists as well as teachers. At first they were chroniclers and copyists, but gradually developed into a teaching group. The rabbi or master was the climax of the development. They preserved the writings, translated them into the language of the people, taught them to the masses of people by various means, and trained pupils to take their places. The rabbinical schools were somewhat after the order of normal schools. A striking individual instance of scribal activity was Ezra's open-air school in Jerusalem where the Scriptures were read, interpreted, and applied to the assembled masses.

There are other instances of educational activity in the Old Testament but these are enough to indicate the didactic emphasis in it. The teaching element runs all the way through it, and gives us an idea of what we should do today. As a matter of fact, education was developed among the Hebrews to a greater extent than it probably was among any other people at the time, even though girls received little consideration. The Talmud placed a great emphasis on the teacher saying: "The world continues to exist only by the breath of the children of the schools."

CHAPTER III

EDUCATIONAL ACTIVITIES IN THE NEW TESTAMENT

As prominent as is the emphasis on the educational method in the Old Testament, it is much more outstanding in the New. Particularly is this true because of the stress which the Master Teacher himself, both by precept and example, gave to teaching. In addition there are a number of other evidences of the prominence given teaching.

CHRIST AS A TEACHER

For a long time we have thought of Christ as a revealer of God, a healer of human ills, and a redeemer from sin. Only in recent years has much consideration been given to him as a teacher, but much has been brought to light in this brief time.

Fact of His Teaching.—Marquis says of Christ: "He was often a healer, sometimes a worker of signs, frequently a preacher, but always a teacher."[1] What are the evidences for this statement?

For one thing he was called *teacher*. While Christ was never in the Gospels called a preacher, yet forty-five times in those records he was called a teacher. Some of the times he called himself a teacher, at other times so-called by his disciples, such as Mary or Nicodemus, and still at other times by his enemies, such as the Pharisees, Sadducees and others. All regarded him as a teacher.[2]

Also he was regularly *engaged in teaching*. We find that he went about teaching in the synagogues, at the Temple, by the roadside, at the sea shore, in the houses, and in fact wherever he was. Teaching was his business and he was at it constantly. He was not an official but rather a self-appointed teacher.

He not only taught the masses but he also *trained a group of teachers* who were to carry on when he was gone. Especially was this true in the latter part of his ministry. In this respect he became a

[1] *Learning to Teach from the Master Teacher,* p. 4 (The Westminister Press, Philadelphia, 1913).
[2] See Williams, C. B., *Function of Teaching in Christianity,* pp. 24-25 (Baptist Sunday School Board, Nashville, 1912).

teacher of teachers, preparing them to continue his work. This was done, as we shall see later, not only by personal instruction but also by the example of his life and by the activities he gave them to do.

Furthermore, he *commissioned his followers to teach*. When he got ready to leave the earth he gave his parting command. All three phases of the Great Commission (Mt. 28:19-20) have to do with teaching—enlisting in the school of Christ, initiating through a teaching ordinance, and continuing the teaching process. The Lord's supper also is a didactic ordinance.

Controlling Aims.—Undoubtedly Jesus did not go about the main business of his life without definite aims and purposes. What were these objectives? How far should they control us today? The answer to these questions will give us not only a better understanding of him but also a better basis for our own work.

From the *negative* point of view it is evident that the Master Teacher was not primarily concerned with inculcating a body of truth. He wrote no books nor did he present at any one place a systematic outline of all of his teachings. He was not material-centered in his emphasis. Furthermore it is clear that he did not seek to dictate or determine the thinking of his pupils. He knew too well the effect of such a procedure on their lives, and was too much concerned about free will and personality development.

On the *positive* side it may be said that he was life-centered in his approach. "His objective was not to impart information merely, but to change and transform life."[3] He sought to develop individuals so that they could face life. Therefore he dealt with life-situations and personal problems. His greatest parable, the one on the Foolish Farmer, grew out of a request made that he divide an inheritance. He was more concerned about developing religious persons than imparting religious truth. To that end he sought to stimulate and direct religious thinking, develop right emotions and attitudes, and lead into practical and vital Christian activity. "I am come that they might have life" (Jno. 10:10).

Literary Forms Used.—Along with other considerations on Jesus as a teacher, it is interesting to notice something of the form in which his teaching was cast. There is artistry even in this.

Probably the most striking form is the *parable*. It is a truth taken from a familiar phase of life to make clear the truth in one that is not so familiar. McCoy says parables are used to secure

[3] Piper, D. R., *How Would Jesus Teach?* p. 41 (David C. Cook Co., Elgin, 1931).

attention, reveal truth to the worthy, conceal it from the unworthy, stimulate thought, and illustrate it.[4] They vary greatly in length, some being germ parables and others long ones. They cover almost every phase of life, including inanimate things, such as soil, clothes, and food; various kinds of plants, birds and animals; and human beings in various relationships.

Epigrams constitute another very striking form of material used by Christ in his teaching. These include short, pithy proverbs and maxims, such as "Physician, heal thyself" (Luke 4:23), and the familiar Golden Rule. Figures of speech including metaphors, hyperboles, and personification were used frequently. All of these are effective and easily remembered.

Along with the last-named come various forms of *repetition and contrast* or comparison such as "Lead us not into temptation, but deliver us from evil" (Mt. 6:13), and the various beatitudes. These striking forms as well as his personality and methods served to drive home the truths he taught.

Methods Employed.—One may go to Christ to find not only the valuable truths he taught but also the best methods to be used. His teaching is our model of method as well as of content. In fact Squires would place him beyond us as indicated in the title of his book, *The Pedagogy of Jesus in the Twilight of Today*.

In spite of the tendency to minimize the *lecture* method we will have to recognize that it had a prominent place in Christ's teaching. The so-called Sermon on the Mount is an outstanding example. It is a didactic discourse rather than a hortatory message. A number of other instances are to be found. These gave Christ an opportunity to set forth his teaching in somewhat systematic form.

Discussion is prominent and probably his most distinctive method. For the most part he did not seek to present formal material so much as to meet life problems. Even the Old Testament was presented not so much exegetically as to throw light on particular problems. Many of his discussions were with individuals such as Nicodemus and were conversational in nature.

Christ also used *questions* frequently (more than one hundred are recorded). Sometimes they were for information, at other times to impress a truth, and on other occasions to provoke thought, deepen conviction, or to secure response. In all cases they served to give life and vigor to his teaching.

[4] *The Art of Jesus as a Teacher,* p. 159 (American Baptist Publication Society, Philadelphia, 1930).

As previously indicated he used the *story* often. This was usually in the form of the parable, and covered a wide range of topics close to the experiences of the hearers. It usually carried its own lesson but might be used to introduce a lesson or clinch a truth already stated.

The *project* method was used to some degree. Christ gave his disciples problems to work out, took them with him on his journeys, and sent them out on missions of their own, thus teaching them through experience. Initiative was always encouraged.

Results Accomplished.—If Christ is to be judged as a teacher according to the results accomplished, he will have to be given first place. Certainly no teacher has ever achieved so much in the life of humanity.

For one thing he trained a group of *leaders* that have carried his message around the world. No teacher ever trained such an effective group of workers. Yet they were from the common people, and he had only a brief time in which to develop them into such an effective leadership.

Also his *disciples* have come to be the largest and most significant group of followers that any teacher ever had. Including all branches there are more than 576,000,000 Christians, which is eighty per cent more than any other group of disciples. They number nearly a third of the population of the entire earth today.

Furthermore his *influence* has gone further than that of any other teacher. His teachings have permeated literature, influenced education, shaped governments, and accomplished reforms in temperance, purity, slavery, womanhood and other lines. Christ's truths have influenced civilization as those of no other teacher.

PAUL AS A TEACHER

Ordinarily we think of Paul as a foreign missionary and evangelist and hardly consider him as a teacher. More careful study, however, reveals the fact that he was very definitely a teacher. In many ways this teaching activity stands out.

The Fact.—Perhaps the strongest evidence that Paul was a teacher is the fact that he *himself says so*. In 2 Tim. 2:1 he says: "I was appointed a preacher, and an apostle, and a teacher." Evidently he knew what he was talking about. Also he refers to himself four times in his epistles as having taught. This includes teaching at Thessalonica (2 Thess. 2:15), at Colossae (Col. 2:7), and in fact at all of the churches that he had established (1 Cor. 4:17 and Col.

1:28). This extensive teaching of young Christians was necessary since they had recently been converted from paganism, lacked the foundation of their Jewish brethren, and in addition were cluttered up with various heathen ideas and practices.

Luke also said that Paul taught. At Antioch, for example, he remained for an entire year and "taught much people" (Acts 11:26). At Corinth he carried on his teaching work for a year and a half (Acts 18:11). At Ephesus he extended his teaching ministry to two and a fourth years, part of the time in the synagogue, and part of it in the school of Tyrannus (Acts 19:8-10). Even while a prisoner at Rome for two years he taught as well as preached (Acts 18:31). From all of these statements it is evident that much of the activity of Paul in his missionary work was that of a teacher.

His Aims.—The first aim that Paul had in mind was to lay a solid *foundation for conversion* and the Christian life. His work was being done largely outside the borders of Judaism where there were lacking the theological and ethical foundations that Jewish teaching gave. In addition to this lack there were added all of the evils which in theory and practice accompany heathenism. A great many corrections had to be made and positive instruction given before an intelligent conversion could take place. It was on the same basis a little later that the catechumenate, about which we shall study further on, was established. And it is because of similar conditions today in foreign lands that the missionary instructs for a period before seeking a profession or church membership.

A second aim was to *develop* in the Christian life. Paul recognized then as we do today that conversion is only the beginning of the Christian experience, and that extended instruction must be carried on if satisfactory development is to take place. He was not contented, therefore, merely to secure a profession. He sought to follow it up with extended instruction "that ye might be filled with the knowledge of his will in all wisdom and spiritual understanding; that ye might walk worthy of the Lord—, fruitful in every good work—, perfect in Christ" (Col. 1:9-10, 28). His ultimate objective in carrying on such an extensive teaching activity was the perfection of Christian character. Within this general aim, of course, Paul includes the specific graces that go to make a socialized, moral and religious character.

Teaching Means.—In general we may think of two types. One was *personal contact*. Sometimes Paul taught privately, going from house to house. At other times he taught publicly, dealing with small groups or larger crowds. Both sexes and all types of people were included. He taught at practically any time of day and any day of the week. His teaching was carried on in synagogues, schools, market-places, and by the river. Kuist says of him: "His life was one teaching experience after another. He taught whensoever an occasion presented itself, wheresoever he happened to be, and whomsoever came within the sphere of his influence."[5] He was a peripatetic and perennial teacher.

In addition to teaching people face to face Paul taught extensively *by letter*. It was impossible for him to be at all of the places all of the time that he desired to be to give the instruction needed. He covered too much territory, had converts in too many places, and needed to give instruction along too many lines. Therefore he instituted the epistle or didactic letter as a means for wider instructional activity. Sometimes these were written to individuals, as Philemon; sometimes to local churches, as Thessalonians; and sometimes to larger groups, as Galatians. Some of these were general expositions of Christianity, such as Romans, and others were largely the answers to particular problems, such as Corinthians, and were especially life-centered. These didactic epistles have been a powerful means of teaching Christianity through the centuries.

Methods and Results.—Prominent in Paul's *methods*, as in that of Christ, is the lecture. There are a number of outstanding instances of such public discourse. Distinctive among them is the famous address on Mars Hill, which is a good example of pedagogical procedure in making the contact, transition, development and conclusion (Acts 17:16-34).

The discussion method gets some consideration, particularly in Paul's writings. Romans is one example. Here he makes his arguments interspersed with assumed questions from his supposed pupils. He is strong on the logical and argumentative.

Exposition is also prominent in Paul's didactic letters, and probably in his teaching in the synagogues. He set forth effectively in systematic, if not in outline form, the teachings of Christianity and their application to the problems of life.

The *results* of his teachings are outstanding. For one thing he secured groups of strong converts in the centers where he labored that formed the basis for church organizations. These worked out into surrounding territory and secured other converts and other churches grew up carrying Christianity into new territory. So Chris-

---

[5] *The Pedagogy of St. Paul*, p. 50 (Geo. H. Doran Co., New York, 1925).

tianity secured a strong footing under the leadership of this Apostle to the Gentiles.

Also through his writings Paul gave the interpretation to Christianity that has greatly shaped Christian thinking ever since his day. Present-day theology is largely the outgrowth of his interpretations. Thus through his disciples and his epistles this great Christian teacher started Christianity on its westward career and greatly shaped the course of civilization.

OTHER NEW TESTAMENT TEACHERS

Although Christ and Paul were the outstanding teachers in New Testament days, they were by no means the only ones. A number of others stand out in the life of the times either in person or in function.

Specific Individuals.—The *apostles* in general were teachers. While the term teacher seems not to have been applied to them, the term "teach" is used two times in Acts to describe their activity. In ch. 5:25 we are told that they were "teaching the people" in the Temple. In ch. 5:42 the writer of Acts says they "ceased not to teach and to preach Jesus Christ." Thus their teaching seems to have been put on a par with their preaching. Furthermore the word "teaching" occurs twice in Acts (2:42 and 5:28) to describe the message of the Apostles, giving further evidence that they were looked upon as teachers.

Peter and *John* are particularly emphasized as Apostles who taught. They are referred to four times by the writer of Acts as being in the act of teaching (chs. 4:1-2, 18 and 5:21, 28). Twice the reference is to teaching in the Temple or teaching the people, and twice we are told that the Sanhedrin either was troubled because they taught, or charged them to "not teach in his name." They seem to have been carrying on their teaching privately and publicly. The results would indicate that they were generally recognized as teachers and that their work was effective, at least enough so to cause the officials to be disturbed.

Another teacher referred to by name is *Barnabas*. Not very much is said regarding him, and his work is connected with Paul. He seems to have been one of the teachers in the church at Antioch referred to in Acts 13:1. He was with Paul in Antioch for a year and "taught much people" (Acts 11:26). This was in connection with planting Christianity in new centers. It is possible that he continued to teach after his separation from Paul.

Still others mentioned by name are *Apollos, Priscilla* and *Aquila.* Again the reference is rather brief. It is simply stated that Apollos "taught diligently the things of the Lord" (Acts 18:25). But evidently he got off the track in his doctrine since he had known only the baptism of John, for in the next verse we are told that Priscilla and Aquila expounded to him "the way of the Lord more thoroughly." Leaving Ephesus Apollos went to Achaia and taught the Scriptures there effectively. Even a teacher may sometimes be taught!

An Official Class.—Along with the names of specific individuals who taught, a *teaching group* is mentioned in the New Testament. In Acts 13:1 we are told: "There were in the church that was at Antioch certain prophets and teachers." Among them were Barnabas and Saul. Apparently here the teacher stood alongside the prophet. There is a possibility that the church at Ephesus had certain elders (bishops) as official teachers, for Acts 20:17 states that there was a plurality of elders there. And we do know that the post-New Testament church had a catechist or an official church teacher who apparently becomes the biblical precedent for the educational director.

Another emphasis which stresses the vocational idea is the reference to a *teaching function.* Says Paul: "God hath set some in the church, first apostles, secondarily prophets, thirdly teachers" (1 Cor. 12:28). In a similar fashion we find in another place a mention of God's having given apostles, prophets, evangelists, pastors and teachers (Eph. 4:11). Not only for New Testament days but for all time the teacher is to be recognized as a functionary along with the pastor, evangelist, and others. This seems to give a further basis for the educational director or minister as a definite functionary in the church. Instead of getting away from the Bible we are probably getting back to its emphasis.

It is clearly emphasized in the New Testament that the *pastor* should be a teacher. In scriptures already quoted teaching was tied up with the work of the pastor. In another place Paul definitely says: "A bishop then must be . . . apt to teach" (1 Tim. 3:2). Nothing could be clearer or stronger. This is just as essential a qualification as that he shall not be covetous, intemperate, or a bigamist, which are referred to in the same verse. Also Paul tells Timothy: "The things that thou hast heard of me among many witnesses, the same commit thou to faithful men, who shall be able to teach others also" (2 Tim. 2:2). This is a fine illustration of what a trained pastor should do for the corps of teachers under him. It is possibly his greatest opportunity as a pastor.

Volunteer Teachers.—There is some emphasis on the work of the unofficial or non-vocational teacher *in the church*. As a matter of fact Priscilla and Aquila were largely in that class, though they did help Paul quite a bit. Paul's exhortations to the Romans include one for the teachers as well as for givers and others, saying: "He that teacheth (let him wait) on his teaching" (Rom. 12:7). James (ch. 3:1) cautions Jewish Christians about becoming teachers too readily because of the responsibility of the task. The author of Hebrews, however, seems to indicate that all mature Christians ought to reach the stage of teachers rather than having always to be taught. Evidently in these references the non-vocational or volunteer teacher such as we have in Sunday school and Baptist Training Union was in mind.

Similarly, unofficial teaching was done *in the home*. Apparently Christ was taught by Joseph as he went about his duties in the carpenter shop, and by his mother who yearned to see the ideals of Judaism implanted in her child. S. D. Gordon has said: "Nazareth is the double underscoring in red under every sentence He spoke."[6] Paul was brought up by loyal Hebrew parents who observed circumcision, inculcated the strictest Pharisaical teachings and caused him to be as "touching the righteousness which is in the law, blameless" (Phil. 3:9). Timothy had the benefit of the teachings of his grandmother Lois and his mother Eunice, and Paul said of him, "From a child thou hast known the holy scriptures" (2 Tim. 3:15). Parents were important as teachers.

EDUCATIONAL TERMINOLOGY

In addition to the examples of various teachers in the New Testament, and the emphasis on the place of the vocational and volunteer teacher, there are a number of other statements which carry a strong educational emphasis.

As to Methods of Work.—A comparison of the terms meaning to *teach and preach* is rather revealing. Dr. C. B. Williams has pointed out that in the New Testament the noun "teacher" translated from the Greek is used 54 times as against 3 uses of the word "preacher." Also the Greek verb for "teach" is used 93 times as against 65 uses of the verb "preach."[7] The Greek noun carrying the

---

[6] *Quiet Talks on Home Ideals*, p. 114 (Fleming H. Revell Co., New York, 1909).
[7] *Function of Teaching in Christianity*, p. 259 (Baptist Sunday School Board, Nashville, 1912).

idea of preacher emphasizes the thought of a herald or one who is hastening with a message. The one translated *teacher* emphasizes the didactic or definitely instructional idea. This is a striking emphasis on method from the viewpoint of the New Testament and the Greek.

If one were to go beyond the New Testament and take the English expressions translated from both Hebrew and Greek he would find some more interesting facts as to the biblical emphasis on methods. The noun "teacher," used apart from persons addressed, is found 21 times in the Bible whereas the noun "preacher" is found only 11 times. The verb "teach" is found 222 times in both Old and New Testaments as against 123 uses of the verb "preach."[8]

In this connection it is rather significant that in the Great Commission Christ says *make disciples*. This means to instruct or cause to become learners. The Christian worker is to make disciples of the peoples of all nations, or lead them to become pupils of Christ that they may study and learn of him. This term undoubtedly involves the teaching idea more than it does the hortatory procedure. It suggests not only the method of activity but also the kind of product, as we shall see later.

As to Followers of Christ.—What word would one most naturally expect to be used to describe Christ's followers? Normally we would think it would be the term *Christian*, for such would designate his sect of believers, just as "Nazarene" characterizes a follower of the Nazarene. As a matter of fact we do find the term Christian employed to designate Christ's followers. But it is only rarely used. In fact it is found only three times in the New Testament, and in at least one of these instances as a term of derision.

Light is another expression used often. It applies not only to Christ, "the light of the world" (Jno. 9:5), but also to the follower of Christ. He said: "Ye are the light of the world" (Matt. 5:14). And Paul said the Christian is "a light of them which are in darkness" (Rom. 2:19). Light is set over against darkness as knowledge is against ignorance. It is a symbol of instruction and understanding.

The word *disciple* is the term generally used by Jesus and others to characterize his followers. It is found 243 times in the Gospels and Acts. It means a learner or a pupil, one enlisted in a certain school of thought or life. Christianity is looked upon as a school with Christ the founder and Master Teacher, the leaders as assistant teachers, the enlisted nations as pupils, and the Bible as the text-book. Thus the educational idea is prominent.

[8] See *Young's Analytical Concordance* (Funk and Wagnalls Co., New York).

As to Message of Christianity.—The expression *wisdom* is used occasionally by Paul to refer to the content or body of Christian truth. This, it is evident, carries the thought of knowledge or learning, and thus suggests the school and educational ideas. The true Christian is expected to be wise.

Light is a term often used to designate the Christian body of truth. The Psalmist said "Thy word is . . . a light unto my path" (Ps. 119:105). And, Paul speaks of "the light of the glorious gospel of Christ" (2 Cor. 4:4). As previously indicated with regard to the Christian being designated as a light, the term emphasizes the knowledge aspect of Christianity.

The expression *mystery* is used a number of times to designate the message of Christianity. This term is more in the realm of the intellectual than it is in the emotional or volitional phase of consciousness. It suggests something hidden or difficult which has become known or understood. A mystery challenges the thought processes, and is suggestive of the educational aspect of Christianity.

But the expression most commonly used to describe the content of the gospel is the word *teaching*. It carries essentially the same idea as the term doctrine, and refers to the system of thought or body of truth held by the disciple after he has been taught. It is in a sense the curriculum of Christianity. Thirty-nine times in the New Testament the different words translated "teaching" are used. So the message of Christianity is a teaching or an instruction.

EDUCATIONAL DOCTRINES AND ORDINANCES

Not only do we have biblical illustrations of teaching, and commands to teach, but also certain doctrines in which education is implied, and ordinances that are didactic in their very nature. Thus by implication and illustration education is stressed.

Doctrines.—Without undertaking to be comprehensive in stating New Testament doctrines, a few *typical ones* may be mentioned. One of the most significant is that of soul liberty and accountability. We believe that each individual is accountable not to parents or priests but to Christ alone and is free to accept or reject Christianity. "Every one of us shall give account of himself to God" (Rom. 14:12). Another vital doctrine is regeneration. Christ very definitely emphasizes that the new birth or conversion is necessary if one is to enter the kingdom of God or Christian life. "Except a man be born again he cannot see the kingdom of God" (Jno. 3:3). Sanctification or Christian growth is another teaching. One does not enter the Christian life full-grown but is first a babe in Christ and must mature in the experience. Character has to be developed. "Work out your own salvation with fear and trembling" (Phil. 2:12). Still another vital doctrine is democracy in church government. Each individual has as much authority as another. Coöperation is the principle on which kingdom activity is carried on. "Tell it unto the church" (Mt. 18:17) is the divine command.

But what is *the significance* of these doctrines for religious education? How is education implied or involved in them? This is very easy to see. It runs all through them. They cannot be carried out without educational activity. If the individual soul is free to accept or reject God, then he must be taught in order to exercise that freedom rightly. Otherwise soul liberty may be a curse rather than a blessing. If regeneration is necessary in order to enter the kingdom of God, then the person must understand that fact and also what is his part in the process. Otherwise he may miss the gateway. Likewise if sanctification or character development is a process rather than an instantaneous experience, instruction must be given in order to develop the proper ideals and activity. Similarly, if democracy in church government is the ideal, information must be had in order to exercise one's Christian citizenship to a proper advantage. In many Bible doctrines education is implied. In fact had it not been for education we would not have the Bible itself!

Ordinances.—There are two ordinances in the New Testament, *baptism and the Lord's Supper*. The former is commanded in Matt. 28:19 and is the immersion of a believer in water. The latter is authorized in Luke 22:19 and is the eating of bread and drinking of wine. They are to Christianity and the New Testament something of what the Passover and other feasts were to Judaism and the Old Testament. They are to be observed by Christian people throughout all the world and to the end of time. Dr. J. B. Gambrell says they are "the two twin fortresses which safe-guard the whole field of saving truth."[9]

But why the emphasis on these ordinances? What is their *significance*? The answer is they are teaching agencies rather than mere observances. The most effective means of teaching is not by the printed page or by the spoken word, but by the re-enacting or dramatizing of a truth. The most important truths to be taught are the atoning death of Christ, his resurrection which proved his deity, our

[9] Love, J. F., and Gambrell, J. B., *The Gospel for the Eye,* p. 41 (Baptist Standard Publishing Co., Dallas, 1911).

regeneration or resurrection to a new life, and the final resurrection of the dead. This most effective means of teaching and these most vital truths to be taught are brought together in the observance of baptism and the memorial supper. They are didactic ordinances of the most significant sort (Rom. 6:4, 1 Cor. 15:29; 11:26) and not mere ceremonials. Hence our emphasis on them.

From the example and commands of Christ, the oral and written instructions of Paul, the activities of other vocational and volunteer teachers, the use of educational terminology, the educational implications of doctrines, and the illustrations through ordinances, it is evident that promoting the kingdom of God by educational procedure is prominent in the New Testament. If we are to be true to the Bible we must go and do likewise.

CHAPTER IV

ACHIEVEMENTS IN CHRISTIAN HISTORY

The emphasis on education as a means of propagating religion, stressed by precept and example in both the Old and the New Testaments, found effective expression in various ways throughout the course of Christian history. It is impossible in the brief space of a chapter to discuss all of them or even some of them adequately. Consequently, attention is directed only to a few of the most significant, and these will be discussed only enough to see their significance for religious education.

Catechumenal and Catechetical Schools

These activities represent the first efforts in early Christianity to utilize educational means for Christian promotion. They are significant not so much for their greatness as for the emphasis they gave to education.

Catechumenal Schools.—In *nature*, they were more of an educational activity than a distinct agency. The catechumenate was more nearly like a communicants' class than a school of any sort. It was a kind of confirmation group, receiving preliminary instruction before being baptized or admitted to the Lord's Supper. The purpose was to prevent unprepared people from getting into the church. It has been termed, "A bulwark of the church against unworthy members."

The *occasion* for this school grew out of the fact that Christian missions had crossed over the boundaries of Judaism into pagan lands and no longer had the foundation of the synagogue Bible school and elementary school on which to build. It was something of the same thing faced by missionaries in foreign lands today. A preliminary training had to be given before church membership could be permitted.

The *activities* included instruction in such matters as Bible history, Christian doctrines, morals, and psalmody. The first text was a little book about the size of Ephesians called "The Teaching of the Twelve Apostles." Containing in orderly form a summary of Christian teaching which would prepare for intelligent church membership, it was thus the first church manual. In early times the bishop or presbyter did the teaching, but in later days a special catechist was employed. The method was largely catechizing with much memory work by the pupils.

The *accomplishments* of the catechumenate were more than we can easily realize now. Through it, ignorant pagans became intelligent Christians. Pupils advanced through the stages of hearers and kneelers to those approved for baptism. Sometimes they were demoted. When they indulged in sinful practices, and persisted in them, they might be dismissed altogether. Often the process lasted as long as three years before they were finally approved for church membership. It was the chief means of religious education in the early days, where synagogues did not exist.

Catechetical Schools.—These were definite schools with specific locations and faculties and were considerably advanced beyond the simple training afforded by the catechumenate.

The *situation* out of which these schools arose is best illustrated by the first one at Alexandria. Here was a great university with a large library, outstanding teachers, and students from many sections of the world. Greek philosophy predominated and a modernistic atmosphere prevailed. In this situation, new converts were over-awed and skepticism arose. To meet these conditions, Pantaenus, about 180 A.D., started the first of the catechetical schools and the movement soon spread into Italy, Greece, and Asia Minor.

The *nature* of the institution at first was more nearly like that of a Bible chair adjacent to the campus of a state university, than anything else we have today. The work often started in the home of the teacher without any institutional or financial backing. Gradually it expanded into the proportions of a theological college including a faculty and a course of study. The teaching, however, proceeded from the point of view of Greek philosophy rather than that of the Bible, and therefore failed to present a pure form of Christianity. It was claimed that philosophy was "a pedagog to lead us to Christ." In their efforts to present Christianity in such a way as to appeal to cultured pagans, they compromised it.

The *constituency* was a somewhat mixed group. Both men and women were admitted, and elementary as well as advanced students included. Some were new converts taking studies preparatory to church membership. They also prepared themselves to meet the subtle attacks of Greek skeptics. Others were idolaters investigating the light of Christianity with a view to the possibility of adopting it.

Still others were prospective religious leaders preparing for Christian service. In this way the institution came to be a sort of theological university, covering both secular and religious subjects.

Although they did not present pure Christianity, the *results* of these schools were outstanding. They helped to meet Greek philosophy on its own ground and thus to stem the tide of materialism and skepticism. Also, the leaders such as Clement and Origen led in shaping the theological formulation of Christianity even though they did cast it in a philosophical mould of thought. These schools served as missionary centers for helping to transform a pagan empire. "Alexandria became the brains of Christendom."

MONASTIC AND CATHEDRAL SCHOOLS

Pagan schools so degenerated that they were closed by official decree in 529 A.D., thus leaving religious schools in possession of the field. In the meantime Catholicism had been developing and with it different systems of education.

Monastic Schools.—These schools got their main impetus from the Benedictine order which largely shaped education from the sixth to the ninth centuries as their institutions spread throughout Europe.

There were three *means* of monastic education. One was through the copying of manuscripts for exchange between the monasteries in building up their libraries. It was a required part of the activity and as the work was done, those doing it naturally learned a great deal about the important documents copied.

Another means of education was reading. When not busy with other things, the monks were required to read. This included two or more hours per day with additional time on Sunday and during Lent. They had reading even during meals.

Formal study was of course the most effective educational method. School systems were developed which became the most effective of their day and were a great influence in the life of the times.

The *scope* of instruction in the schools was broad. There were the elementary grades composed both of children designated for the religious life and of those who came in from the outside for daily instruction.

Then there were secondary grades, in which were taught more advanced subjects including religion as well as the seven liberal arts. These were for outsiders and those who were in training for the order.

Finally came the specialized or vocational training for those who planned to be monks. Here special emphasis was given to the Bible, doctrines, church decrees, prayer and music. For them, it was essentially a theological seminary. Attention was also given to the practical arts.

The *accomplishments* of monastic schools were far-reaching. In these institutions located in out-of-the-way places, there were preserved from the barbarian invaders the choice manuscripts including the Bible, sermons, other religious materials, and the Greek and Roman classics. Also in addition to training a monastic religious leadership they gave general training to the future princes, kings and other leaders of Europe, and through them gave a religious and moral coloring to European life for generations.

Cathedral Schools.—Although not as prominent as monastic schools, the cathedral or bishops' schools played an important part in the educational life of the times.

Their *origin* was due in part to the decline of cathechetical schools and the need for some kind of school to take their place. The development of churches in large centers together with the sending out of workers from these to the surrounding communities also seemed to call for special training agencies. And, too, the distance between monastic schools made it needful to have other schools more readily accessible. All these conditions contributed to the development of the cathedral schools.

Their *activities* were distinctively religious, probably more exclusively so than monastic schools. They were primarily vocational and intended for the training of the secular clergy as the monasteries were for the training of the religious. Likewise, the curriculum being more definitely religious and moral, was better fitted for religious leadership. However, as time went on they broadened their activities to include other than religious leaders thus placing stress on the rudiments of learning as involved in elementary education and the liberal arts which were characteristic of secondary education.

The *results* of these schools seemed to justify amply what was put into them. Through their development of elementary and secondary education, they came to be, in a measure, the fore-runner of the public schools of Western Europe, at least more so than did the monasteries. Likewise, they developed more than did the latter institutions, the spirit of free inquiry and discussion which helped to pave the way for the Renaissance and the Reformation. From these schools came some of the greatest thinkers of the day in the realm of religion; men like Abelard, for example. The movement for universities developed more from these schools than it did from the monasteries.

MEDIAEVAL UNIVERSITIES

By the time of the Reformation, universities had grown up over a wide area and were exerting a tremendous influence over the religious life of the times. As a matter of fact, they were one of the leading forces causing the Reformation.

Rise.—Several forces converged to bring about universities toward the close of the mediaeval period. One was the influence of commerce and travel which broadened contacts and stimulated thought. Particularly was this true with the Crusades which brought into contact the Mohammedan learning with that of the East. Another was the stimulus brought about by the rise of the professional spirit. In fact, the universities usually specialized in some one of the vocations such as law, medicine or theology. Still another influence was the Cathedral school with its spirit of free thinking. In fact, some of these schools grew into universities.

Among the outstanding schools were Bologna, specializing in law; Salerna, emphasizing medicine; Paris, stressing theology; also Oxford, Cambridge, and Heidelberg. They had such outstanding teachers as Abelard, Roger Bacon, and Thomas Aquinas.

Activities.—These universities attracted large numbers of students from their own and surrounding countries. The students often lived in communities, carried on their studies and exercised quite an influence over both the schools and the towns where they were located. The course of study included the seven liberal arts and in addition, law, medicine, and theology. Emphasis was given to preparation for teaching. Much of the instruction was in Latin and by the lecture method. Debates were engaged in frequently.

The school life was related to religion in several ways. The majority of schools were chartered by the Pope and therefore had an obligation to foster the church. Some of them were a development from church schools and the others had some theology in the curriculum. Most of the teachers were outstanding church men who permeated their teaching with religion. Mediaeval universities were, therefore, primarily Christian.

Achievements.—These schools did much for moral and religious progress. For one thing, they stimulated *inquiry* and freedom. The investigative spirit was much more evident than it was in monasteries. Monarchs listened to what the students had to say thus making the students influential to some degree along with the nobility and the clergy. This contributed to democracy and progress.

More significant, however, was the fact that they produced great *thinkers* and leaders who were independent and progressive in their activities. Among them were men like Dante, Wycliffe, Copernicus, Newton, Luther and Calvin. These men through their translating, teaching, and writing, helped to usher in the Renaissance and the Reformation. But for the universities, these movements might have been atheistic instead of religious.

THE REFORMATION

The Reformation was one of the outstanding examples of the effectiveness of education in moral and religious activity. It is, in fact, one of the strongest apologetics for the value of religious education as a means of social progress.

Growth.—The *beginning* of the movement which we ordinarily call the revival of learning, or Renaissance, started in Southern Europe as a literary reform. In Italy in the early part of the fourteenth century, under the influence of Dante and others, the study of the Latin classics was revived. As the movement spread northward into France, Germany and Holland, Hebrew and Greek were added to the studies and it took on more of a religious nature. In England, Wycliffe translated the Bible and the Lollards popularized its study. These activities were preliminary to the religious revival.

The *development* of the Reformation proper came under the leadership of Luther in Germany. After studying and translating the Bible, he broke with the Catholic Church, opposed its teachings and practices, and precipitated a crisis. Almost simultaneously in Switzerland, Zwingli led in an emphasis on New Testament religion and in an opposition to Catholicism. His work was followed by that of Calvin who consummated the movement and whose theological treatises have greatly shaped Christian thinking since that time. In England, Henry VIII broke with Rome and established the Anglican church, and the Puritans carried forward the reforms. Other countries in Europe took up the crusade and the influence spread even to America.

Causes.—The *schools* stand out prominently among the originating forces leading to the Reformation. Both Cathedral schools and universities played a large part. The free-thinking spirit and investigative attitude of teachers like Abelard went a long way in preparing a favorable atmosphere. The study of Hebrew and Greek helped much.

Another contributing influence was *popular Bible study*. Wycliffe's translation of the Bible in England and the Lollards' teaching it throughout the country gave a new vision. Luther's translation of the Bible in Germany and his popular presentation of its doctrines, as opposed to those taught by the Catholic church, created ideals and public sentiment. People were taught to read in order that they might read the Bible.

Other literature helped greatly to bring on the Reformation. Luther published in pamphlet form an address delivered to the nobles and in five days 5,000 were sold. His ninety-five theses nailed publicly on the door of the church at Wittenberg with the explanations and discussions growing out of them served in shaping public opinion. Calvin and other leaders carried on similar educational activities all of which helped to determine the movement.

Results.—The Reformation led to the instituting of extensive educational activities in the various countries where it spread. These were soon seen to be necessary if the movement was to be other than merely a temporary reform.

Strong emphasis was given to the establishment of *school systems*. Public education today is in a measure the ultimate outcome of the emphasis of Reformation leaders on education. Luther wrote the mayors of the cities of Germany: "There is no other outward offence that in the sight of God so heavily burdens the world, and deserves such heavy chastisement as the neglect to educate children." Also he said: "Next to the ministry, it (the office of school-teacher) is the most useful, greatest and best: and I am not sure which of the two is to be preferred."[1] Others made similar emphases and strong Protestant school systems were established in Germany, Switzerland, England and elsewhere.

Educational literature likewise resulted. Luther prepared a "Short Catechism" and a "Large Catechism." Zwingli wrote a treatise on *The Christian Education of Youth*. Calvin produced his famous *Institutes*. More than a score of religious texts of the nature of catechisms and handbooks appeared in a little over a decade. Some of the books were even illustrated. Portions of the Bible were printed separately. Even elementary treatises in psychology and pedagogy appeared. The Reformation not only was initiated by educational

---

[1] Painter, F. V. N., *Luther on Education*, pp. 131, 143 (Concordia Publishing House, St. Louis, 1928).

means and carried on through educational procedures, but also resulted in the establishment and perpetuation of educational systems.

CATHOLIC EDUCATION

As the Reformation progressed and the Catholics saw what was
being accomplished by educational means, they set out to counteract
it. Schools under Protestant control were condemned and Catholic
schools instituted. In other words, Protestants and Catholics fought
each other with rival school systems. This activity has been termed
the Counter-Reformation.

Jesuit Schools.—The *organization* of Jesuits founded by Loyola
in 1534 operated in the field of secondary and collegiate education.
Somewhat military in form, it is headed by a general, with a graded
system of officers over provinces, individual schools, and groups
within the schools. Discipline stands out prominently in the system.
It has been characterized as a "Catholic Salvation Army." In forty
years it spread over the world and still carries on.

The *aim* is "All for God's greater glory" and the educational
activity leads definitely in that direction. The aim all along has been
to train the leaders rather than the masses and thus shape civilization. The priests take the three-fold vow of poverty, chastity, and
obedience and devote their lives with missionary zeal to Christian
education. They stand ready to go anywhere at any time at the
superior officer's command, to train both those preparing for the
order and those planning to go out into other activities.

The *studies* include the work of the lower school with a five or
six year course largely literary in nature, and an upper school running seven to nine years emphasizing theological studies. A "system
of studies" was worked out in 1599 to guide even in the most minute
details of activity and it has been changed very little even to the
present time. Latin has been the prevailing language used. Reviews
and drills are frequent, emulation is stressed, and discipline is severe.

The *results* have been significant. The Jesuits have been a power.
Their effectiveness has been outstanding among school systems. For
three centuries they trained most of the leaders of Europe. They
carry on effectively throughout the world today. Painter says: "A
more formidable foe never faced Protestantism!"[2] And Quick concludes: "Since the Revival of Learning no body of men has played
so prominent a part in education as the Jesuits."[3]

[2] *History of Education,* p. 167 (D. Appleton and Co., New York, 1896).
[3] *Educational Reformers,* p. 33 (C. W. Bardeen, Publisher, Syracuse, 1896).

Parish Schools.—The *rise* of these schools is observable through a considerable period of time. They originated long before the Reformation, received a new emphasis in the Counter-Reformation, and have had an extended history both in Europe and America. From time to time church councils authorized their establishment and decreed that pupils be required to attend. Finally they were attached to almost every church, attended by millions of pupils, and constitute one of the significant educational systems—Catholicism's right arm.

The *philosophy* underlying the system is the belief that religion is promoted more effectively in childhood than later and by the educational rather than the inspirational method. They believe, furthermore, that it must permeate all of education rather than be tacked on to an educational system secular in nature. "That philosophy is false which attempts to . . . . . instruct the mind of the child in geography and grammar and reading and history . . . . . and keeps God outside of it."[4]

The *characteristics* of these schools are distinctive. They are for the pupils of a church or parish, are supported by the church and free to the pupils. They usually include the elementary grades only. The religious, and particularly the Catholic elements in geography, reading, history, civics, literature and other subjects are definitely emphasized. In addition a period is given each day in definite instruction in religion with graded catechisms. Additional time is given to prayer and religious exercises. Thus "the cure of souls" is central in the entire system.

Significant *results* have been achieved. By means of these schools primarily—since little attention is given to Sunday schools or to mass evangelism—the Catholics have been able to hold their ground in a time when the entire trend of the times has been away from their autocratic and authoritative system. They have also succeeded in making new inroads particularly among negroes and foreigners. These results are due not to superiority in doctrines but rather to their capture of childhood through the educational method. In this we may well learn from them.

THE SUNDAY SCHOOL MOVEMENT

Probably the most far-reaching educational activity in the field of religion since the Reformation is the Sunday school movement. It has

[4] Curley, Archbishop, *The Church and Education,* p. 7 (National Catholic Welfare Conference, Washington).

reached the largest number of people of any religious-educational organization, and in the most many-sided ways.

Beginnings.—Prior to Robert Raikes there were many individual activities, yet it remained for his efforts to give real impetus to the movement. Raikes was a printer in Gloucester, England, and for some time had been interested in moral reform. Going one day into a poor section of the city called "Sooty Alley" to hire help, he was struck by the miserable condition of the children. He saw their needs and set out to remedy the situation. In July 1780 he hired some women at a shilling a day each to gather the children into one of the homes and teach them for about two hours in the morning and about three in the afternoon, and in addition take them to church for preaching. They learned to read and studied the Bible, catechisms and other materials. It was not a Sunday school as we now know it but did great good and transformed the community.

Growth.—Raikes published the result of his activities in his paper the *Gloucester Journal*, arousing great interest. Many schools were started as a result. For a while there was opposition to the movement, but as prominent people, including the Queen, became interested, it spread rapidly over a wide area. Promotional organizations and publishing houses were started to aid the cause. The movement spread from children to adults, poor to rich, city to country, and to other nations.

In the New England and Middle colonies of the United States schools were started early, and local organizations formed to promote the work. Later the American Sunday School Union was organized and sent missionaries into the South and West to establish schools. Gradually our denominational agencies were established, more extensive promotion was carried on and great numbers enlisted, until today the Sunday school has come to have the largest attendance of any service of the church. There are over a third of a million schools and more than thirty million pupils enrolled.

Improvements.—As Sunday schools grew in numbers they improved in *quality*. From an unorganized institution it has grown into a well-graded and departmentalized one. Beginning with no text-books it now has a variety of them for all ages. With no meeting place at first, it now has splendidly equipped buildings for classes as well as departments. Training course materials covering a wide range of subjects have been prepared. Standards have been set up, and definite aims worked out.

It has developed extensively in its *activities*. Originally teaching was the main function. Now it has come to include worship as a regular weekly activity. In many churches it is used as the main agency for developing in giving. Evangelism and service have become important parts of its work. In short, almost every church function is carried on through the Sunday school. This is a far reach beyond the beginnings under Raikes.

Achievements.—It would be impossible to catalogue the achievements of this religious-educational organization. In *enlistment* it has brought untold members into touch with the life of the church. In fact the Sunday school has come to be the church's main outreaching agency.

In *character growth* it has been most powerful. Most of those converted are through its instrumentality. Worshipful attitudes are cultivated most effectively through its departmental programs and stewardship is likely getting its best development through the Sunday school.

As an agency for *moral reform* it is accomplishing more than Raikes ever dreamed of or most of us even now realize. One prominent daily paper in America stated in an editorial that the Sunday school is the greatest antidote for crime. Prohibition was largely won through its teaching on temperance.

Furthermore the Sunday school has contributed much to the *development* of its workers. It uses more workers than any other church agency, gives them a manifold activity and thus furnishes laboratory training in Christian life and service.

Other Religious Education Agencies

Since the beginning of the Sunday school movement, developments in the field of religious education have been rapid. Many agencies have sprung into being, especially in recent years. We can here discuss only a few of them and each rather briefly at that, leaving out entirely the Pietists, Moravian, Brothers of the Christian Schools and others.

Christian Colleges.—Many of those who led in settling our country held degrees from Oxford and Cambridge, some even the M. A. degree. The ministers especially were college men. Soon after arriving, the fear arose that there would be left an illiterate ministry "when our present ministers shall lie in the dust." So Harvard was founded in 1636 to train them and to "educate Indian and American youth in knowledge and godliness." Following this came the establishment of Yale, Princeton, Brown, and others. All except one founded before the Revolution were Christian and even it had the Bible in its curriculum.

Since the Revolution most of the major denominations have established academies and junior and senior colleges for training religious leaders and christianizing the community. Methodists have established such institutions as Boston University, Northwestern University, University of Southern California, Duke University, Emory University and Southern Methodist University. Northern Baptists founded the University of Rochester, University of Chicago, and the University of Redlands; and Southern Baptists the University of Richmond, Mercer University, Baylor University, and others. Other denominations have done likewise. These institutions have been effective missionary agencies in influencing lives for Christ. They have served also as leavening influences in the field of higher education, and they have trained an effective religious leadership for the home and foreign lands. Without them the kingdom of God would have suffered irretrievably.

Training Organizations.—Since the middle of the past century individual churches here and there had young people's meetings for prayer, temperance study, and missionary activity but the Young People's movement did not begin until 1881. In that year Rev. Francis E. Clark started in his church at Portland, Maine, an organization to help young people "pray and read the Bible every day" and "endeavor to lead the Christian life." Reports of it were published in religious papers and the movement, taking the name of Christian Endeavor, began to spread throughout the nation, into Canada and around the world. It is interdenominational in nature.

As the various denominations observed its activity they became interested in establishing organizations of their own. As a result, the Epworth League was established by the Methodists in 1889, the Baptist Young People's Union of America in 1891, and in 1896 Southern Baptists officially launched the B. Y. P. U. which later on took the name of Baptist Training Union. Lutherans, Episcopalians, Catholics, Jews and others have formed somewhat similar organizations. These young people's societies have capitalized on youth leadership and expressional activities, and have done much to develop young church members in prayer, Bible study, temperance, missions and service. Especially have they created spiritual morale through their assemblies and conventions.

Vacation Schools.—One of the moral hazards of our times, particularly in the cities, is created each year when hosts of boys and girls are released by the public schools for the vacation season. Realizing this, various organizations in different cities have sought for many years to sponsor some sort of summer activity for them. Not until 1901, however, did a definite movement get started. In that year Rev. R. G. Boville, Executive Secretary of New York City Baptist Missionary Society, having observed the school of Rev. H. L. Jones which had operated for three summers previously, began to promote the work in the city. Later he gave his entire time to this work, making it interdenominational and international in scope.

Gradually the different denominations took it up as a distinct part of their own programs. Presbyterians were first, beginning their activities in 1910; Northern Baptists were next in 1915, and Southern Baptists third in 1923. Methodists, Disciples, Congregationalists and others have fostered vacation schools. These schools running from two to four weeks in the summer, with no textbooks or examinations, and with much stress on hand-craft, recreation, and dramatics have been powerful agencies in counteracting the temptations of vacation periods by giving wholesome instruction and building moral character.

Week-day Schools.—Closely related to the vacation church school is the week-day church school. While the former operates only during the summer the latter carries on through the school year. It has grown up out of the secularization of public education to supply the deficiency through more extended instruction and closer correlation with the public schools. Some efforts have included all grades but the trend is toward the high school grades only, with the teaching done by the churches either separately or together, and time given and credit allowed by the schools. Gary, Indiana, gave impetus to the movement in 1914. It has spread widely through the nation and done much to put the missing "r" (religion) into education.

Similarly there has developed a movement to provide religious instruction for students in state universities, agricultural schools, and teachers colleges. This is done by denominations separately or jointly. It began as early as 1893 at the University of Michigan, but most of the development, especially in the South, has come during the last ten or twenty years. As the proportion of students in denominational schools decreases, and that in state schools increases, it bids fair to become one of our most far-reaching and effective educational activities.

Missionary Education.—Women have taken the lead in this. Prior to the Civil War little interdenominational activity had been carried on. Following that conflict came organizations for training in missions by the Congregationalists, Methodists, Northern Baptists and others. The Woman's Missionary Union of Southern Baptists was officially launched in 1888, with organizations, graded materials, and programs of activity for the various age groups. These agencies have done more than any others among us to put the missionary emphasis into religious education.

Starting in 1906 as an interdenominational movement, laymen organized to develop more effectively fraternal life, stewardship ideals, and the missionary spirit among the men of the churches. The Southern Baptist Laymen's Missionary Movement was launched in 1907, and in 1926 it was changed to the Baptist Brotherhood. It has helped considerably in giving religious morale to men.

Similar in purpose to the above organizations is the Church School of Missions started in 1923 which seeks to give vision and interest in missions to every one in the church through special training classes for a week or so, for all age groups and both sexes, with texts adapted to all groups.

From this brief survey of achievements in the field of religious education by the various agencies during the period of Christian history, it is easy to see that education has played a large part in the development of Christianity throughout the centuries. Progress in missionary achievement, moral reform, and church growth have come largely because of the emphasis placed on the educational method. These developments illustrate and verify the striking statement of Benjamin Kidd: "Give us the young and we will create a new mind and a new earth in a single generation."[5] And they constitute a tremendous challenge for the future.

[5] *The Science of Power*, p. 309 (G. P. Putnam's Sons, New York, 1918).

CHAPTER V

DEMANDS OF MODERN SOCIAL CONDITIONS

The example of educational activities in the Bible, and the inspiration of achievements in the course of Christian history are not the only incentives that we have to carry on religious education today. These are positive and emphatic. But there are negative emphases just as strong. They come to us from the challenge of unsolved problems in our present social order which we must face more seriously than before if we are to clear up the present chaotic conditions.

PHYSICAL TEMPTATIONS

Some of our most serious problems pertain to the physical life, and must be confronted by each individual. While trying our best to eradicate them from society, we must at the same time prepare our youth to face them individually and not be overcome by them.

Tobacco.—Within recent years the widespread use of tobacco particularly in the form of the cigarette has become a problem. Especially is this situation accentuated since women have begun to smoke. We are told that the increase in cigarette consumption has been 900 per cent since 1915, having reached a total of 162 billions a year. It is said that 60 per cent of men now smoke, averaging 20 cigarettes per day each, and 20 per cent of women, averaging 11 per day.

Seemingly it is a rather harmless habit. But when we remember that the nicotine in one cigarette if concentrated and taken would kill a person, and that there is in addition carbon monoxide gas, acrolein used in poison gas, marsh gas or fire dam, formaldehyde used in preserving specimens, and furfural which is fifty times more poisonous than alcohol, we can see that there is some reason for calling the cigarette a "coffin nail." It is recognized that tobacco affects the stomach and its activities, the heart and blood vessels, the lungs, and the nervous system. It is proverbial that regular tobacco users are unable to resist disease or stand an operation as well as those who do not use it. And the offspring of tobacco users are affected.

Although there is no natural appetite for tobacco, the high-powered advertising in papers, on bill-boards and over the radio; the natural

64

desire for thrills and appearances; and the influence of social pressure have helped to cause the alarming increase. In 1935 five American cigarette companies spent $30,000,000 in advertising. The propaganda is definitely educational, one state university reporting that every student received a free carton of fifty cigarettes. Some students have made their way through school by distributing cigarettes.

Liquor.—The use of alcohol as a beverage in the various forms of beer, wine and whiskey has increased in alarming proportions in recent years. The drink bill in 1937 was $5,000,000,000, or more than a ninth as much as our national debt. Arrests for drunkenness increased more than 100 per cent from 1932 to 1937, and convictions for drunken driving increased nearly 75 per cent in the same period. In 1936 girls employed in liquor-serving establishments numbered 1,350,000, or twice as many as are attending college.

Without going into details as to results it is enough to say that alcohol affects the stomach and liver, tending to preserve rather than aid the digestion of foods; the heart and blood vessels, contributing to Bright's disease and pneumonia; and the brain and nervous system, resulting ultimately in local paralysis and dementia. It handicaps perception and the higher mental processes, and contributes to immorality and to crime. Drunkards are never good life insurance risks nor safe subjects for operations.

While there is probably no natural appetite for liquor, one may soon be acquired. The accessibility and respectability given to liquor by the sale of it in grocery and drug stores, the influence of the crowds, and the widespread and pleasing publicity given to it, have greatly increased drinking. In 1936 in newspapers alone $562,000,000 were spent in advertising liquor. The strongest kind of educational propaganda especially aimed at youth, and utilizing the shrewdest sort of psychology, has been carried on.

Immorality.—Another serious personal problem faced today, especially by youth, is that of immorality. It was serious in biblical times and has been ever since. All races, ages, and sexes are affected by it. From almost any community tragic instances within recent months could be mentioned. In one grammar school fifteen children between the ages of nine and twelve were found to be immoral. Immorality is an evil "clutching this very minute at the throat of the nation," according to a prominent physician.

Immorality affects every phase of the life of the social order. Physically the very blood stream of the nation is affected. Five per cent of the American people are said to have syphilis, ten per cent gonorrhea, and to make bad matters worse the second generation also suffers the consequences. Socially the harm is greater still. Each year 50,000 unmarried mothers are registered in the United States, and 10,000 girls and young women lose their lives from abortion.[1] Figures alone cannot begin to give the whole story of blighted lives and anguished spirits.

Here again a type of educational publicity has greatly accentuated the problem. To be sure, the instinctive drive serves as a powerful stimulus. But this has been augmented a great deal by movies portraying the unnatural relation of the sexes, by magazines with stories making much of the sex appeal, and by books which capitalize on sex. Sex appeal has come to be used in advertising almost every kind of commodity. And of course saloons and dance halls have played their part.

But what bearing on religious education have all these problems of tobacco, liquor, and immorality? If all of these evils are increasing in alarming proportions, then the people at large need to know about it, and those interested mainly in the moral aspect of education are responsible for giving out the information. If the effects produced are detrimental to the physical and moral life of the people, then these results also need to be put before the people, and those primarily interested in moral problems are the main ones to do it. And if these problems have gained their footing mainly by means of educational propaganda carried on among the young, then it is high time that religious education create a counter-system of propaganda to stem the tide. In other words the present situation constitutes a tremendous challenge to religious leaders of youth to bring up a generation who will use their bodies to the glory of God.

RECREATIONAL ACTIVITIES

Closely related to the personal problems just discussed are certain recreational activities. They are very largely personal, though fostered by financially-interested people, who are more concerned with cash than with character.

The Motion Picture.—The motion picture business is now a major industry in the United States. Tremendous sums of money are invested in the big companies which foster it and it has become our most popular institution. Because of its dramatic features, its appeal to natural interests, its availability, and its inexpensiveness,

[1] See the *Readers Digest* for August, 1937.

the motion picture has come to be the most patronized institution in America. It is said that around 88,000,000 people attend weekly the 16,000 theaters in the United States. This is three times as many people as attend public schools and colleges, or churches. The motion picture is indeed the people's university.

The institution is by no means all bad. There are many valuable educational features, particularly of a geographical or historical nature. Also there are many wholesome amusement elements which furnish relaxation to tired nerves and bothered minds. But along with these features there are many harmful elements. In the first place the movie industry generally disregards the Sabbath, even lobbying at legislatures to keep the day open. Also they foster bank night or buck night, both of which are forms of gambling. Worse still, they stimulate immorality and crime through the things portrayed on the screen. A study of one hundred thirty-three pictures revealed seduction, adultery, and other immoral features in one hundred seven, and murder, gangster activities and other lawlessness in eighty-one!

The Dance Hall.—In recent years the commercialized dance hall has become a serious problem. Shorter working hours have given more leisure time, and good roads and automobiles have eliminated distances, so that in addition to the halls in cities, dancing places have sprung up generally out in the country—often at out-of-the-way places. In many instances high-school gymnasiums are used for dancing and the activity becomes an official affair. A study of one high school revealed that young people often learn dancing at school functions, and then patronize the commercialized places. Countless numbers of young people attend these places throughout the land.

While many good people patronize these institutions, the influence is generally bad. This is true for various reasons. For one thing the dance itself is inclined to stimulate the passions. One cannot engage in the embrace involved and not have the sex instinct strongly aroused. Henry W. Stough has well said: "What is ethically wrong *off* the dance floor is not ethically right *on* the dance floor and music and motion cannot alter this principle."[2] Also the association is usually bad, these halls often being adjacent to a drinking place, if not a house of ill fame. Even if one is not personally harmed, his influence in Christian service is compromised when he patronizes such places.

[2] *Across the Dead Line of Amusements,* p. 114 (Fleming H. Revell Co., New York, 1912).

Games of Chance.—Games of chance involve the recreational and quite a bit more. In recent years the gambling spirit has spread even to children as new forms of activity have come into being. A growing practice which borders on the gambling spirit is the advertising activity of business concerns and picture shows, with their punch boards, drawings and similar methods which constitute a sort of kindergarten in gambling. Beyond these are the slot machines, marble boards and other games of chance. In addition there is card-playing and dice-throwing for gain. Betting on horse races, and various kinds of raffles and lotteries which are sometimes national in scope, can also be included.

All of these develop the gambling spirit or the desire to get something for nothing. The fundamental principle of life is to earn our living by the sweat of our brow or give value received for whatever we get. Games of chance violate this principle. In fact much of the social security emphasis does the same thing and appeals to the spirit of selfishness in man. Furthermore, gambling in its purest form develops the attitude of getting not only at the expense of, but also to the hurt of, the other fellow because in a lottery involving one hundred people, if one gains, ninety-nine must lose. This is positively sinful.

As we think of movies, dances, and games of chance, the question emerges again—what can religious education do about them? At least three things. One is to develop in the coming generation the kind of ideals and attitudes which will cause them to participate only in the things that will neither harm their lives nor cripple their influence for doing good. Another is to lead them not to participate even in legitimate amusements at the expense either in time or money of things more valuable. And a third is to create in them a desire to eliminate from society those amusements that are harmful to Christian character. These things may be done by the Christian teachers in our homes, churches, and schools.

Educational Developments

Turning from a somewhat negative to a more positive problem, we come to education. Probably the outstanding recent development in America has been its educational system. It has been the major emphasis during the past third of a century. We have come to depend upon education much more than upon government. In many ways it offers a challenge to religious education.

Accessibility.—There was a time when school houses were few and far between, often in out-of-the-way places and with roads approaching them none too good. The writer remembers walking regularly nearly a mile and a half to school along a branch bottom with frequent crossings and through a muddy lane that more than once pulled his "Brogan" shoes off. Sometimes pupils had to go three or four miles. Now there are more schools, at points more nearly central, and for the most part on good highways. Besides, buses operate in many rural and village sections, enabling pupils to get to school easily. Especially is this true of Junior and Senior high school students.

Attendance.—Growing out of the greater accessibility of schools and also their compulsory attendance laws, many *more people* are now in schools. From 1880 to 1930—a period of half a century—attendance in elementary schools increased from 10,000,000 to 25,000,000, and in high schools from 100,000 to 5,000,000. In forty years college attendance grew from 60,000 to 1,350,000. It has been said that one person out of every four in the nation gives his time daily to study or teaching.

Not only do more people attend school, but they attend for a *greater length of time*. Fifty years ago many schools ran only three to five months, and the average aggregate attendance was 582 days, or the equivalent of third grade education. Now they run seven to ten school months, and the average attendance is over 1200 hours all together, or the equivalent of a sixth grade education.

Efficiency.—Not only are there more schools and more people attending them, but they are also much more efficient. For one thing the *equipment* is much better. The writer's father attended school in a log house with split logs for seats, a dirt floor, open window, and fire place. Now one finds a school building like the Phillips High in Birmingham, Ala., occupying an entire block, three stories and a basement in height, with auditorium, class rooms, laboratories, cafeteria, and provisions for teaching not only the regular literary studies but also all phases of domestic science, mechanical arts, business, photography, journalism and other special lines. Provision is made now for elementary schools, junior and senior high schools, and in cities for junior and senior colleges.

The *curriculum* has broadened from the "three r's" to include all phases of literary studies, together with practical and vocational training. The course of study in the modern high school is in many cases beyond that of the college fifty years ago, and in some cases probably equivalent to an M.A. degree then. And the end is not yet in sight, for constant improvement is being made especially in the direction of projects and creative learning. Wide ranges of specialization are developing.

Furthermore, *teaching standards* have improved. A generation ago one could teach school by making an average of 65 per cent on a special county examination with no grade below 50 per cent, whether he had ever gone to school a day in his life or not. Now one must be a graduate from high school at least, usually from junior college, and frequently from a senior college before teaching school. And enough courses must be taken in the field of education to assure familiarity with pupil life and modern methods.

Results.—If we look at some of the results of modern education the scene is both striking and challenging. For one thing the *knowledge of the outside world* has been greatly extended since the beginning of the century. Through the microscope and the telescope man has greatly broadened his view of the universe, and this understanding constitutes a real problem unless his knowledge of God has grown at the same time. Otherwise there is a strain on the individual's faith. Powhatan James has well said: "Science must draw from religion those principles of reverence, and honesty and sincerity, and even faith, without which it cannot succeed in its task."[3] Without such, the developments in science may prove a curse rather than a blessing.

But the *knowledge of the world within* has been just as amazing. The study of psychology has revealed much knowledge of human life and the understanding of sex and the mysteries of life has made a new problem morally. Junior high school pupils know more about those matters today than their grandparents did a generation or so ago. But what direction will such knowledge take? Will it uplift or degrade human life? To say the least, it constitutes a strain on the power of self-control. The outcome seems to depend on other forces than those inherent in the school system itself.

As Christian citizens we cannot face the tremendous developments in the field of secular education, whether from the standpoint of provisions made, numbers taught, or results achieved, without being aware of the fact that we have not made corresponding developments in the field of religious education. If we are to match the developments made, we must reach more people, have them a longer time, provide better equipment, have a more nearly adequate curriculum,

[3] *Reasons for Christian Education*, p. 153 (Texas Baptist Education Board, Waco, 1915).

and do more efficient work than we have thus far done. Nothing less than this will enable us to challenge American youth, provide adequately the fourth "r" in education, and so Christianize thinking as to cause students to maintain their faith in God and power of self-control in an era of widened knowledge.

DOMESTIC ISSUES

Prominent on the horizon of social problems today are those that have to do with the home. In many respects the most serious issues center here, for as it goes, so goes civilization. Society can never rise much above the standards of the home. And all thinking people recognize that the life of the American home is seriously endangered.

Marriage.—Too frequently when this topic is mentioned the response is laughter. It is not looked upon as serious enough to merit thoughtful consideration. Yet more serious errors are made in the matter of selecting a life companion than in almost anything else. One needs only to observe any community for only a few years to be convinced of this fact. Too often young people marry on the spur of the moment after only a brief acquaintance, and with little or no opportunity to study the background and characteristics of each other's life. Too often marriage is the outcome of mere passion or a dare rather than true love and thoughtful consideration. As a result many people are mismated and much anguish and sorrow is likely to follow in the wake of these tragic and fateful experiences.

Divorce.—Growing out of mismating in marriage, and undeveloped or unadjusted personalities, is the divorce problem. There are now nearly a quarter of a million divorces annually, an increase of over 1500 per cent in half a century, which is about five times that of the population. Our nation now leads the world in divorces. A third of a century ago only one out of every twelve marriages ended in divorce. Now it is one of every six, in some states one of every five, and in some counties twice that ratio. If this same ratio of increase continues, divorces will balance marriages by the end of the century. Instead of the single ground recognized by Christ—that of adultery— there are now more than fifty. And in one or two states a residence of only sixty days qualifies one for a divorce. Without question it is one of our major social evils.

Parenthood.—Much that has been written in recent years relative to marriage has stressed birth control and trial marriage rather than parenthood. Consequently, the attention and emphasis have been turned away from the parental idea. Marriage has been looked upon as a sort of permanent holiday affair and the emphasis has been more on the physical rather than the spiritual side. The reading of questions propounded and answered by the daily columnists, as well as divorce court proceedings, is evidence of this fact. There is need for a new stress on the possibilities and advantages of parenthood today. For it has tremendous values for the parent as well as for the race. Says Harry E. Fosdick: "What nature is getting at is not the pleasure of the path but the goal of children, and anybody who makes it his principle of action to steal the gratification of nature's lure without fulfilling nature's purpose is committing a psychological theft on which nature wreaks inevitable vengeance."[4]

In relation to marriage, divorce, and parenthood, religious education has a large part to play. For one thing we need an educational emphasis both to counteract the wrong ideals and to build up wholesome ones. To this end there is an opportunity in the curricula of the various educational organizations in our church, for such discussions along these lines as will give the youth of the land the biblical concept of marriage, divorce, and parental responsibilities. Also pastors may give helpful discourses from the pulpit on these topics. And our Christian colleges should offer courses to prepare for this phase of life. Fortunately, we are beginning to have some helpful studies in this field.

Not only should instruction be given to guide individuals away from the wrong ideals and into the right ones, but such teaching should be given as will also help to crystallize public sentiment so as ultimately to issue in legislation that will make it easier for youth to go right in these matters. Particularly is there a need for tightening up the laws on the conditions for marriage, such as minimum age, public notice, and medical examination. We also need stricter laws relative to the grounds and conditions under which divorces may be granted. These laws would need national uniformity to protect states that do try to be strict. These results will come through religious education.

ECONOMIC PROBLEMS

It would not require any argument, especially during the past few years, to convince even the most skeptical that things are seriously wrong with our economic order. The nerve connecting with the pocket-book is a very tender one. The needs are evident, though

---

[4] Quoted by E. T. Dahlberg in *Youth and the Homes of Tomorrow*, p. 94 (The Judson Press, Philadelphia, 1935).

the cause and the cure may not be so clear, and many may not connect the problem with character.

Capital.—The modern machine age, together with the concentrating of the population in cities, has helped to bring about a situation favorable to the rise of big business. Economy in production and distribution has also helped, for people always want bargains. As a result tremendous business concerns controlling multiplied millions of wealth have sprung up. This is one of the most significant facts of modern society. It has resulted in a number of ills. Among them are freezing out the small competitors, keeping down the price to the producer, raising it unduly for the consumer, long hours and low pay for labor, and big profits for capital—sometimes more than 1000 per cent. Added to these problems in recent days has been the displacement of hordes of laborers through the use of machinery. The final outcome has been serious economic maladjustment with bitter feeling and suffering. Professor Ross was entirely right in saying: "The master iniquities of our time are connected with money making."[5]

Labor.—With the rise of capital has been that of organized labor. In fact labor practically had to organize in order to protect itself from the evils just mentioned, especially bad working conditions, long hours, and low wages. Organized labor sprang up alongside organized capital—an organized labor which met and solved many of the problems. But as it began to have power and realize its strength it seemed to forget the evils done to it, and to retaliate in return. Consequently we have had extreme demands for high wages and few hours, an unfair protection of inefficient union laborers, violence during strikes to those who were not members, and "picketing" of concerns who chose to employ non-union labor. Organized labor can be as heartless as organized capital. Much bitterness of feeling and lack of Christian consideration have been shown, manufacturing concerns have been unduly interfered with, and often the masses of people have suffered from high costs and scarcity of products due to the locking of the wheels of industry. These conditions have furnished fertile soil for the seeds of communism and other "isms" that have seriously threatened the unity of our country.

Government.—Since so many people have been out of work, it has been necessary for the government to provide for them. This it has done through all kinds of organizations planned for different groups. The results were that some evils were added to the already

[5] *Sin and Society*, p. 97 (Houghton Mifflin Co., New York, 1907).

complicated situation. For one thing the government has become in some instances a competitor to business. This has a tendency to work a hardship on business recovery. For another thing it has paid wages so much higher in many cases than private business could pay, especially in rural communities, that it has had a tendency to wean many people away from private industry and make them permanent wards of the government. Dependence thus becomes a habit rather than an accident. Also there has been encouraged a disposition to "soldier on the job" and not return a fair day's labor for the pay received. Self-respect and self-dependence have been seriously impaired.

How far religious education can remedy the economic evils growing out of capitalism, organized labor, and governmental activities it is impossible to say. Probably only a little can be done directly, for much of the solution is in the hands of these agencies themselves. A great deal may be done, however, in building right ideals and attitudes into the rising generation through the various organizations for moral and religious instruction. Something of that old-time sense of honesty, industry, and economy may be so instilled into the youth of the land that they will want to take care of their country rather than have their country take care of them. Elsie Robinson was absolutely right in saying recently in her daily article: "America was built by . . . the sweat and pride and prayers of common citizens who paid their way as they went . . . and would rather have starved than accept the hated dole of charity . . . Men need work for the good of their souls as well as the good of their pocket-books—and all the pension plans on earth won't alter that fundamental human necessity." Religious leaders in class-room, pulpit, and press may well join hands in one strenuous endeavor to develop the kind of character in the youth of America that will correct, both personally and collectively, our economic ills.

Civic Evils

Already we have touched the civic side of life in dealing with the social problems discussed, for nearly all of them are finally rooted in the civic order. There are, however, certain immediate and evident governmental tasks that call for special attention.

Crime.—For a number of years crime has been on the increase in the United States. This has been particularly true since the World War. During recent months it has reached enormous proportions. We are the most criminal, civilized nation on earth. Ex-Gov. Neff of Texas has said: "Organized and commercialized crime is now an established and paying business . . . More people were murdered in Texas in one year than in the entire British Empire." Good roads, fast automobiles, and large cities seem to give a new feeling of ability to evade the law. Hijacking is worse than Jesse James ever conceived it. Kidnaping has reached positively alarming proportions. Crime is organized with lawyers, doctors, and policemen and judges to help out. The average age of the criminal has dropped from over forty years of age to under twenty in a period of ten years. The president of a large life insurance company states: "Life was never as insecure in the United States as it is today."

Politics.—Political life has always had its elements of corruption. This has been true among all peoples, and under all forms of government. A more thorough knowledge of human nature and better means of handling the masses seem to have added to the problem. Citizens are not only often dominated by personal favoritism and partisan politics, but also frequently sell their influence and votes during political campaigns in order to secure the election of a relative or a friend or secure a job. Politicians may not only buy votes, and sell their own in legislative halls, but may be even bribed in their decisions as judges or in the administration of the law as executives. The wildest kind of governmental scheme can find an advocate if it is felt that votes can be gained by it. No attention is paid to the effect of the scheme on character. Selfishness was never more manifested in political leadership.

Race Antipathy.—The social inheritance of race prejudice and antipathy is readily and effectively handed on from one generation to another. While children of all races play together without antipathies, the attitude of older people soon carries over to them. In the eastern part of our country the prejudice is probably manifested most toward Greeks, Italians and others from Central Europe. In the Southeast it exists toward the Negroes as a hold-over from the days of slavery. In the Southwest the Mexican comes in for his share of ill will. And in the far West Chinese and Japanese are disliked. In recent days due to agitation in Europe and elsewhere, the Jew has become the object of prejudice. This attitude is contrary to the spirit of Christianity, is harmful to the person exercising it, and makes for constant trouble in the social order. It is one problem that even Christians have to reckon with constantly.

War.—One of the gravest problems in our civic life is the war spirit. It is very difficult for the average person to realize that there are forces deliberately working to bring about war. But such is the case. Those interested financially in concerns that profit by it sometimes go to the extreme of creating public sentiment in favor of war or lobbying to bring it about. Furthermore the ambition of self-seeking rulers to control large areas and make great names for themselves or hold on to power they would otherwise lose, contributes to fomenting the war spirit. It has been estimated that one battleship (which becomes useless in a few years) costs enough to build and equip three great universities such as the University of Michigan. More than three-fourths of our national disbursements during our American history have gone for war or things related to it. And the cost in killed and crippled men is beyond calculation, for war takes "the blood of the nation." Truly has it been said: "War converts mankind into two classes: beasts of prey and beasts of burden."

If the evils of crime, political crookedness, race hatred, and war are ever eliminated from human society, they will have to be done by our educators. The public school system can do much to train a generation of citizens who will be fair with their fellowmen, loyal to their country, just with all races—citizens who would constantly seek to eliminate war. The exchange of students between countries and correspondence between those of different nations will help. Our relations with China are a good example. But if these civic evils are ever fully eliminated, it will come as the love of Christ is implanted in the lives of the coming generation. This must be done by our teachers of religious education in home, church, school, and through the press. There is no greater problem facing us today than that of undergirding and interpenetrating our civilization with the ideals and spirit of Christ, and establishing, as far as it is humanly possible to do, the kingdom of God on earth. This is enough to arouse the best there is in us.

Such, then, are some of the problems in the physical, recreational, educational, domestic, economic and civic life of our land that call for a program of religious education adequate to meet the needs. It was out of such considerations that Woodrow Wilson was led to say: "Our civilization cannot survive materially unless it be redeemed spiritually." And Roger Babson has said: "We do not need more commerce or battleships. We need more religious education." There is no greater task confronting the citizenship of America.

CHAPTER VI

DEMANDS OF MODERN RELIGIOUS CONDITIONS

In this chapter we come to the last of our studies presenting the challenge to religious education from the Bible, from history and from modern conditions. In some respects it will probably constitute the strongest appeal, since religious needs are seemingly the most evident and without question the most significant. Religion is at the heart of all our problems. Solve it adequately and we will take care of all else.

ELIMINATION OF RELIGION

The Puritans came to this country because of a religious motive. Religion, therefore, was at the heart of every phase of activity. The churches fostered it, schools taught it, business problems were settled by it, and legislation was passed in order to promote it. Gradually, however, conditions changed.

Materials.—In the early days schools were established primarily to promote a knowledge of the Bible. In Connecticut in 1650 they resolved to establish schools, "It being the chief project of that old deluder, Satan, to keep men from the knowledge of the Scriptures."[1] A Pennsylvania law passed in 1683 required all parents and guardians to have their children "instructed in reading and writing; so that they may be able to read the scriptures."[2] Similar reasons were given in other states for the establishment of public schools. All along the religious motive was dominant.

Naturally, the textbooks carried a large content of biblical material. The Horn-book, which was a sort of paddle covered with transparent material, contained the alphabet, the Lord's Prayer, the Ten Commandments, and the Apostles' Creed. The New England Primer, a small vest-pocket book, 3,000,000 copies of which were used, had the alphabet in scripture verses, the Lord's Prayer, questions on the Bible, the Shorter Catechism and other materials. The American ("Blue-back") Spelling Book prepared by Noah Webster, about 24,000,000 copies of which were sold, had on 36 of the 166

[1] Quoted by S. W. Brown in *Secularization of American Education*, p. 6 (Teachers College, New York, 1912).
[2] Ibid., p. 21.

pages, statements on religion, Bible facts, Bible characters and Christian doctrines.

Due to the influences of certain liberal groups, the multiplicity of denominations, and the principle of separation of church and state, a gradual process of eliminating these materials was carried on until now we have practically a secular curriculum. Prof. M. L. Perkins investigated 1291 readers and spellers published during our national life, and of those printed from 1776 to 1825 he found 22 per cent religious, 50 per cent moral, and 28 per cent otherwise. Of those published from 1826 to 1880, 12 per cent were religious, 27 per cent moral, and 61 per cent neither. Of those published from 1881 to 1920, 4 per cent were religious, 7 per cent were moral, and 89 per cent of other types. During the last five years of the last period 0 per cent were religious, 3 per cent were moral, and 97 per cent were secular. Thus we have reached a secularized curriculum in the public schools.

The meaning of this is clear. Pupils no longer get the Scriptures as a part of the curriculum of our general school system. Though valuable materials may be given, the Bible itself will have to be learned through other channels. Moreover, the natural tendency will be for the pupil to discount religion. Dr. Weigle says: "When the public schools provide for the education of children in every other sound human interest except religion, the suggestion is unavoidable that religion is a negligible factor in human life."[3]

Teachers.—In the beginning of our national history, the teacher was usually either the minister of the community or some one licensed by him to teach and even if the Bible as such had not been included there would have been a definite religious element. In fact the teacher was quite an ally of the pastor, often seeing that the children went to church, and catechizing them on the preacher's sermon. The contract of a teacher at Flatbush, New York, called for him to help look after the church services in addition to his public school teaching. He also instructed in the Bible and the Catechism and had prayers in the school.

But this situation has changed. Now no religious obligation whatever is placed on the teacher by school authorities. Recently in Texas and probably elsewhere, the trustees are not even permitted to ask about the religious life of the applicant, at least in any official

[3] *Education for Christian Service* (Symp.), p. 311 (Yale University Press, New Haven, 1922).

capacity. The teacher may be an active Christian, negative religiously, or even antagonistic to religion.

This means, of course, that church people may no longer count on the teacher officially for any assistance in the matter of Christian teaching. And all of us know that the influence of the public school teacher who is with the pupil five days a week may more than counteract that of the pastor or Sunday school teacher who is with him only one Sunday. He is the church's greatest ally or handicap.

Schools.—Formerly most of the schools themselves were under Christian auspices. Especially was this true of secondary schools and colleges. Many of the academies and other high schools were founded by religious organizations and were Christian in teachers, texts, and atmosphere. This continued until recent years. The same was true of colleges. Harvard, the first college, was thoroughly Christian in the beginning. Its seal bore the motto "Christ and the Church," and before graduation the student had to "read the originals of the Old and New Testaments into the Latin tongue." Others such as Yale, Brown and Princeton were founded by Christian leaders, conducted under Christian auspices, and held religious services. Columbia's charter still requires a chapel on the campus open daily. Nearly all early colleges were Christian.

As time went on many Christian schools were gradually eliminated and secular institutions took their place. The modern high school has practically supplanted the denominational academy. Much the same result has come to the college. The Federal Land Grant of 1862 allotting lands to agricultural schools helped to further the wave of state colleges and normal schools, as well as A. & M. colleges. Municipal junior and senior colleges have also grown up. Denominational high schools and colleges have been pushed off the map. More than 300 such institutions founded in Texas before the Civil War have disappeared. Southern Baptists had 119 schools of all grades in 1919 and twenty years later not over 69 remained. The majority of youth from Christian homes are now being trained in secular institutions.

The significance of this trend to eliminate religion from education is evident. If Christian teachers, biblical materials, and even denominational schools themselves are set aside, a generation of youth will grow up without their values. If, therefore, we are to provide religious instruction for the coming generation comparable to that of the past, we must build a more comprehensive system of religious education. This involves religious literature, adequate educational organizations in the churches, better support of Christian colleges, and religious activity at state and independent institutions. Probably the strongest definite challenge to religious education comes from the elimination of religion from educational institutions.

ANTI-CHRISTIAN TENDENCIES

Not only do we face the elimination of the religious element from much of our educational life, but in addition we confront the promulgation of certain views that are definitely opposed to Christianity. Some of this is in the field of religion and some of it relates more definitely to the moral life.

Behaviorism.—Certain psychologists seeking to be scientific in their studies introduced the laboratory method of study. This meant that instead of introspection they resorted to observation. As usual they began with the white rat or dog. The result was that the extremists concluded there was no such thing as mind or soul and that everything could be accounted for on the basis of stimulus and response. According to this view man is merely a neural mechanism, the product of internal response to external stimuli, and therefore the result of habits rather than ideals.

The effect of such a view on religion and morals is evident. Man is purely physical and not a soul. So there is no such thing as immortality and no place for God or religion. Since there is no mind or consciousness, moral accountability is left out and one is not responsible for what he does. Thus the spiritual and the ethical are eliminated from life. This sort of teaching in some degree or other finds its place in many institutions of higher learning. Not so long ago the writer heard a professor in a nationally-known teachers' college say to his class: "Do not use in your papers any more, the term soul. Psychology knows nothing about it." This is as dangerous a view as atheism.

Expressionism.—Psychology in recent days has put much emphasis on the subconscious. A phase that has received particular attention is the *complex*. By this is meant some thwarted desire or problem thrust back into the subconscious mind without an adequate solution. The result is a center of disturbance often resulting in a nervous breakdown or some other ill effect on the body or mind.

The cause most emphasized is sex desire. The thought is that if it is not allowed expression a dangerous complex arises. Therefore provision must be made for its free expression. Hence early marriage is advised by some, trial marriage by others, and sex expression apart from marriage by others still. Based largely on the teaching of Freud, this phase of life is put as almost the sole basis of love and marital happiness. As a natural result much stress is laid on birth control.

The inevitable outcome of this emphasis is the giving of free rein to natural desire, which inevitably means much immoral living. Without question a great deal of the cause of the wide-spread wave of immorality in our country is due to the emphasis on sex life in books and magazines. An evidence of the radicalness of the emphasis is seen in the fact that two prominent men who were trying to eliminate such books from a certain state university, and printed a tract giving excerpts from the books, were indicted by a Federal grand jury for sending obscene literature through the mails![4]

Atheism.—In the scientific and philosophical fields of thought the idea is frequently advanced that man is the product of blind forces of nature operating in the universe, and that there is no personal God back of the universe. This is the view of materialistic evolutionists. They seek to explain the beginning and continuation of the universe on the basis of matter and motion. When the idea of a god is mentioned at all in some educational centers a pagan or mythological god rather than Christ is stressed. Says an editorial in the Literary Digest: "In school, it seems, every pagan god in history may be the subject of the day's lesson but not the God of the Bible."[5]

Furthermore, certain independent organizations have been formed to promote the advancement of atheism through the schools. One of these was named "The American Society for the Advancement of Atheism," with branch societies in various universities taking such names as "The Damned Souls." Similarly a Junior Atheistic League was formed with a former Christian Endeavor worker as its head for the purpose of establishing branches in the high schools of the land. Some of these local societies have taken such names as "God's Black Sheep" and "The Society of the Godless." To be sure, such organizations have never been general and are usually short-lived, but their even getting started shows an ominous trend.

The result of these anti-religious tendencies does not end merely with skepticism about God, the Bible, and immortality. It carries over into every-day living. Much of the crime, economic and political

---

[4] See Squires, W. A., *Educational Movements of Today*, p. 49 (Presbyterian Board of Christian Education, Philadelphia, 1930).
[5] Quoted by J. C. Roper in *Religious Aspects of Education*, p. 78 (Cokesbury Press, Nashville, 1926).

crookedness, and immorality grow out of such a background. This is natural. Eliminate God, make man a mere animal, give free rein to instincts, and the jungle life is the inevitable result. If we are to deal with causes rather than symptoms, we must go back of the moral and religious ills to the things that inspire them.

This means that these "issues" having to do with God, the soul, and moral living, need to be met with a positive program of Christian teaching. Much of it will have to be done in the Christian college and by the teacher of Bible in the state and independent school. Since quite a bit of the problem is related to high school, the local church can do much through organized classes, training unions, and week-day church schools.

THE UNTAUGHT MASSES

The American home is handicapped in giving anything like thorough instruction in the Bible because of the fact that one or both parents may not be Christians, neither may be capable of effective teaching, or the time element may be lacking. Since not more than 3 per cent of our young people get to Christian colleges, a heavy responsibility falls back on the churches.

Number Unreached.—One of the most tragic facts in American life is the large number of people now remaining away from church on Sunday. Dr. Walter S. Athearn says: "There are in the United States 42,891,850 Protestants and nominally Protestant youth under twenty-five years of age. Of this number 14,361,900 are reported enrolled in Protestant Sunday, Parochial, and week-day religious schools; 1,225,740 are on Cradle Roll or Font rolls, and 27,275,110 or 66.5 per cent of the total are not enrolled in any religious school."[6] He shows further that 75 per cent of Catholic youth under 25 years of age, and 95 per cent of Jewish youth receive no systematic religious instruction. He concludes: "Taking the country as a whole seven of every ten children and youth of the United States under twenty-five years of age are not being touched in any way by the religious-educational program of any church."[7] In the light of this fact it is easy to realize the difficulty in carrying through a moral reform such as prohibition. There are enough who have never been taught religiously to defeat it.

[6] *Character Building in a Democracy,* p. 26 (The Macmillan Company, New York, 1924).
[7] Ibid., p. 26.

Irregular Attendance.—Not only are great numbers unreached for religious instruction, but of those who are reached many are absent a major portion of the time. Few Sunday schools have much more than half as many present as they have on their rolls. A survey of 1420 Sunday school pupils in a typical small town showed 5.1 per cent attended 97 per cent of the time, 11.5 per cent came 67 per cent, 10.6 per cent were there 37 per cent, and 12.6 per cent showed up only 6 per cent of the time. Others attended at varying rates in between. In other words, not only are fewer than one-third of the youth of the land enrolled in church schools, but also fewer than two-thirds of those that are enrolled are there regularly. Of course no adequate results in religious instruction can be given under such circumstances. We would not think of allowing public education to be carried on under such irregular and unfavorable conditions.

Brief Time.—If all of our youth were enrolled in the Sunday school and Training unions on Sunday, and attended every session there would still be an unsatisfactory situation because of the brief amount of time actually given to instruction. The average Sunday school class or Training Union group does not devote as much as half an hour per week to a discussion of the subject assigned. This is very meager when we realize that there are 112 waking hours per week. It is also very poor in comparison with the public schools which have almost thirty times as much time. Catholic children get on the average approximately four times as much religious instruction as do Protestants, and Jewish children over six times as much. To be sure much good comes from the worship periods of our educational organizations, but frequently they are not very definitely educational.

Inadequate Curriculum.—If all of our youth attended church school all of the time, we would still face an insufficient system of religious education due to an inadequate curriculum, at least so far as the Sunday school is concerned. From 1872 through 1917 when the old Uniform Lessons were used, only 35.1 per cent of the Bible was included. In other words if a child had entered at five years of age in 1872, attended every Sunday and studied every lesson, at fifty years of age he would have had little more than a third of the Bible, and this mainly historical. Nine books would never have been touched. The Improved Uniform Lessons have corrected this somewhat in that 40.1 per cent of the Bible is included, but it is still top-heavy with historical material. The Closely Graded go considerably further and include 62.4 per cent of the Bible, with material much better adapted to the younger age groups, but stop short with the

Intermediates, seemingly forgetting that Young People and Adults also need material adapted to life problems.

If the American people are ever to handle adequately crime and other national problems they must face seriously this matter of the masses of people being untaught religiously, for religion provides the stimulus for proper conduct. This means that a more aggressive effort must be made to reach the unenlisted for our church schools; that the enlisted must be led to attend with more regularity, and that religious education must be extended into the week-day so that more time may be given to instruction and a wider range of curriculum provided. To do these things there will probably have to be a closer correlation with public schools so that more may be reached, more time be available, and probably credit given. Every possible opportunity must be used to give the rank and file a chance at religious instruction.

IGNORANCE OF THE BIBLE

A natural consequence of the fact that the masses are untaught is shown by the gross ignorance of the Scriptures. After a century and a half of Sunday schools, a half century of young people's societies, and many years of other activities the sad fact still remains that the average person still knows very little about the Bible. Hosea's statement is as applicable now as in his day, "My people are destroyed for lack of knowledge" (Hos. 4:6).

American Soldiers.—From various angles studies as to religious knowledge were made of American soldiers during the World War. Dr. Frederick Lynch says that in fifty books written by chaplains and Y. M. C. A. secretaries during this time there is "absolute unanimity as to the appalling and almost complete ignorance of Christianity." American chaplains made such statements as these: "The average young American knows very little about God, Christ, prayer, faith." "Not one in a hundred had ever heard of the kingdom of God." Summing up the results of its investigation among chaplains, Y. M. C. A. workers and others "The Committee on the War and the Religious Outlook" concludes: "If there is any one point upon which chaplains agree it is in regard to the widespread ignorance as to the meaning of Christianity and church membership . . . If a vote were taken among chaplains and other religious workers as to the most serious failure of the Church, as evidenced in the army, a large majority would agree that it was the Church's failure as a teacher. We have not succeeded in teaching

Christianity to our own members, let alone distributing a clear knowledge of it through the community at large."[8] These youth were from all kinds of homes throughout the nation and represent a fair cross-section of our life.

College Freshmen.—A study was made of high school graduates who were just entering a state university. They had come from the best homes and schools throughout a state, and should have been above the average. They took the test voluntarily and naturally were those who felt fairly capable in the biblical field. There were 139 freshmen participating. There were eight questions calling for the naming of ten books of the Old Testament, ten of the New, the divisions of the Old Testament, identifying five Bible characters and similar matters. Twelve made as much as 75 per cent, 91 got less than 50, and the average was 40 per cent. Ten could not name a book of the Old Testament, and only 68 named ten. Old Testament books mentioned were "Hezekiah," "Phenecians," "Gentiles," and "Xerxes." Twelve could not name a New Testament book and only 46 named ten. New Testament books mentioned were "Paul," "Thelesians," "Lazarus," and "Samson Agonistes." Twenty-seven made no effort to name the "Apostle to the Gentiles," 72 replied correctly, and others mentioned "Methusaleh," "Moses," and "Judas." Twenty did not even try to name "The Beloved Disciple," sixty-eight answered correctly, and names given were "Abraham," "David," and "Peter." "Apollos" was thought to be a heathen god, and "Cana" was the promised land. And yet all of these had graduated from high school and were now in a state university!

Religious Workers.—From time to time information has been gained in various ways from those leading in various capacities in religious work. The results have been rather startling. One is reminded of the biblical emphasis on the blind leading the blind. A business man who was Sunday school superintendent asked the writer in a training class one night if it was definitely known *who* Genesis was. A farmer who was also a Sunday school superintendent in answering a question in a training course examination as to what the Book of Judges told about said, "the General Judgment." A public school superintendent and Sunday school teacher who had graduated from a Christian college did not know whether the book of Ephesians was in the Old Testament or the New. Many pastors

[8] *Religion Among American Men*, pp. 13-15, 131 (Association Press, New York, 1920).

have shown ignorance of the Bible just about as great as the above. The spiritual illiteracy in the land is indeed appalling. It is of more consequence than literary illiteracy, though it arouses much less excitement.

When one realizes the wide-spread ignorance of the Bible not only among the masses but also in the ranks of college students and even voluntary and vocational religious leaders, he is made to realize that a new crusade is needed. If the generation now in our colleges, including vocational and non-vocational workers, will set themselves to the task of remedying the situation, the evil can be eliminated almost in a generation. It will require creating public sentiment, setting up organizations, enlisting the people and consistently teaching them. "An aroused church, a nation-wide program of religious education, and technically trained, professional leadership will not only remove the menace of spiritual illiteracy that now threatens the life both of church and state, but it will prevent the recurrence of spiritual illiteracy in the future."[9]

UNDEVELOPED CHRISTIANS

Too often in our zeal to reach the last unconverted person and "evangelize the world in this generation," we forget to give proper attention to those who have made professions. Consequently they fail to develop. One prominent evangelist has emphasized "the ministry of conservation" along with "the ministry of rescue" saying: "Two hundred new members are two hundred new liabilities until they are properly lined up in their respective places in the church." A few years after the famous Northampton revival Jonathan Edwards said: "Multitudes of fair and high professors have backslidden . . . Experimental religion is more than ever out of credit."[10]

In Attendance.—It is a noticeable fact that many who make professions of faith during an annual revival meeting do not show up again until the next revival, if even then. The average church, and particularly the large one, will do well to have one-fourth as many present at the Sunday morning services as it has members. At the Sunday night services probably one-sixth will be a good percentage for the big church. What about the other three-fourths or

[9] Athearn, W. S., *Character Building in a Democracy*, p. 42 (The Macmillan Company, New York, 1924).

[10] Quoted by Davenport in *Primitive Traits in Religious Revivals*, p. 130 (The Macmillan Company, New York, 1910).

five-sixths? They are becoming a matter of increasing concern in many sections of the country. This derelict group has been referred to by Dr. John R. Sampey as the "lost sheep of the house of Israel." (Matt. 10:6). The situation has become so serious in some places that the churches have set up special organizations and put on special campaigns to get their own members back to church. In at least one instance the churches of one denomination of an entire state have taken that as their primary task.

In Giving.—Just as noticeable as the matter of failing to attend church is that of failing to support it and its work with one's means. In fact the latter naturally grows out of the former. It is proverbial that about one-fourth of the church membership carry practically all of the financial burdens. Many never give anything at all for religious purposes either for work at home or in foreign lands. Many others who contribute some, do it meagerly and spasmodically, when they "feel like it." Southern Baptists give less than a dollar per capita per month to all purposes. Not a tenth of our members give as much as a tithe of their income, when this should be the starting point rather than the stopping place. Only two of a B. Y. P. U. membership of more than twenty, after giving a splendid program on tithing, were found to be tithers. Often religious leaders are short in their giving. Many of the poorest people spend more on soft drinks, shows, and tobacco than they do on the church and its work. And not only does the kingdom of God suffer thereby, but their own characters are dwarfed, for we live in God's world, enjoy his blessings, owe him a part of our income, and cannot short-cut a moral obligation without suffering the consequences in character.

In Service.—When one considers the matter of religious leadership in church life the problem is still more serious. Even in cultured centers and large churches it is extremely difficult to find enough people to carry on all of the responsibilities of church life without greatly over-working a few. Many who will promise to teach a class in Sunday school or lead a group in the Training Union soon quit or are irregular in their attendance. Often those who are prominent in other phases of community life are incapable or undependable in church work. Many who can teach in public school or speak in political life cannot or will not perform similar duties in church. Few, comparatively, can intelligently guide an inquiring soul to Christ. Many cannot even lead in public prayer. Some are still so ignorant or prejudiced as to be opposed to some of the educational activities of the church and missionary enterprises on the foreign field. Either we have brought too many people into church membership or failed to do for them what we should.

It is almost needless to say that the great host of undeveloped church people whether as to attendance, giving, service or whatever it may be, furnishes a situation that calls for a new emphasis on the educational method. Probably we should begin by following a sounder psychology in leading people to make professions of faith, to promise to give sums of money, or to undertake church responsibility. Possibly these results should be sought more through individual conviction than crowd pressure. But whatever may be true as to that activity, we certainly need to put forth greater efforts to develop those we do get into our churches. Without question it is true that most of our troubles come out of a lack of training. The ministry of conservation must follow that of rescue if we are to have converts who are substantial.

Lapses in Faith

Going still further in our consideration of the challenge of religious conditions, we confront the problem of the large number of people who go back on their professions completely or switch their alignment to an entirely alien group. Sometimes the defection is even to the point of skepticism or atheism.

Backsliding.—Many who make professions simply ease out of religious activity altogether, or perhaps it would be more nearly correct to say that they never get started in it. The fact is that many who attend revivals and are baptized into church membership never show up again. As an example of such defection consider Southern Baptists. In a twenty year period 2,330,000 were baptized. The net gain during the period was 1,216,000 or 52.5 per cent. Deaths totaled 361,000 or 15 per cent. This left 756,000 or 32.5 per cent unaccounted for, which was twice the number of deaths and nearly a third of the total number. Such a loss in the educational or business world would be counted very serious. The country boy was about right who told the writer that in his church "about a third of the ones that profess in the revival one summer have to refess the next." Either we are getting a great many unconverted into our churches or failing to develop young converts. At any rate, we have certainly failed to introduce control into conduct, as education is supposed to do.

Heresies.—Not only do many drop out of evangelical church life, but others go off into groups that are far from central in their Christian beliefs. One illustration is the number that go over to Russellites, for most of their gains come from the ranks of the churches rather than from the ranks of the lost. By means of their highly-advertised lectures and wide circulation of dirt-cheap, many-colored books, they have made tremendous gains in recent years. Similarly the Christian Scientists through their newspapers, lectures, and distribution of free tracts in hotels, depots, and on trains have drawn many from the ranks of evangelical Christianity. But perhaps the most noted instance is in the case of the Mormons. In spite of their wild theology and questionable ethics they made a gain of 87 per cent in a ten-year period. Undoubtedly their house-to-house distribution of free literature, and carrying on of week-day schools of religion adjacent to the public high schools in Utah, as well as regular Sunday instruction, help to account for the gains. Gains in the ranks of the Spiritualists and Buddhists are other instances.

If these lapses in faith, particularly backsliding and the inroads of heretical groups, are to be counteracted, it must be done not only by sound instruction prior to profession in order that a sane experience may be had, but also by continued efforts at teaching and training, that the new life may become intelligent and the individual habituated in the Christian faith. Especially should more attention be given to teaching the fundamental doctrines. Undoubtedly we should give much attention to the converts already made as well as to those yet to be won. Dr. W. E. Hatcher was eminently right when he said: "It is at least as important to save what we have as to save the lost." And this definitely involves religious education.

If in this chapter on the challenge of religious conditions the picture has been made a bit darker than some feel it is, let it be emphasized that it has not been done pessimistically nor to criticize what has been accomplished, but rather to make emphatic the need for more thorough training in religious matters. If the public schools are not to be depended upon to teach Christianity but instead often present things opposed to it; if, after what our churches have done, the majority are still untaught religiously and are ignorant of the Bible; and if undevelopment is common and lapses from the faith frequent, then without question the supreme religious task of America is a program of religious education in Sunday church schools, week-day church schools, Christian colleges, and state universities sufficient to correct these conditions.

A SELECTED BIBLIOGRAPHY FOR CLASS USE

Athearn, W. S. *Character Building in a Democracy*. The Macmillan Co., New York, 1924.

Athearn, W. S. *The Minister and the Teacher*. The Century Co., New York, 1932.

Betts, Geo. H. *The New Program of Religious Education*. The Abingdon Press, New York, 1921.

Brown, A. A. *A History of Religious Education in Recent Times*. The Abingdon Press, New York, 1923.

Cady, M. E. *The Education that Educates*. Fleming H. Revell Co., New York, 1937.

Coe, Geo. A. *Education in Religion and Morals*. Fleming H. Revell Co., New York, 1904.

Drummond, N. R. *Educational Function of the Church*. Baptist Sunday School Board, Nashville, 1924.

Eby, Frederick. *Christianity and Education*. Baptist General Convention of Texas, Dallas, 1915.

Fickes, T. H. *Principles of Religious Education*. Fleming H. Revell Co., New York, 1938.

Fiske, G. W. *Purpose in Teaching Religion*. The Abingdon Press, New York, 1937.

Horne, H. H. *Jesus the Master Teacher*. Association Press. New York, 1925.

James, Powhatan. *Reason for Christian Education*. Baptist General Convention of Texas, Dallas, 1915.

Kent, Chas. F. *Great Teachers of Judaism and Christianity*. Eaton and Mains, New York, 1911.

Kidd, Benjamin. *The Science of Power*. G. P. Putnam's Sons, New York, 1918.

King, H. C. *Moral and Religious Challenge of Our Times*. The Macmillan Co., New York, 1917.

King, H. C. *Personal and Ideal Elements in Education*. The Macmillan Co., New York, 1904.

Kuist, H. T. *The Pedagogy of St. Paul*. Geo. H. Doran Co., New York, 1925.

McCoy, C. F. *The Art of Jesus as a Teacher*. American Baptist Publication Society, Philadelphia, 1930.

Piper, D. R. *How Would Jesus Teach*. David C. Cook Co., Elgin, 1931.

Price, J. M. *Christianity and Social Problems*. Baptist Sunday School Board, Nashville, 1928.

Price, Carpenter and Chapman (Editors). *Introduction to Religious Education*. The Macmillan Co., New York, 1932.

Roper, J. C. *Religious Aspects of Education*. Cokesbury Press, Nashville, 1926.

Sherman, H. N. (Ed.). *Education and Religion*. Cokesbury Press, Nashville, 1929.

Squires, W. A. *Educational Movements of Today*. Presbyterian Board of Publications, Philadelphia, 1930.

Stough, H. W. *Across the Dead Line of Amusements*. Fleming H. Revell Co., New York, 1912.

Swift, F. N. *Education in Ancient Israel*. Open Court Publishing Co., Chicago, 1919.

Trumbull, H. C. *Yale Lectures on the Sunday School*. John D. Wattles, Philadelphia, 1893.

Wilm, E. C. *The Culture of Religion*. The Pilgrim Press, New York, 1912.

Part II

Principles of Religious Education

CHAPTER VII

PSYCHOLOGY

The problem of the religious educator is that of translating ideas into conduct, and transmuting conduct into character. The average teacher, to the contrary, has assumed that there is a separation between the idea presented and the conduct expected. He thinks in terms of two processes, one of imparting truth and the other of building character. Experience has demonstrated that the habits and attitudes of growing youth are actually being shaped by every experience in the lesson process and by his associates in the throbbing atmosphere of life itself. It has been well demonstrated that the ideas of the lesson will more likely control conduct when definitely linked with the experiences of the lesson period and with practice in living these ideas with associates whose approval he values. The task of a religious educator in achieving a character result embraces the utilization of the lesson material, the teacher himself, and community approval of the conduct proposed.

THE LEARNING PROCESS

Learning as suggested by the statement of the problem, is largely adjustment to the conditions of life. This learning may be secured through a trial and error process in which the successful reactions are linked together in a unity of experience. Likewise learning may be secured by the use of ideas growing out of the experiences of others and accepted by the individual as experience. This enables one to gain practice in the absence of the situation. It is also true that the learner may acquire certain skills by observation. By watching others perform he may abridge the trial and error process to a noticeable degree. In any case the individual learns the reactions which he makes in his adjustment to the conditions of life.

91

The process of learning looks to the four achievements—knowledge, skill, attitudes and appreciations. Knowledge has been defined as "familiarity with facts, events and principles with an understanding of their meaning." Skill has been defined as "an ability to do an act with ease and accuracy." An attitude has been defined as "an habitual way of thinking and feeling about persons, relations and things." Appreciation has been defined as "the ability to assign values."[1] The concern of the teacher is primarily that of the development of skills, attitudes and appreciations. The human organism, however, approaches these results through knowledge.

In the process of translating knowledge into skills, attitudes and appreciations certain well known principles of teaching have been established and laws formulated by which the mind functions. A brief statement of these principles will clarify the general laws of teaching.

Action Urges.—These urges reside in the individual by inheritance. These are needed for the protection of the individual, and when they act it is for the satisfaction of a particular need. It appears to be true that man's behavior is a reflection of his striving for various forms of satisfaction. Man has certain legitimate wants or needs which give direction to his actions.

Situation Response.—The situation response is the testing ground of an urge. Trial and error is the timid advance on an environment, and the first learning. When an urge arises the child responds with one of these instinctive modes of behavior. The world is not always friendly to the way in which the mechanism responds. For this reason the child early in life discovers that his innate modes of behavior have to be modified, if they are to find satisfaction in the environment. This modification to secure satisfaction constitutes learning. Social tradition is the tested pattern by which an urge should act for the sake of the fullest benefit to the future self. The responses to a situation may consist of a split reaction, one being called primary learning, and the other incidental. All learning arises from a local situation, and its effects are associated in the mind with the local situation. The incidental learning may be in the nature of a maladjustment, and result in unseemly behavior. It is in this area that attitudes are formed.

Motivation of Urges.—The motivation of urges is the dynamic step in learning. Purposeful guidance of learning requires the locat-

[1] Corzine, *Looking at Learning*, pp. 21-22 (Baptist Sunday School Board, 1934).

ing of the fundamental urges responsible for activity, or that actuate the individual to get on in life. One who would control another must adapt himself to the interests of the individual. The most potent motives have their roots in the dominant urges. For the purposes of learning the urges within the social bracket are of most value. Achievement of one's self, or of beating a record, or of competing with another, or of securing the approval of others are based on human urges. Stated differently, the major control motives are fear or blame, rewards or prizes or approval, duty, and love. Man responds favorably to that which has the greatest appeal to him. The key to controlling behavior is knowing what another's interests are at a given moment. Change of response results from establishing within the individual a sense of higher values in the proposed conduct. The desirable conduct must be made appealing to the individual. Among these incentives are the will to live, health, hunger, perpetuation of the race, companionship, social approval, power of control. Every failure in an attempt to win an individual to an ideal behavior is an indication that adequate incentives have not been discovered or applied.

Effects.—The effects resulting from activity of these urges are definitely educational. An act of learning takes place only when the individual is motivated. When the organism acts simply, satisfaction results unless some element is introduced into the experience which sets up dissatisfaction. In order to regain satisfaction repeated efforts at adaptation are undertaken until a satisfactory result is obtained. This process is learning.

Guidance stimulates the reactions that tend toward right conduct, and suppresses those that tend toward wrong conduct. The problem of profitable instruction is largely that of correctly motivating the study so as to secure a satisfying outcome. Repetition of the act will depend on the previous satisfaction in performing that act. Specific habit depends upon that repetition with satisfaction.

General Habit.—General habit, or an ideal covering all situations, results from the application of specific habits in various situations. The specific habit must be learned in the process of reacting repeatedly to a specific situation. Virtues and vices are specific, not general. They become general as their repetition under widely different conditions gives them a set as an ideal of conduct. The principle involved in the process is known as transfer of training. Unless the individual is directed to the conscious adoption of a general ideal there is no assurance of a transfer of training.

On the basis of these general facts there are certain laws that have been formulated:

The Law of Use.—The principle of activity may be stated in terms of a law as follows: "Those elements in our environment to which we make response are learned, and those to which we do not make response are not learned. Those learnings which are put to use are retained and strengthened; while those which are not put to use are weakened or lost." (Corzine p. 58) An act that is once performed is more easily repeated whether good or bad. William James' laws of habit formation rest on this law. "Launch a habit with zest." "Never allow an exception."

Two corollaries to the law of use and disuse are the law of frequency and the law of recency. The law of frequency as generally stated is: "Other things being equal, the more frequently a connection has been exercised the stronger the connection." The law of recency as generally stated is: "Other things being equal, the more recent the exercise, the stronger the connection between the situation and response." The more frequently and intensely a learning is put to use the more permanent it becomes.

The Law of Readiness.—The principle of motivation may be stated in terms of a law as follows: "When an individual is ready to act in a certain way, for him to act in that way is satisfying and for him not to act is annoying. Conversely, when an individual is not ready to act in a certain way, for him to act in that way is annoying."[2] An individual acts when action is desired. One will learn when the learning is related to his felt needs. When there is no felt need efforts to learn are drudgery.

The Law of Effect.—The principle of satisfaction may be stated in terms of a law as follows: "Those experiences which are satisfying we tend to repeat and those that are not satisfying we tend to avoid. Learning is stimulated by a satisfying outcome and is hindered by an unsatisfying outcome." (Corzine p. 67) Whether one wishes this result or not, the result is present. There is something about the effect which accompanies the act that determines future attitudes. The more satisfying the result the more certain is the reaction to be repeated. Incidental learning, which may be the opposite to the lesson, often has its origin in the satisfier or in the annoyer.

The Integration of Personality

The task of the Christian teacher is so to direct the innate urges that they will result in a unified person. It is the object of Christian

[2] *Ibid.*, p. 66.

education to introduce control into the experiences of living in such a way as to lead to responses in the direction of Christian faith and life. When these are rightly guided they will build up a system of habits, attitudes, motives, and knowledge which will integrate into character. This total way in which one thinks, feels, and acts constitutes his personality. The Christian teacher is primarily concerned that this personality be Christian, that the moral decisions of the individual be in harmony with his Christian ideals.

The art of personality building, which Kulp[3] defines as "the organization of habits and attitudes and emotions around certain life purposes that create a status in life," is one of providing a balanced realization of the fundamental urges. The quest is for human happiness, and it is acquired by a legitimate realization of these life needs. Failure to provide legitimate satisfactions for these needs produces maladjustments of personality through the thwarting of the satisfactions to which the urge is entitled. Disciplining of these maladjustments would consist of seeking for the causes of the unseemly behavior, and the finding of more acceptable outlets for one's interests. The critical concern in personality development is, therefore, the type of attitude that the particular discipline would produce.

Three types of personality are classified in terms of the extent and nature of their integration.[4] First, is the psychopathic personality, one that tries to satisfy each instinctive urge upon its appearance. There is a lack of purpose, a resulting unhappiness, and a conflict with society which withholds approval. A second type is the inhibited personality, resulting often when the child is taught that some of his instinctive urges are sinful. Although he banishes these appetites from his immediate consciousness, he cannot banish them from his personality. They emerge in some malignant fashion. Certain sources of power seem to be extracted from that personality. The third type is the integrated personality, the individual who succeeds "in forming such a harmony of healthy emotional attitudes, that all of his energy is united into one common purpose, moving in one direction. It is he who has developed the strongest personality for which his native endowments fit him."

When the wrong methods of satisfaction are used, the result is disintegration. The theory of child training which concerns itself with the future development of the child rather than with the immediate behavior is most important. Of greatest importance in childhood years is not so much external behavior, but the emotions that

[3] *Educational Sociology*, p. 198 (Longmans, 1932).
[4] Ligon, *Psychology of Christian Personality*, p. 15 (Macmillan, 1935).

are developed. Abstract ethical principles are not so significant in the early years. Temperament, on the other hand, is formed during these years. The child may not learn from punishment that a certain course is wrong, but he may have instilled within him a fear which will contribute toward his becoming a weakling in his maturity. If he is forced to be generous toward one whom he dislikes he will not learn generosity, but he may learn to resent discipline. To the religious educator, then, the future development of the child is the important concern in childhood experiences.

The integration of the personality requires the development of faith in an invincible cause, and with that a sense of dependence, which is a faith in parent and in God to help achieve the results. This faith releases all one's power for the achievement of his vision, without a hampering fear of defeat. This faith rests ultimately upon the belief that the ideal which will give the best personality is Jesus. One who accepts Jesus as the guiding ideal of his life, and identifies himself with him, can hope to stand against overwhelming forces of life.

Native Urges and Their Influence on Character

Education must begin somewhere. The body is the gateway to the self. Personality is reached through the native endowment, which Hocking calls "the permanent ingredients of our being." Each child has inborn responses to environment, corresponding to the oak tree that dwells in the acorn. These are called instincts or urges, reflexes and capacities.

Nature.—Instincts are the starting point in education. They are urges, drives or stings to action and hence dynamic in nature. They are the unlearned tendencies to act in certain ways. Their recurrence results in habits, and habits are basic in educational procedure. These self-starters naturally react upon themselves and aid in accelerating the work of learning.

Kinds.—The grouping of instincts or urges is a mechanical aid in handling these impulses. A simple classification would consist of individualistic, perpetuative, social, and projective urges. The first group includes the protective tendency to feed, fear, and fight. The second group has reference to the sex or racial urges. The third group includes tendencies to flock together, to compete, to seek approval, and to communicate. The fourth group embraces those tendencies to establish standards of conduct and to regulate interests that effect the utmost expansion of the self. This includes efforts to reach and prevail with the Determiner of Destiny.

Modification of Tendencies.—The directing of instincts is the problem of the trainer of character. Unmodified, these pure impulses trail to the wild man. Modified, they lend themselves just as freely to the constructive program of society. It satisfies them just as well to help as to hinder. Learning is possible through the modifiability of urges. This is true for three reasons. First, modification means basic plasticity. Heredity does proportionately less for man than for the animal. It provides him with the raw materials and challenges him to complete the work. Second, modification means a tendency to act. Like cement it is ready to conform. Instincts are not snobs, they accept the first influence as correct. This is the teacher's challenge. Third, modification means responsiveness to guidance. Like cement it is ready to set. Because of this willing impulse it is comparatively easy to establish control. The danger and the strength lie in power developed by auxiliary forces.

The character outcome of handling urges lies in the understanding by the religious educator of these potentialities. These tendencies are willing to enter into an alliance with the teacher for moral and spiritual ends. They yield readily to a process of pattern weaves which are called habits. They lend their power to modes of thought which are called ideas. They conform to socially approved standards of action which are called ideals. The builder of character uses this wealth of urges in introducing social patterns into the life of the individual.

In building character the skillful teacher knows the need for control of these urges. Some tendencies need to be confirmed, others suppressed. Confirmation is achieved by associating some satisfaction with the instinctive act. Pleasurable results lead to repetition of the act. Elimination is achieved by so managing the child's environment that the impulse will atrophy through disuse. The association of dissatisfaction with the wrong response tends to weaken its recurrence. The boy jeered by his mate for showing "yellow" will face fire rather than be rebuked again for fear.

In redirecting these innate tendencies, "instinct, as a guide, shows a fatal lack of sense of direction." Real guidance for these "urges" is sought outside of the tendency itself. Like Jochebed, who offered to nurse young Moses, the teacher or parent proffers the guidance of maturity. The method is to find a better outlet for the impulse than is being sought. Psychology names these two: "substitution," and "sublimation." The wise father urges the child to substitute stroking the cat's head for pulling his tail. The wise junior teacher says, "Wiggle thus," instead of "Don't wiggle." The "gang" leader goes "hiking" rather than rob a peach orchard. By sublimation the instinct finds expression through helpful channels rather than through selfish ones. The fighting instinct is sublimated when it defends an unselfish cause.

THE UNFOLDING LIFE AND ITS IMPLICATIONS

Not all of the urges appear at birth. Many are deferred for months, some for years. Their unfoldment covers the period usually referred to as immaturity. Education for character, and in religion, is most effective as it observes the "seasons of the soul."

The Periods of Unfolding.—The span of life is divided into three general periods of twenty-four years each. Immaturity covers the first twenty-four and is itself divided into two periods of approximately twelve years each, called childhood and adolescence. Each of these periods is divided into three parts designated as early, middle, and later.

Early childhood embraces the pre-school years. These years are largely under the control of basic urges, of organic needs. Mentally the child is receiving stimuli, very suggestible, and largely imitative. There is little interpretation of sensations. Deeper emotions are not yet possible. Self-control is yet in the offing, for the representative powers known as memory and imagination have not yet assumed control. He is unable effectively to inhibit natural tendencies.

The teacher and parent will provide controls for the child under six. Careful direction will protect the child from dangerous practices. During this period specific good habits will be cultivated upon which ideals are built and upon which the religion of later years will depend.

Middle childhood begins with school life at six. The representative faculties, memory and imagination, are coming into control of the experiences. Sense perceptions are especially subject to recall. Imagination is more constructive and more subject to experience. The wings of fancy are clipped by a growing sense of reality. Attention shifts quickly and centers largely around the child's interests. A growing independence of the home upon his initiation into school means an expanding social nature.

Later childhood begins about nine years of age. It continues the development of the earlier period, intensifying some of the tendencies. No new powers and no new kinds of interests arise during this period. It is the time for mastering the tools of learning and for developing the habits and skills needed in using them. Memory of the verbal and the mechanical type is prominent and lends itself to drill in those matters that need to be routinized. A good memory is due to his growing power of attention, perhaps not prolonged, but close. This is also the time of growing independence. His sense of mastery of the tools of learning gives him a sense of superiority over the "kids." A certain willfulness is replacing the plasticity of earlier years. He is increasingly rebellious against authority, though he respects true authority. This is also the time for a fuller social life. The child is more intensely cultivating a group of chums. He is becoming a worshipper of the heroic in men.

Parents and teachers will select those forms around which habit shall gather its skills. Religious habits, moral habits, personal habits of thrift, punctuality and the like will be formed now. They will also recognize the need for authority, but will guard against the ultra-arbitrary type that lacks the undergirding of reason and leaves wrong attitudes in the child. They will, further, give attention to the friends of the child, both immature and mature, and surround him with persons who will challenge the heroic in the child.

Early adolescence begins about twelve years of age. Most of the instincts which mean so much to later life are deferred for development to this period. The real character of the individual is now establishing a "set" for life.

Early adolescence has been called "physical" adolescence because "all other phases of growth and development for the time being become subordinate to the unfoldment and flowering of sex functions." The body undergoes tremendous strain as it is being modified for the demands of maturity.

"Stress and strain" mark these years. The youth is learning to do moral deeds by reflection and by deliberation. By choice he selects principles of character and conduct. There may result premeditated wrong or premeditated right. An unfortunate association may overpower all the work of years, or fine associations may save as quickly. Naturally conversion would become a conspicuous experience of this age. This is further a time for transfer of control from without to within. External restraints must be applied through ideals, not by arbitrary authority. "Psychological weaning" becomes imperative where the parent has refused to let the child grow up. Now that he must "be a man" he needs the removal of direct authority in favor of developing inner control. This is, further, a time of finest idealism.

It is the nascent period for the unfolding of the deeper moral nature. Personal loyalties grow up here that are stronger than armies.

Middle adolescence begins about fifteen years of age. This has been called "emotional" adolescence because the affective instincts are in the ascendency. The emotional life of the adolescent is doubtless far more determinative of the youth's future than is his intellectual development. The rational processes of the next period will tone down the excesses of emotional life, but they will not change their power. Now he is "just spilling over with interests." Spiritually these ebullitions of emotion are of eternal value. This is the peak of religious idealism and the high tide of conversion.

Later adolescence begins about eighteen years of age. As the earlier period covers junior high school, and middle adolescence covers senior high ages, so this period begins with entrance into the college circles. It has been called "intellectual" adolescence for the reason that the rational or the intellectual faculties are in the ascendency. The personality is developing full power of mastery over self and over environment. Action is more often the outcome of deliberation. If a well-poised manhood is not developed now it is due to some mental or physical defect, or to vicious educational processes. The task of the teacher is to help personality to "find itself" and, progressively, "to develop itself toward its highest conceivable form."

Adulthood is that period from about twenty-four years of age, known as maturity. The theory that learning ability ends at maturity has been discarded. The processes of learning are as real at this stage as earlier in spite of excessive practical demands on the individual. The maturing of the crop sown and grown through earlier years now ripens for weal or woe.

Problems are numerous among adults. Unsocialized habits pass over unbridled into inner controls. "Spoiled children" are now "short-horned deacons" and obstinate neighbors. Criminal tendencies of youth, conceits, riotous and profane living, extroversions, introversions, are well formed. These adults are society's problems. They are not only their own enemies, and menaces to society in some cases, but they are walking patterns for youth of the type that should not be. A new integration of personality is possible. The "new birth" of religion performs such miracles of reintegration. Unfolding has no end else immortality has lured us into error.

Implications for Religious Education.—Unfolding of new life means hope for religious educators. It is not the small number of criminals, but the large number of respectable persons who are morally unenlightened, and religiously orphaned, that inspires pessimism in moral and religious leaders. In the new generation there is hope. Hope lies in their plasticity, and its willingness to conform to pattern. For practical purposes the surface implications of this unfolding for religious education may be listed.

For grouping. For social values in education children must be grouped and will group themselves. Genetic psychology advises us as to certain general principles to be observed in grouping.

(1) The unit in grading should be a group of pupils nucleated around a central experience. "Homogeneity" is the educational term involved. Unfolding brings certain interests to the fore, and character building grows faster by using the central areas of interest as motivation. It is common knowledge that certain years are conspicuous for their uniqueness. The girl of sixteen is marked. The awkwardness and related experiences of early adolescence fall around thirteen. The sophomore is notorious, and counts his years as nineteen. The principle would take these years as representing a stage of development, and urge the value of grouping around them as pivotal experiences.

(2) Unfolding life has taught that nascent characteristics should be handled early for the sake of fullest individual development. The most successful training is that which utilizes the plasticity of a newly arrived instinct. Since the pubertal changes of early adolescence are so significant in life development that period may be used as an example. The application of this principle would mean an early effort at influencing the child as his nature demands. Provision must be made for the arriving of new interests rather than have the new interests arrive unprepared for. This would mean the allocation of twelve-year-old children to the thirteen-year-old group.

(3) Genetic psychology teaches that the need of the child is the primary determinant in grouping. Two cases will illustrate the point. In the control of children autocratic authority prevails largely with junior ages. Early adolescents are rapidly growing into inner control, and resent the earlier authority. Wisdom would recognize the change and place the latter under the control of ideas. Again, precocious or mentally retarded children should be grouped with their finest adjustment in mind.

For method. Growing a person is like farming. The farmer plants and cultivates. The growth comes from the inside. The religious educator simply offers favorable conditions for growth that the life within sends forth. He must provide the environment that will bring the proper response. This we label method.

Psychology has parted with the method of selection of materials and procedure by individual judgment. Psychology through experimentation will present those phases of knowledge that are within the comprehension of the child and in harmony with the mental stages through which the child is passing. The approaches to his interest and control centers are a matter of method, and their laws are fairly definitely formulated. A discussion of method appears later in this book.

For conduct control. The introduction of control into experience in terms of religious ideals is the theory of religious education as defined by the late President W. S. Athearn. Three forces for control are at the disposal of the teacher of religion, namely, habit, ideals, and religion.

(1) Habit means that the tendency to act has been encouraged to act in ways that have been pleasant. The teacher will use methods of habit formation for setting up the skills of moral living that make for character. The habit of prayer, for example, is a distinct control. Church attendance habits become controls. Training conscience is training a control. The more widely and deeply constructive habits are cultivated, the more promise there is for control in personality.

(2) Ideals control when conduct is governed by self-approved standards. Conduct becomes amenable to ideals by stages. Instinctive behavior is first modified by pain and pleasure. Behavior is controlled by anticipation of the praise or blame of society. Behavior is controlled by an ideal of right or wrong without regard to the mandates of society, which is the control desired by religious educators. Control was established in the full when a Luther stood, and said: "I cannot do otherwise."

(3) Religion as conduct control transcends all other motives. Religion lifts habits and ideals into the control of a Person. Belief that certain conduct is according to the will of God is strong undergirding for control. Conscience rests upon a feeling of obligation to that Being above man. The projective instincts find no satisfaction short of their completeness in that Person. His will and favor are final for control. The religious educator must impart knowledge of that Person directly and effectively and completely.

For conversion. The unfolding life offers the religious educator a supreme concern at the point of personal relation to the Supreme Being. It seems that man does not become capable of religion at any specific age, for he is always capable. But "he is not always capable of it in exactly the same sense, nor does religion connote at every age exactly the same kind of ideas and feelings. There is such a thing as the religion of an immature mind, and there is such a thing as the religion of a mature mind; and each of these has about it some distinctive features."[5]

Conversion follows in the course of the "seasons of the soul." In the first place it is seldom experienced before the full instinctive development has been attained. Somehow God has made himself all but indispensable to the supreme synthesis of life. In the second place the climax rests in the period of maturing emotions, where love is strong. Studies of conversion ages show that sixteen is a most favored year. Thirteen and eighteen or nineteen are also well pronounced. These are located at the peak of three psychological experiences. In the third place it is evident that these conversion experiences differ with the psychological experiences of the individual. Late conversion is likely to take the form of a sense of spiritual ruin or personal guilt before God. Adolescent conversion is likely to grow out of a conviction of "personal failure to realize an ideal," or sins of shortcoming. Another type has a sense of lack of harmony which is attended by great distress of soul. The differences in type are due psychologically to differences in temperament, in childhood training, and in the life that they have lived. The way of the religious educator is plain in view of these facts. He must utilize every contact between the youth and the finest Christian men and women for reaching the central objective, a personal surrender of his powers to God.

For worship. The attainment of full Christian personality requires power and vision. These come through worship as mystical union with God. The church at Jerusalem first met for spiritual renewal and experience, then a revival broke out. Personal power in the Christian life has come only as men have found reality in their devotional life.

Religious educators will find the implication of unfolding for worship to mean: first, that there is but one way to God, and that is by experience. Second, that experience of God is possible for every age in terms of its own development. Third, that the media of worship must be adapted to the stage of experience of the worshipper. This includes hymns, Scripture, prayers, and ceremonies. Fourth, since worship is the meeting point of God and men, worship is a matter for Christian economists to safeguard by capitalizing its power and by tabooing slovenliness in its conduct.

[5] Tracy, *Psychology of Adolescents*, p. 186 (Macmillan Co., N. Y., 1920).

CHAPTER VIII

OBJECTIVES

The educational process includes objectives, curriculum, and method. Objectives are the results that we wish to achieve. The curriculum is the subject matter offered as the vehicle for reaching the objectives. The method is the way in which the curriculum is manipulated. An objective without a vehicle is a dream. An objective without a method is a hazard. A curriculum and a method without an objective is folly. The process is like a tailor cutting out cloth by a pattern but without a customer. Such a process is wasteful. A tailor with a pattern and a customer but lacking cloth is useless. A tailor with cloth and a customer but with no pattern would waste his material and disappoint his customer. In the religious educational process these three elements are so interrelated that one without the other is useless.

Years ago some observer remarked that if our foresight were as good as our hindsight we would be a longsight ahead. An intelligent objective provides against the tragedy of an untrained foresight, and uses the wisdom of our hindsight to guarantee better outcomes of foresight. An objective has been defined by Vieth[1] as "a statement of a result consciously accepted as a desired outcome of a given process." Objectives are the "statements of desired outcomes to be achieved through the process of education."[2] They are to education what orders are to a transport convoy sailing without lights or signals to a predetermined port, or what the blue-print is to a builder.

THE FUNCTION OF OBJECTIVES IN RELIGIOUS EDUCATION

It is most important to blaze the trail for childhood by the poles of the Christian compass. Supreme values lie in the purposes and ends of religion. Waste, and aimlessness in religion are economically and spiritually vicious. To avoid these evils it is imperative that leaders should understand something of the functions of objectives.

An Objective Furnishes the Pattern for Modeling the Curriculum.—The formation of the curriculum is determined by

[1] *Objectives of Religious Education* (Harper and Brothers, 1930, p. 18).
[2] *Ibid.*, p. 19.

the product desired. For example, the instructions of Jesus assign definite objectives as "making disciples," and "teaching them to observe." The master passion for the Christ was that all men might see and love God as he saw and loved Him. To this end the curriculum is formed.

An Objective Scales the Method to the Process.—Method is the technique of the process. Its function is to approach every problem with an open mind for the discovery of truth. Its function is to ferret out the meanings of the truth in human relations and problems. Its function is to achieve the task of carrying over into deeds and changed conduct, the ideals of the curriculum. An objective functions when it employs method to give meaning to subject matter that may be requisite to the knowledge, attitudes and skills needed in a Christian society.

An Objective Sets the Pattern for Leadership Training.— Insurance men train their salesmen after a different manner from asparagus growers, or watch manufacturers. Neither group would be effective in the other fields. The materials handled, the processes, and the purposes are different, and training takes these into account. The leader in the teaching of religion must be trained so to interpret religion that men may be won to Christ, and so to motivate religion that men may apply his principles to daily life. Training for public school teaching does not suffice for this service. The objectives of the two types of teachers have much in common, and much more that is distinctive. The leader in religion has his pattern of training implied in his objective.

An Objective Motivates Christian Endeavor.—Tests made among average Sunday school teachers disclose an inadequate or indefinite sense of direction in the teaching function. Lack of interest, absence of enthusiasm, lifeless performance, weariness in the work, carelessness in preparation and attendance, discouragement in outcome, usually result from failure to set out objectives. A tangible and real goal stimulates effort, and encourages endurance. The workman who sees a cathedral in a pile of stones is more fortunate than the fellow-laborer who sees only an opportunity to earn his bread. The Christian teacher who senses in the life of the boy in his class a potential prophet of a new day, or a spiritual workman in the daily toil, knows no bounds to his zeal.

An Objective Conserves Energy, Spirit and Life.—The tragedy of life is its wastes. Confusion, uncertainty, destruction of materials and loss of efforts are rare where men know what they are doing. Courts have sometimes confirmed youths in criminality by inadequate and incorrect ideas of the reason for law and of the meaning of justice. Likewise many parents and perhaps many Sunday school teachers have aided and abetted malformation of character through lack of understanding of the nature of the child and of the objectives of genetic processes. Artillery practice may produce noise, satisfy the powder manufacturers, and give a type of pleasure to the gunners as they train their guns toward open space in night target shooting, but the purpose of practice is defeated and the procedure wasteful because they do not see a target, or know its location. Likewise much Sunday school teaching is as prodigal of effort as night target practice because there are no visible objectives. A religious objective avoids waste of energy of teacher and pupil, and possibly a waste of human life.

An Objective Provides a Measuring Instrument for the Determination of Progress.—In making an automobile trip to a distant city in a limited time, one drives with confidence as he checks his daily mileage against his total mileage and the allotted time. In college a degree at the end of four years enables the youth to know his daily progress. A failure at one point may defeat the end. The whole course moves forward with certainty as it is checked daily by its objective. Sunday schools set up standards of excellence as objectives in administration, organization and teaching. These register good or poor performance. Of more vital concern is the setting up of objectives for the class-room and the home. The determination of such aims as conversion, change of habits, reshaping of malformed personality, knowledge of Bible facts, decision for Christian life-callings, will provide measurements of progress. The more definite these objectives the greater will be the satisfaction in checking results. Without these objectives there is no valid basis for choosing or evaluating much of the curriculum material and procedure. Without them attempts at directing class instruction are likely to lean toward lesson learning rather than growth in understanding.

THE DETERMINATION OF OBJECTIVES

Three methods have been used in arriving at objectives. In the past curriculum construction was left to tradition, hit-or-miss efforts, and the whims of lesson writers. Rather glibly these individuals discoursed on "knowing the Bible," "character building," and other general terms whose only virtue was indefiniteness. The objectives that used to be set up certainly have the appearance of being a kind of "New Year resolution," conforming to the spirit of the occasion but not to be taken seriously under any condition. Today we are concerned with determining specific objectives which bring education into more vital relation with life.

The first method for discovering objectives has been called the *consensus of opinion method*. It is a kind of questionnaire procedure. This is the practice of asking our equally perplexed friends who have given little thought to the matter, to help us solve our problems. Out of our "collective ignorance" we attempt a solution. The judgment of thoughtful men, however, may help to formulate a philosophy, and aid progress. Its value in determining objectives will depend upon the training of the men and the nature of the product sought.

The second method may be called *analysis of life experiences*, or *the scientific method*. Sociologists refer to such a plan as "job analysis," which will show the abilities, attitudes, habits, appreciations, and forms of knowledge that men need. The educational sociologist, by a more systematic study of everyday life, has discovered social needs and educational values. Each educational activity must prepare for some situation that will likely be faced by the pupil. To meet these requirements impersonal scientific investigations of the needs of society must be made. Peters[3] proposes the following needs: 1. "Fundamentally we need to know, on a scientific basis, what are the abilities that are needed in a society, the fitnesses that individuals must have if they are to be socially efficient in maximum degree. 2. Next we need to determine scientifically what is the subject matter that can make largest contributions toward these desired ends. 3. Then we need to know, on an experimental basis, what are the methods of handling subject matter that will be most economical of time and energy. 4. Finally, we need to have some adequate measuring instruments that will enable us to tell whether or not, and how largely, we are succeeding in actually attaining these ends."

The church has done little in this area. Hartshorne and May opened a new approach to character education through their "Studies in Deceit." They turned trial and error into a prescribed method. Vieth enriched the field of religion by his scientifically conducted study of the writings of approved religious leaders, the results of which were submitted as comprehensive objectives. No doubt there are values for religion awaiting further careful investigations. It is a question in the minds of some whether the Christian college should

[3] *Foundations of Educational Sociology*, p. 81 (Rev. ed., 1930, Macmillan).

not be specifically entrusted with many investigations in the field of religion that would yield superior values to the church. One college, for example, undertook a limited study of Biblical material with a view to determining certain values for citizenship building. Another test based on recognition of a quoted passage, location of passage, memorization of passage, and personal observance as a philosophy of life, established the priority of certain passages as lesson materials. Another investigation covered a study of specific hymns in a selected group of churches over a period of weeks. The results became a basis for a possible reëducating of those congregations in hymn usage. These unpretentious experiments suggest the possibilities of church colleges in applying scientific methods to religious uses. Out of such study valuable sets of objectives might be produced.

A third method of determining objectives may be called *the philosophical method*. Philosophy has been referred to as "the attempt to think consistently about the meaning of life as a whole," or "an answer to the problem of human values." Vieth[4] maintains that the ultimate aims of education can only be determined by philosophy. Bode[5] contends that education and life are more than scholarship. He observes that many of our educational leaders seem to "approach their task without any definite point of orientation, without any clear consciousness of whence we have come and whither we ought to go." The development of a program to meet this need of social, ethical, moral, religious living is an undertaking in philosophy. The proposed program, Bode points out, tells us the direction in which education should move: "It furnishes the standards or objectives by which we may be guided in the scientific determination of 'immediate objectives,' i.e. the objectives which serve as means for the realization of more ulterior ends." All of this means that the objectives determine "what sort of facts are needed in order that a program may be built."

What are life's supreme values? What is the ultimate purpose of life? The philosophy which correctly answers the questions is theistic, not humanistic. It believes in a controlling personal deity, concerned about human values, and requiring certain ethical conduct after a divine pattern, dwelling within the spirit of man, accessible to the spirit of man, yet transcending human reach. Humanism leaves God out of life, or identifies him with human ideals. The objectives growing out of such philosophies differ widely. Theistic objectives involve

---

[4] *Objectives in Religious Education*, p. 45 (Harper & Brothers, 1930).
[5] *Modern Educational Theories*, pp. 333, 347 (Macmillan, 1927).

an acceptance of the fact of God, an experience of God, a committal to God's way, religious ideals of living, and an intelligent knowledge of the Book of God. They recognize the existence of a soul, and of a destiny known as personal immortality. The Christian faith proclaims a living Christ, offers comfort in bereavement, ennobles the present life, and plants the conviction that the crown of life is the wealth of eternity. Naturalism and humanism have offered no adequate substitute. The Christian faith further believes that man can choose between good and evil, and that every individual is accountable for his conduct. The Christian philosophy based on that of Jesus exalts the good life, accepting the doctrine that losing one's life is the way to find it.

Ultimate objectives must be determined by Christian living. The choice among the many values contending for primacy in life will be made in the light of one's philosophy of life. The scientific method is useful in the defining of immediate and specific objectives in religious education, but the determination of the ultimate ends can be made only through philosophy. It is probably true that the best results are obtained through a careful integration of the results of the three methods.

TYPES OF OBJECTIVES

A road trip to a distant city is not so difficult today because our objective has been anticipated by experienced travelers. We are advised to take a certain marked route, and the road map will provide all further information as to intersecting roads, cities en route, points of special interest, and definite mileage. Reaching the destination depends upon taking the right road and keeping on the road. Along the way further planning is necessary, setting daily distances to match the total time allowance, reaching hotels at the end of the day, stopping at points of interest along the way. In terms of objectives the first would be called ultimate, while the second would be immediate objectives. The attainment of the first depends upon the second. The validity of the second depends upon the reality of the first. Neither without the other is complete. Yet ultimate and immediate do not define objectives. They simply indicate the order in which we wish to reach a goal. Other groupings are more definitely purposive.

Both the scientific and philosophical determination of objectives break up the aims into cross-section statements, as the following indicate.

Social Science.—Social science urges utility as the determiner of objectives. The greatest amount of good in the time at our disposal is the ideal. How to live in the widest sense, ability to think reflectively, to be cultured in mind and heart, to be spiritually effective, and to be socially capable and Christian, are to meet the utility purpose. The relative value of the time spent, of the subject matter mastered, of the benefit to be derived should determine objectives. Utility makes no charge against any curricular elements that in themselves have value, but insists that they be compared with other subject matter that might be used instead. Objectives formulated by utility provide for those needs most frequently occurring in the life of the pupil, requiring the most critical adjustments, touching life at most points, and which hold most meaning for the individual.

Society.—Organized society urges protection of group solidarity as the determiner of objectives. Society has the right to protect itself against the dangers of ignorance and vice. Society sets as objectives for its safeguarding, the training of the individual to active participation in the social process, the sense of social responsibility, the recognition of honest social debt, thrift, the spirit of artistry, respect for law and finally, the spiritual motivation of social, national and international relations.

Race Experience.—Race experience urges conformity to established values as determiner of objectives. The fathers built the sound society in their day upon memorization of the Scriptures, respect for authority in home, church, and state, the mastery of doctrinal statements and conformity to adult patterns. These are made central in any plan of education. The great inherited faiths are waiting to serve the seeker and to indicate the lines he will need to take. These ardent experiences of humanity still have at the heart of them "some inescapable command." Professor Atkins has well said, "Religion can say with more truth than any other human institution, 'They reckon ill who leave me out.'"

Class-Room Method.—Class-room method urges the teaching situation as determiner of objectives. Sluggish children will respond to activity methods perhaps. Restless children, problem children, average children and adults will respond to elastic methods. Through these situations the teacher is setting up objectives for each lesson. The objectives which the teacher himself states, and labors to validate in the class-room are practically the real objectives of his course. They surpass "any hand me down statements he is likely to secure."

The Curriculum.—The curriculum urges a philosophy of education as determiner of objectives. The church school curriculum follows one of two points of view—the subject matter point of view and the conduct-response point of view. According to the first position the objectives are either to protect the traditional teachings or ritual or symbolism of the church by incorporating them into the subject matter, or to preserve rigorously the Bible text as the only material for study. According to the second point of view the objective is the development of the spiritual life of the child. Subject matter is stressed only as it serves this end. The curriculum objectives are to bring together all materials that will further religious experience in the individual. They will set up proper goals and provide the means for actual experiences in situations such as the pupil normally meets in the routine of his life.

Public school and church school leaders urge the character trait as determiner of objectives. Specific traits are recognized as desirable or undesirable. The traits singled out are the essentials in the development of an intelligent respect for the conventions of society, the development of personal ability to think reflectively, the development of a sense of responsibility of membership in society, and the development of an integrated personality. Christian character has become definite enough for us to lift out of Christian conduct certain qualities of acting which we call Christian traits—such as coöperation, dependability, faith, forgiveness, love, loyalty, reverence. Such traits are specific and can be easily used in interpreting the individual's experience, and in checking conduct as Christian.

The church urges discipleship as determiner of objectives. Committed as it is to making disciples, and to teaching them to observe the instructions of Jesus, the church finds its general objectives defined. Winning the individual to Christ, indoctrination in the Christian message and program, cultivating Christian graces, making real the fellowship with God in worship and faith, are among the objectives set out as religious.

ULTIMATE OBJECTIVES

The term "ultimate" does not mean final, but long range. Ultimate objectives are aims that cannot be achieved in the present. Possibly they are never achieved. Christian character, good citizenship are of this type. Ultimate objectives are difficult to locate because they are intangible. They are like the kingdom of God that men search for widely but to find it within. They are life's perspective. Compared with the immediate objectives they are the ideal as contrasted with the active objectives. They mark out the direction of life, while the specific aims mark out the daily efforts. They are the teacher aims while the latter are the pupil purposes. They are the curriculum concern while the latter are the method concern.

The source of ultimate objectives in religious education is the ideals of the Christian religion for individuals and for society. The formulation of these ideals may be determined in one of three ways, or in combination. The usual source of the statements of objectives has been consensus of opinion. A second way consists of a research analysis by trained observers of the experiences of life for the discovery of life's greatest needs. A third approach to the determination of objectives is through a philosophical study of religious values. The best proof of the soundness of any philosophy of education is its product.

The areas of ultimate objectives, as defined by the second method, a scientific technique, appear to be at least seven in number. Paul H. Vieth arrived at this conclusion after studies of the writings of the foremost leaders in the church field in America. While prepared primarily to meet a graduate school requirement, and then published under the title, "Objectives of Religious Education," his statement of aims has been accepted by various church bodies as the general basis of the curriculum. As representing such the International Council of Religious Education states them as follows (The International Curriculum Guide, Book One, pp. 10-15):

(1) Christian religious education seeks to foster in growing persons a consciousness of God as a reality in human experience, and a sense of personal relationship to him.

(2) Christian religious education seeks to develop in growing persons such an understanding and appreciation of the personality, life and teachings of Jesus as will lead to experience of him as Savior and Lord, loyalty to him and his cause, and manifest itself in daily life and conduct.

(3) Christian religious education seeks to foster in growing persons a progressive and continuous development of Christlike character.

(4) Christian religious education seeks to develop in growing persons the ability and disposition to participate in and contribute constructively to the building of a socal order throughout the world, embodying the ideal of the Fatherhood of God and the brotherhood of man.

(5) Christian religious education seeks to develop in growing persons the ability and disposition to participate in the organized. society of Christians—the church.

(6) Christian religious education seeks to lead growing persons into a Christian interpretation of life and the universe; the ability to see in it God's purpose and plan; a life philosophy built on this interpretation.

(7) Christian religious education seeks to effect in growing persons the assimilation of the best religious experience of the race, preeminently that recorded in the Bible, as effective guidance to present experience.

The areas of ultimate objectives as determined largely by a Christian philosophy will cover in general the same needs. They are grouped naturally under the divine relationship, the social relationship, and the personal growth. The first covers the Creator, the Redeemer, and the revelation of divine will. The second group covers the institutional relations of men of brotherliness in a church fellowship, and of men of good will in a human society. The third group covers the character traits, and the integration of personality in a philosophy of life that guides to the ideal destiny.

DIVINE RELATIONSHIP OBJECTIVES

The Creator Aim.—"Thou shalt love the Lord thy God with all thy heart." Religion meant for Jesus the assurance of God as Father, of God's will as the law of life, and the ability to see Him everywhere. The objective of the religious educator is to bring the individual into the confidence that we live in "a reasonable world; that we are a part of a just and moral order." The teacher seeks to create a sense of need for what religion has to offer as well as to show how religion meets that need.

The Redeemer Aim.—"Believe on the Lord Jesus Christ, and thou shalt be saved." These words express the faith of church people. The teacher of religion sets as his dominant purpose the winning of the child to Christ. To leave the living Christ out of instruction is to destroy every reason for the Christian movement.

The Revelation or Bible Aim.—"The sower soweth the word." We are the creatures of the past as well as of today. Religious experience has produced its philosophy, and has well tested its right to claim the loyalty of men to the spiritual control of life which it proclaims. The teacher's objective is to plant the Bible truths in the mind and affections of the youngest and of the most seasoned veteran, to teach the meaning of these truths, and to lead men to test every act and every thought by their precepts.

THE INSTITUTIONAL RELATIONS GROUP

The Church Aim.—"In whom ye also are builded together for habitation of God in the spirit." Jesus did not make the church an end in itself. It finds its meaning as a means to the end of the Kingdom of God. It is the Master's great missionary society. The objective of the religious educator is to enlist every disciple of Christ in the church, and to develop every member into an efficient apostle. The teacher regards every pupil as potentially a missionary, and sets about training him to assume maximum responsibility.

The Kingdom in Society Aim.—"Thou shalt love thy neighbor as thyself." The first century Gnostics branded all matter as evil. The only two escapes from the flesh, which was matter and therefore evil, were through withdrawal from life, or through utter disregard of the flesh. Contrary to the teachings of this sect Jesus ordered his followers, "Go ye into all the world," for "ye are the salt of the earth." A better understanding of the meaning of Jesus will reveal to men a closer correlation between the Kingdom of God and the good society. Men grow in Christian virtues as they mingle with society rather than as they withdraw from society. The objective of the teacher is so to guide the child in the midst of his daily experiences that he will come to discover God in the streets, and to find the purposes of God increasingly effective in human relations.

THE PERSONAL GROUP

The Character Aim.—"Be ye therefore perfect, even as your Father which is in heaven is perfect." Christ thus concluded instructions touching human relations. Christianity entrusts its adherents with a spirit of life. Character consists of socially approved attitudes, habits, and appreciations, but Christian character consists of the same characteristics and traits fashioned after the Christian pattern, and governed by the Christian motive. The objective of the religious educator is to bring the individual to govern his conduct and thoughts by the Christian ideal.

The Personality Aim.—"Abide in me, and I in you." The Christian philosophy of life grows out of this Christ-centered outlook. The pattern of life which we accept gives shape to our personalities. The materialist thinks of life as a treasure-house for him to possess, get it as he can. He crowns might king, and accepts the spoils as belonging to the victor. The Christian looks at life as God's greatest value, and has learned that its highest riches are obtained through love. The objective of the teacher is to build a philosophy of life which discovers its meaning and value, and opens human eyes to see spiritual reality.

In general ultimate aims should satisfy the following demands: (1) They should dove-tail into practical, daily life. (2) They should cover religious, social, and personal needs of the individual. (3) They should be true to the accepted revelation of divine truth. (4) **They** should be true to the best ideals of human experience. (5) **They** should mould changing society by the pattern of the society that wisdom decrees should exist.

SPECIFIC OBJECTIVES

After determining the direction of education the immediate **and** continuing function of the teacher is to locate specific or immediate aims. These constitute the objectives for each lesson period, **and** for each unit of work. They are selected on the basis of their fitness for instilling the knowledge, developing the abilities, and creating the attitudes that are required for building the major objective. These aims are within the reach of a day or a period. They seek to meet today's problems today. Their educational value lies in their direct relation to and contribution to the more remote purposes. Mastery in teaching consists in ability to see the ultimate objective through the specific aim.

Nature of Specific Objectives.—The nature of specific objectives appears when one remembers that there is a reason for performing every act. In every life situation there is a goal which the individual desires to achieve. That goal is a Christian objective when it rests upon the ideals of the Christian religion. The religious educator recognizes this fact, and seeks to arouse a motive for doing the specific act in a Christian manner. The specific Christian act becomes a specific objective. Honesty, for example, is inclusive of honesty in a wide variety of situations. The teacher seeks to produce specific habits of honesty in speech, in play, in work, and in all other relations. The Christian motive lifts the act out of mores into morals.

Specific aims grow out of immediate pupil needs. For greatest educational value the teacher will adapt his objectives to his discoveries of these needs. His discoveries will be made on the play ground, at camp, on a hike, in the home, or wherever the child reacts naturally. The reactions of pupils to various situations will reveal personal needs. The questions he asks, the friends he seeks, the interests he manifests, will provide a clue to his thinking and living, hence a basis for setting up specific objectives.

The determination of specific objectives is arrived at through at least three channels, a trained judgment, a diagnosis of needs, and scientific research. Trained judgment grows out of experience in locating the elements that constitute a Christian ideal, and the detailed steps involved in the process of attainment. Diagnosis is **an** analytical process of splitting up ultimate aims into their components, or a process of stepping down the intangible ideal into the tangible action situation. More specifically it ferrets out the maladjustments and other needs and makes them the objectives of specific correctives. The adult, for example, may be found to hold to erroneous interpretations of the facts of religion or of life. He may possess untrustworthy knowledge of doctrines which has been accepted as truth. It is the function of immediate objectives to seek to remedy the error. Scientific research is the technique of the sociologist in setting up objectives. More progress has been made in blue-printing the maximum citizen than in studying his moral needs. Studies have been made, however, on the basis of the needs discovered in the child, and on the basis of the characteristics possessed in common by great men, as fundamental human needs. Extended surveys have been made of school children of specific ages as they study and play with a view to determining the core experiences of each age. Likewise studies of great men in all ages will reveal character traits held in common by all of them, and regarded as essential to great living. Objectives are formulated on the basis of such findings.

Principles in the Use of Specific Objectives.—Certain general principles should guide in the use of specific objectives. (1) Specific objectives must point toward the ultimate ideal. Pupil purpose, pupil interest, and pupil background, should be guided toward the ideals for which religion stands. (2) They must provide as complete as possible coverage of the component elements of the ultimate aim. Varied areas of application of a principle encourage transfer. (3) They must provide reflective thinking, or the relating of cause and effect. Thinking goes on at the point of a dilemma. A decision formed in the face of a felt difficulty prepares one to select a course in subsequent new situations. (4) They must be tangible. Religion is peculiarly subject to abstractions. The founder of Christianity employed the concrete in much of his teaching. (5) They must reflect the immediate needs of the pupil. To ignore the principle is to lose vital contact in instruction. (6) They must be stated in terms that are meaningful to the teacher. "Salvation," "faith," and other terms are sometimes hazy, and therefore meaningless, to pupils because they are hazy to the teacher.

CHAPTER IX

CURRICULUM

In his *Song of Hiawatha* Longfellow wrote "As unto the bow the cord is, so unto man is woman. Though she draws him yet she follows." Differently stated, the figure might read, "As unto the bow the cord is, so unto the curriculum are the objectives. Though they draw it yet they follow." The curriculum gives value and tautness to the objectives. The objectives drive the strength of the curriculum to the mark.

Traditionally the curriculum has been thought of as an organized body of desired knowledge. According to Bower[1] it becomes "an instrument in the hands of the religious community for preparing persons to live religiously in a complex and rapidly changing world." For Betts[2] it means all of the "organized educative influences brought to bear upon the child through the agency of the school." The scope of the curriculum is therefore made to include instruction, worship, expression and all the planned activities that take place in the church school.

In the field of morals and religion such a curriculum occupies the place of importance next to the child, and consists of the posting by mature society of markers along life's highway for the guidance of the immature. It is hoped that this knowledge of life based upon human experience will enable younger members of society to make safe and happy human adjustments. Experience came out of life. The curriculum proposes to return it to life, and that with interest.

THEORIES OF THE CURRICULUM

The theory and practice of religious education as it applies to the curriculum has passed through a long and changing history. There has been little agreement as to the nature of the child, the meaning of character in the Christian sense or of methods in the field of procedures. Consequently no permanent solution of the problem of the curriculum has yet been agreed upon. A statement of several points of view will be interesting and helpful.

[1] *Curriculum of Religious Education*, p. 254, Charles Scribner's Sons, 1927.
[2] *The Curriculum of Religious Education*, p. 239, Abingdon Press, 1921.

Education as Discipline.—The first theory to take form was that of education as discipline. The thousand years before Luther were characterized by authority and discipline. This was the order in church and state. The few imposed their wills upon the masses, and demanded obedience and submission. The teachers of Luther and Ignatius Loyola encouraged the performance of hard or distasteful things in order to achieve victory over sinful natures. Any personal satisfaction was felt to be of the Devil, hence to be avoided. Naturally these conceptions colored educational theory and set disciplinary materials at the center of education. The more difficult a subject the more value it held for education. Individuals who had been subjected to rigorous mental processes of memorization or reasoning in one area were by virtue of that discipline likewise capable in all other fields. The educated man was one who had applied himself to the disciplinary subjects, and submitted himself to the repressive measures of the authorities.

Knowledge as the Foundation of Education.—A second theory stressed instruction or knowledge as the foundation of education. Herbart came to the conclusion that there is not an intellectual and a moral education: there is only one education, and that founded upon instruction. There is no education apart from instruction. Knowledge is not an ornament but a builder of mind. Feeling and willing, or moral and spiritual states spring from objects of knowledge.

The cumulative experiences of the race have crystallized into customs, and their violations into taboos. Thus these have grown into a treasured body of knowledge. The protective urge of maturity has prompted the parent to teach these facts to the child as the Shema of the Hebrews so well illustrates. This organized body of knowledge therefore becomes society's curriculum. It follows that the preparation of every child for later responsibilities requires that this subject matter of learning be imparted by instruction. Fixing knowledge in the mind, this theory holds, is the open door to character and faith. "Knowledge is power" has been an honored motto in many a school-house.

This theory had its effect on the curriculum in religion. Men must know the doctrines. The gravest error consisted of ignoring or refusing sound doctrine. Creeds must be planted in the minds of men. The catechism was an attempt to break down these massive doctrines into child-mind portions. Subject matter presented with interest and thoroughness was depended upon to produce character. The fallacy of the theory, so Bower points out[3] lay in the forcing of education to the patterns of race inheritance, with an adjustment to the past rather than to ongoing life. The curriculum became Bible centered, with the courses limited to the history, biography and theology of the Book, the purpose of instruction in religion being to transmit the recorded inheritance of the past.

The Child at the Center.—A third theory of the curriculum puts the child at the center. Begun by Froebel in an unhappy childhood, his philosophy of education discovered the child. In his "cosmic evolution" "creation is not an act performed once and for all; it is rather a continuous process of productive activity." Education becomes "an element in the process of cosmic evolution." The Herbartians developed this theory under the title "culture epoch." In biology it was called the "recapitulation theory." Froebel's educational system was a protest against the idea that learning could be imposed upon the child from without.

The curriculum in this theory rests on the belief that the child learns by doing and through doing, and that learning is the result of his self-expression. The object of learning is not knowledge but the building of habits, skills, attitudes. The material to be used in education must be drawn from the ideas, customs, and institutions at the culture level experienced by the child. Boys' clubs at one time projected their programs largely on the "culture-epoch" theory. Little "savages" were let loose to tear apart the household furnishings of a civilized father and mother. To correct them would be to impound the pent-up savagery that must at some time be released. The difficulty arising from this approach to the curriculum is that it anchors its material in the past, and fails to anticipate progress.

Maximum Development of the Individual.—A fourth theory places the maximum person at the center of education. The interest of education is not so much in the child as an immature human being, but in what the child may become. The objective is the achievement of the maximum development of the individual. The educator sees the integration of the self taking place, as Bower advocates, through purposeful experience, in the midst of an environing society. The teacher's part is to help the child find meaning in his experience, and guide him in recognizing a purpose in it all.

The curriculum aims to provide for such a person an opportunity to find experience in contacts with ultimate value, but accepts the tested experience of the race as to the direction of ultimate achieve-

[3] *Ibid.*

ment. Society guides as the individual ascends, and society has fulfilled its end when the individual has arrived at fullest self-realization.

Religion is vastly concerned with this theory. But one must keep in mind the fact that if morality and religion are to function effectively as control in experience, they must be taught as a part of the experience. The habits and attitudes of the growing child are being shaped by his experiences with his associates in his play and social life, and by the actual practices which he observes to exist in the community. One learns what he practices and not necessarily what he is told. When instruction in the Sunday school consists of words, such as "be good," what the child learns is to listen to words. Physicians, lawyers, and skilled workmen in many arts, have attained superior performance through practice under trained supervision. This is no new fact, yet many teachers forget that mere knowledge of facts of the Bible will not insure Christian conduct. This theory of the curriculum is exceedingly valuable because it assumes the necessity of guided experience in producing a maximum Christian person.

THE CURRICULUM BACKGROUNDS

In answering the question "How are we to get children to want to do what they know they ought to do but what they do not want to do?" various devices have been proposed from "spare the rod and spoil the child" to cramming his mind with Bible verses. The early Sunday school movement inherited the religious convictions of the Reformation, which placed the Bible at the center of the church and of life. Luther taught the Bible to the masses. From his day to the present the curriculum has been constructed with varying relations to the Bible. Some leaders look upon the Bible as the text book of religion, and question the validity of any type of lesson material drawn from any other source. Others go even further than allowing Bible centered lessons, and demand "the Bible only" for instruction.

The Bible alone has never remained for long periods the sole curriculum. In order to understand and enrich its meaning organized courses of study have come into existence. At least four steps have been taken in the development of the traditional lesson courses.

(1) Before the American Revolution the churches were bent on destroying heresy. Since correct doctrine was so important, the Bible must be interpreted in terms of accepted statements of truth. The "catechism" arose as the instrument of instruction in doctrine.

(2) When the movement for general education in America became

widespread, the schools dropped religion from their curriculum because of the separation of church and state. Likewise, the secular element was dropped from the Sunday school course, and the Bible again became the sole textbook.

(3) The first attempt at organization of Bible study took the form of Bible verse memory contests. The discovery was soon made that the memory was tricky, and that there was no great instructional value in this recital of Scripture. Churches keeping careful records reported a falling off in moral and spiritual conduct. To meet the practical need of bridging between the Scripture and the child a "question book" was prepared for the purpose of stimulating explorations into the Bible.

(4) Prior to the middle of the last century it dawned upon the leaders that the wide use of catechisms and question books was evidence of a definite need that the Bible be organized into lesson plans, and be adapted to individual differences. As early as 1823 certain passages of Scripture were selected as the basis of a course of Biblical "lessons." Their value was apparent, and the selected lesson has remained popular for a century.

TYPES OF CURRICULA

Confusion arose in the early experiments with an organized study of the Bible because no aims had been devised, and no leaders were trained in the principles of curriculum making. The acceptance of the Bible as the sole subject matter of the Sunday school limited any attempts at the formation of a curriculum. It soon became obvious that some thread of purpose must be run through the Bible to give the serial studies uniformity of length, sequence and usefulness. Truman Parmele, as early as 1823, offered the churches of Utica, New York, a group of lessons based on the historical portions of the New Testament. The earliest permanent effort at an organized curriculum was made by the American Sunday School Union in 1825, by enlarging their two-year course based on Biblical materials to a five-year cycle. The school year of nine months seems to have determined the number of lessons annually.

There followed a number of similar or improved courses which are more or less familiar to the present Sunday school worker. They may be grouped as the Uniform Lessons, the Graded Lessons and the Elective Courses.

The Uniform Lesson.—By 1872 Sunday school associations, denominational promoters, and private publishers, brought to maturity the "uniform lesson." In the same year the National Sunday School Association met in Indianapolis. Mr. B. F. Jacobs, a Baptist layman of Chicago, offered the resolution that formed the International Lesson Committee. The resolution provided for the appointment of a committee of five clergymen, and five laymen, to select a course of Bible Lessons for a series of years not to exceed seven. Alternation between the Old and New Testaments was to occur semi-annually or quarterly. The Convention by this resolution recommended the adoption of these lessons by the Sunday Schools of the whole country. The function of the committee was limited to the selection of the lesson title, the Scripture passage, and the memory verse. The materials thus selected were sent to each denomination wishing to use the uniform lesson, and each publishing board prepared the lessons with comments for distribution in "quarterlies."

Advantages and disadvantages cluster around the uniform lessons. During its more than sixty years of existence the plan has increasingly sold the world on the value of systematized instruction in religion. It has made the world Sunday school conscious but the limitations of the plan in this day of public school enlightenment make its continuance questionable. Its disconnected order, "hop-skip-and-jump" method will never unfold the maximum of spiritual facts of the Bible. The Book so taught, in the words of a devoted Sunday school teacher, "will remain too largely a source book for moralizing and preaching. No one would undertake to teach any other great literature by such a scrappy method."

The Graded Lesson.—Fifty-five years ago, Doctor William Rainey Harper prepared his Hebrew texts on the inductive study plan. His method was transferred to general Bible study. Through his pupils the plan spread in popularity. The public schools gradually added strength to the idea by their experiments in a graded course of study. Many teachers in the public schools were teaching in the Sunday schools, and trying out in the Sunday schools principles employed by them for five days a week. These forces operated to create a definite demand for lessons more suitable to child needs.

Conservative leaders objected to grading the materials of the Bible. A late pastor of great wisdom contended that the Bible was the same for seven-year-old Mary as it was for seventy-year-old great-grandmother. But public school leaders, disillusioned teachers of primary children who had seen the harm of uniformity to younger pupils, and educationally minded parents, directly and indirectly forced an issue on a graded Sunday school curriculum. "If graded lessons about the Bible are necessary," objected a prominent Sunday school superintendent, "then why not graded lessons in the Bible?" The International Graded Lessons resulted.

The Closely Graded Lessons consisted of a separate unit of subject matter prepared for each year to be used as textbooks are used in the public school. These lessons were "pupil-centered" rather than material centered, the aim being in terms of the needs of the child rather than with the thought of covering any particular section of the subject matter. In plan the lessons are intended to be consecutive and accumulative; that is to say, the lessons of each succeeding age-group presuppose the training afforded by those of the preceding group, thus creating a continuous series of steps upward through the curriculum. "Up to the ninth year the lessons were organized on the topical plan. For the four years from nine to twelve inclusive the courses were based on biblical chronology. From the thirteenth to the sixteenth year inclusive biography and history supply the basis of materials, but without emphasis on chronological sequence. From seventeen to twenty the courses deal with sociology and historical materials, chronological order being observed in two of the courses."[4]

In addition to the International Graded Series there are several independent graded studies in use. Among them are "The Constructive Studies in Religion," published by the University of Chicago Press, and "The Completely Graded Series," published by Charles Scribner's Sons. Denominational closely graded lessons are published under trade names, and as publishing board series. Among them are Keystone (Northern Baptists), Pilgrim (Congregational), Bethany (Disciples), Augsburg (Lutheran), Berean (Methodist), Westminster (Presbyterian).

The Elective System.—The former rigidly organized curriculum has suffered severely in public school circles of late. Larger liberties are granted local groups for the determination of content and arrangement of curriculum. The introduction to a state bulletin begins: "The school must give a larger place to realities; it must develop in youth, through actual experience, greater initiative, greater willingness to accept responsibility and to face reality; greater powers of leadership, of organization and of dealing with problems on the basis of data and objective interpretation. The curriculum must provide for individual pupils, as well as groups, upon the basis of inborn capacities, background of experience, present

---

[4] Betts, *Curriculum of Religious Education,* p. 362, Abingdon Press.

needs, and predictable future needs." (Alabama Department of Education, Curriculum Bulletin No. 5, 1938, p. v)

The church must develop a type of curriculum in addition to the uniform lessons better to meet the needs of men today. The Bible is a closed book to many, except as familiar writings yield select passages for moralizing. The increasingly higher level of intelligence in many churches would warrant the use of background studies, and correlative courses as illuminators of the Bible. Studies in religions of the world, Greek philosophy, the development of Christian churches, philosophy of religion, are within the grasp of many church members today, and would enrich their lives. Such human variables can be provided for only through a system of the electives supplementing the regular courses.

The range of electives beyond the uniform lesson, or the strictly Biblical studies, covers such areas as missions, church history, Christian apologetics, Christian hymnody, Christian biography, Christian industrialism, Christian parent guidance. A case in point is described by Grace H. Patton in "Character," (Vol. 1, No. 2). The curriculum for parent education in Riverside church, New York City, was the experiment reported. The aim of this school is "to find a satisfactory approach to every moral and ethical problem which the average parent of today has to face in dealing with children. It aims to lead them to some practical and helpful conclusions regarding these problems." In this way parents with wide ranges of problems become beneficiaries of the contributions of religion to every day living.

Certain secondary values are also attached to elective courses. One thoughtful teacher believes that their introduction will improve the quality of teaching, just as specialization has improved the quality of teaching in the high-schools and colleges. Further it is believed that the use of textbooks will result in an improved scholarship over the requirements of the lesson leaflets or quarterlies.

The Demands on a Curriculum of Religious Education

A curriculum of religious education means more today than the subject matter of the Sunday school. Every spiritually cultural contact falls within the scope of the curriculum. "As culture materials have sprung out of life and arisen out of the processes of everyday experience," Betts (p. 203) reminds us, "so they must be built back into the life of each succeeding generation if culture is to persist." The church receives a steady moving stream of fresh blood into its body from year to year. The processes of orientation, of absorption, of idealization, of spiritualization are entrusted to the curriculum.

The Individual.—The individual makes the first demand. The child of the race needs his potential self developed and nurtured. He has a right to the religion that has controlled human conduct through the ages. He needs to know of the faith that steadied his forefathers in peace and strife. He has a right to be led into the way of God. He has a right to a working knowledge of the time-approved and tested human values.

Society.—Society makes demands on the curriculum of religion. Betts[5] reminds us that the contribution which society has made to each of us is not meant "as an out-and-out gift, but as a loan." "The individual must pay back, not only the original principal, but this with interest." The curriculum must cultivate the sense of social responsibility. It must cure the desire to get without giving in return. Society therefore expects the curriculum to Christianize the institutions of society. The spirit of service in public office, national and international peace, respect for law, justice in human relations, are some of the products expected of the curriculum.

The Church.—The church, likewise, looks to the curriculum as the chief agency through which it fulfills its teaching function among men. Jesus commissioned this institution above all others to "make disciples," and to "teach them to observe whatsoever things I have commanded you." The accomplishment of these tasks is the result of the church school curriculum in action. The church expects every member to know its meaning and message. Christian zeal, mission-mindedness, loyalty, evangelism, training workers for local leadership and for world service, are entrusted to the curriculum. The interlocking relations with the school and the home involve the church in a responsibility for an integrated curriculum which builds up to and into the Christian college curriculum in religion, into and along with the home, and into the life of the public school.

Some Principles of Curriculum Construction

The race moves forward on the shoulders of the father generation. No set of youths begin and move on in their own right. There is the inheritance of yesterday to thank or to recognize. To forget the past is impossible, and to ignore it is suicidal. Yet that generation that accepts the conventions of yesterday without testing their validity

[5] *Ibid.*, p. 281.

for today has played traitor to God's plan of discovery. A curriculum in the making, therefore, should be governed by the principles of adjustment to the present, adaptation to the individual, validity of past experiences, varied application and a consciousness that a definite end must be approached.

Adjusted to Life.—The effective curriculum will consist of materials that apply the pattern objectives to actual life experiences. The curriculum is the agent of the objectives, and must be patterned by the objectives. Objectives to be valid must be stated in terms of life situations. Parents usually succeed in establishing desirable habits by training the children in the habit patterns of daily living. Table manners are learned at the table. Peaceable attitudes are formed on the ball field. Regularity in churchgoing is formed in the practice of going to church. In their moral and religious life the changes to be expected will be realized as training takes place in the midst of, or in terms of, real situations.

Thus the curriculum becomes and must be increasingly creative by drawing from real life the patterns for experience. The problems for religion come from real life. Abraham learned the value of faith in Jehovah in the midst of the famine, and at the improvised altar on Mt. Moriah. The early Christian church learned the meaning of the risen Christ as they faced the taunts of an unbelieving Judaism, producing the prophets and the gift of the Holy Spirit as evidence of their faith. Virtue is born in the midst of temptation, and temptation is real when virtue is challenged. The curriculum will set forth clearly the moral and religious experiences that await every man.

Such an experimental curriculum seeks a "center of interest," as Mildred Hewitt[6] calls the controlling purpose. This interest is developed through units of work, which are major experiences taken from the life of the child or the community arranged into extended lessons that may require two or three months for completion. The center of interest, for example, may be some principle of Christian living. The unit of work may be a study of the personal and official practices of men in public trusts who are observing or violating that principle. The study would lead to an understanding of Jesus' standard for the practice of men. Whether or not the curriculum in a particular church or denomination can be adapted to the unit plan, the fact remains that the selection of subject-matter should be determined on the basis of its fitting into the present needs of the pupils.

[6] *The Church School Comes to Life,* p. 50 (Macmillan, 1932).

Adapted to the Development of the Child.—Students of child life remind us that at each new level of development "the problems of life are reset in different forms and upon a larger scale." If the curriculum is to enrich the child it should reach the child through his interests. One is seldom interested in ideas outside his experience. Many studies have confirmed the claim that the child is not a miniature man. He is in the process of becoming a man. His ability to maintain control in experience will depend upon the instruction falling within his experience. This variable includes age, social experience, the attitudes of association groups, and individual capacities.

The most effective curriculum is the graded curriculum that is adapted to the capacities, needs and experiences of the learner. Paul fed his "babes in Christ" on "milk," and not "meat." The whole Bible is the Word of God, but some of its meanings are beyond the child's understanding. The effective curriculum avoids the unintelligible materials, and adapts its content to the age and experience of the child.

The experimental curriculum admits that it was made for the child, and not the child for the curriculum. Every new section of experience begins where the earlier section ended, but it is not mechanical joining. When there is forcing of application too far in advance of the child's interests, or out of the ranges of interest, or the using of materials foreign to the needs of the child, the educational process fails. The harm that results is disinterestedness may end in permanently injuring a sensitive nature. Middle aged persons who have suffered in Sunday school at this point reflect sadly, "I never learned anything in Sunday school." The child does not begin with principles and work to problems as an adult might, but begins with his problems and works to the principles needful for his age. Coe[7] pointed out years ago that enterprises in which the pupil felt the need for certain conduct brought into being the problem of how to perform accordingly, and that in so doing the school "becomes a place where the child acquires not merely a set of standard ideas but likewise a varied experience of living."

Tested by Race Experience.—The theory is current that it does not matter greatly what facts the pupil learns just so he becomes forward looking. Such a doctrine may be good for trial and error procedure, but it may be expensively wasteful. One may grant the

[7] *Religious Education*, 1922, p. 147.

right to others to explore in morals and religion, but he wants his own boy to follow the approved trails to clean, honest, upright living. In ministering safety to life, the curriculum must check its offerings by the tested and accepted experience of the race.

The effective curriculum is thus the guided curriculum. The race has looked to its religious books for authoritative guidance. Christians have found their Bible to be a sufficient and approved guide. Their confidence rests back on the nature of God so strikingly proclaimed by Isaiah. Isaiah proclaimed for Jehovah, "My word shall not return unto me void." Isaiah's confidence in the validity of his word to man did not rest on a conception of God as a dictator but on this superior knowledge of the hearts of men, and of their needs. Isaiah interprets God as wishing to guide men not by His will, but by His infinite wisdom. This reflects the spirit of the Bible and gives it an irrefutable claim to acceptance by men. A guided experience, then, means an experience patterned by the superior wisdom of God.

A curriculum, therefore, that enters into individual experience must recognize the race experience in the setting up of codes of ethical conduct, and in the giving of form to faith. Ethical neutrality negates even the most artistic life, for less than the Biblically approved code will lead by its own fruition to defeat, disillusionment, disgust, and death. Ethical conformity leads naturally into richer life. Optional faith or belief in God disqualifies the most profound philosophy, and confusion marks humanistic lessons as lacking in spiritual dynamic, and as confusion of sense of direction. Intelligent faith enheartens and glorifies life. A curriculum tested by the experience of the race will incorporate materials of faith and worship which the race has "practiced and prized." The experiences that have established a right to govern undoubtedly arose out of situations that have "common elements with the present situation." No better code of conduct or of faith has been devised than that contained in the Book.

Many-sidedness of Application.—The outcome of a specific lesson depends on the way it is taught. Careful surveys and wide observation have destroyed the notion that "telling" guarantees doing. Psychologists have pointed out that there is no transfer of training where there are no common elements of content in the two types of activity, and a clear understanding of the universal element in the activity that is to be carried over.

The effective curriculum will provide for many-sidedness in the application of its truth. When honesty, for example, is taught the teacher naturally expects the child to live honestly. In teaching honesty the stress might be placed on theft, and the commandment "Thou shalt not steal" well impressed. It might happen that the same pupil would cheat on examination on the following day without thought of having violated the lesson, or later he might be elected to public office and rob the public treasury "as everybody does," or in official position he might "shave" the salaries or wages of dependents in his employ without the slightest sting of conscience. The principle of varied application would lead the teacher to make an application of the truth in several possible situations. Naturally the process would not be complete until it had been tested by the sanction of Jesus, and measured by the character of the Kingdom of God.

The experimental curriculum, therefore, will connect the instruction with definite experiences of the individual. The use of parallel areas of life will afford an opportunity for the application of the principle to other life experiences. The whole of life's relations, personal honesty, intellectual honesty, social honesty, honesty with God, must be canvassed in connection with the lesson taught before there can be reasonable certainty of transfer. The question asked of every curriculum might be, "How far into the various areas of life does the subject matter reach?"

The Content Patterned by the Objectives.—A well defined goal makes possible the selection of suitable instruments for the attainment of the end. The effective curriculum will contain subject matter selected with a view to maximum suitability to the objectives. The average church has set conversion, church membership, stewardship, training for leadership, recruiting for professional leadership, as definite objectives. The lesson content should reflect these purposes.

A practical criterion for judging curriculum materials was prepared by C. C. Peters[8] as a score card for the Indiana Survey of Religious Education. The scale for measuring content covers these points:

1. Fitness of materials to appeal strongly to pupils of the age for which the lesson is intended.
2. Fitness of the materials to meet the needs of the pupils as defined by child psychologists and by sociology (age levels considered).
3. Fitness to meet the specific objectives of the particular church (or other group) for which the material has been prepared.

[8] Athearn, *Indiana Survey of Religious Education,* vol. 2, p. 114 (Harper & Brothers, N. Y.).

Mildred Hewitt[9] suggests the following additional tests:

Is our curriculum leading our pupils to appreciate Christian values, and to make them their own?

Is it helping them to think of the church as an enterprise to which they wish to give their best?

Is it leading them to approach life situations in the mind and spirit of Jesus?

Is it helping them to find help and enjoyment in Christian worship?

Is it leading them to take their places as Christian citizens in the world today?

By means of all these, is it bringing them into continuously closer relationship with God, and His Son Jesus Christ?

[9] *Ibid.*, p. 74f.

CHAPTER X

METHODS

Educational science has shown that growth takes place through experience, and that experience will develop most satisfactorily under a set of tried conditions. Educational art is simply good method in providing opportunities for these conditions to be realized. It will be observed that this conception of method commits teaching, preaching, and worship to the one task of guiding the experience of the individual toward the objectives of the Christian religion.

THE CONTROLLING FACTORS IN TEACHING METHOD

From the standpoint of the teacher there are four controlling factors in the educational process. The pupil, the objective toward which he is to be guided, and the curriculum by means of which the objective is to be gained, are the major factors, the equipment entering as the fourth. There must be a way of connecting up the curriculum and the individual. This is method, and when it is in harmony with the laws of growth it may be called educational.

The Pupil Factor.—To be efficient, method must understand the pupil. His development results from experience. Experience is built out of his reaction to environment. Through reacting to life he learns the ways that are better for him, and the ways that are worse for him. Attitudes, skills, and appreciations are formed, and these aid him in making later responses. The educator must so understand the pupil that he may be able to direct these growth processes toward the Christian objectives.

The primary challenge of the pupil to method lies in individual differences. These differences are due to age, sex, and psychological variations. The age differences definitely change method. Certain methods for boys are different from those for girls. Differences in capacity, interest, and needs of individuals call for an adaptation of method.

Method in dealing with individual differences must recognize the fact that learning is the purpose of teaching, and is an individual experience. The transfer type, the lesson learner, and the direct learner type must be dealt with differently. This means a rethinking of the old lesson-hearing method of teaching, and the substitution therefore of direct teaching of the ends to be learned. The old tests, instead of fathoming information, will be used for checking effectiveness of teaching, and for correction of method. These differences in capacity are to be met by variations in the rate of progress, in the quantity of material, and in the quality employed. Differences in interest are to be met by variations in strength of motives, and in the type of reward. Differences in need are to be met by offering incentives that will satisfy those needs.

The Objective Factor.—Method is not a free agent. It is under compulsion to find the way to the objectives. The teacher with an objective is teaching for a verdict. His methods may be varied, individual, or peculiar, but they are methods when they produce a verdict. Having determined what kind of training the subject taught proposes, method determines the kind of training the pupil should get from the subject.

The objective will vitally affect method in that it is the determinant of the worth of a process. The objective no longer serves as inspirer to renewed effort, but admonishes, "if at first you don't succeed find out why your method has failed." Since the aim or objective is not knowledge so much as a change in conduct and ideals, it is apparent that definite aims must be met by definite methods.

The type of objective will definitely affect method. (1) One objective, for example, might be a mastery of Biblical facts. Outline texts might be memorized, scrap books made, "work books," developing the main teachings of the Bible, might be followed, tests and the like would be a part of method. (2) If the objective is the application of Bible messages to men of today the method might include a discussion of current philosophies, national and social questions, scanning of the daily press for challenges to religious education, visits to the alms houses, juvenile courts and other institutions of dependency and correction, correspondence with selected groups of foreign children, and further pursuits of some project. (3) If the objective is concerned with committing individuals to Christian decisions the method might include guided conversations with vital Christians about their experiences, talking to older persons who have failed to commit themselves and are grieved because of it, collecting figures on "conversion probabilities" for various ages, the assignment of Christian service "in the name of Christ."

The Curriculum Factor.—Method cannot ignore **materials.** Since the modern curriculum includes in addition to text books "all the agencies within the school organization which combine to produce the educational results," the sources of religious materials are as broad and rich as the experience of the race. Biblical material is varied in its rich treasures, and varied in its forms. Here lie historical backgrounds, ethical and moral precepts, and a philosophy of Hebrew monotheism and Christian trinitarianism. In addition to Biblical materials is a rich heritage of extra-biblical materials, covering Christian biography so powerful for ideals, Christian literature expressing the yearnings for reality, Christian art expressing the conflict of the ideal with the elemental forces of life, and Christian music reflecting spiritual release from enslaving passions and powers. These materials are available for religious instruction, but lend themselves in different ways and to distinctive techniques.

Subject matter definitely determines method. Where the objective is competence in the individual, habits of courtesy, promptness, respect for the rights of others, devotion to truth, love of the church and the like, there is a general goal for teaching regardless of the subject matter. Where the objective is the adjusting of the instruction to the goal of the Christian church and to the atmosphere of the Christian religion, there is a function calling for specific subject matter methods. Training for church membership, for example, calls for training in the purposes, values, responsibilities, and philosophy of church life and function. Such training should develop a love for the ideal, and for the fellowship of its wider ministry in a world fellowship. The materials used for the acquiring of these ideals, beliefs, skills, and attitudes, are largely printed matter for the representation of facts. The method varies with the materials used.

Method is the way the pupil learns subject matter, and not the way the teacher teaches it, yet the way the teacher teaches it helps the way the pupil learns. Consequently there are principles implicit in the process that are serviceable. (1) Subject matter should be taught in the spirit of its content. Geography is intended to interpret the environment of the people, and not teach their faith. History is intended to explain the manners, customs and ideals of a people, and not their faith. Religion as the philosophy of a race is intended to account for their faith and their aspirations. Each of these subjects requires a different method, though the purpose of each converges in the other. (2) Subject matter should be taught by a method that will develop its underlying purpose. Biography is not taught as art, but to teach religion. Biblical material grew out of an experience of concrete truth, for the purpose of imparting spiritual values, of inspiring Christian ideals, and of stimulating religious faith. The methods used should discover these purposes and follow a technique that will replant them in current life. (3) Subject matter should be adapted to the pupil experience. Unless the curriculum fits into the experience of the learner it loses effectiveness. Things that belong together should be learned together. Bible experiences that fit the present experience inspire a sense of truth and reality of the Bible experience. (4) Subject matter incorporated into a unit of work should offer manysidedness of application. Materials draw to themselves wide ranges of related truth, and reach out to widely expanding experiences of life. Through weeks of study and application the truth of the unit comes to a richer and wider dominance in the pupil's life.

The Equipment Factor.—The traditional classroom is a place for hearing lessons. As such it is a bare sort of place. Under the hearing-recitation plan the desk and the chair were enough. Under the first hand experience plan of teaching the pupil needs a workroom in which are collected the materials essential to the immediate study. Equipment for research, handwork, visual aids, graphic implements, auditory mechanisms, are regarded as essential and often indispensable appurtenances to effective education.

Method will be changed to utilize the available equipment. Instead of question and answer, or drill, or other verbal procedures, the lesson will be conducted by studying maps, graphs, models, concordances, reference books, by making of scrap-books, preparing reports, and observing pictures of scenes or incidents. In each case a method will be used that will fit the teaching situation.

Specific Methods

While dependance should not be placed upon one method to the neglect of another, there are several specific methods which have a place in the practice of the church. In general these may be classified in terms of the technique employed. (1) Individualized methods are those in which the teacher alone participates. (2) Socialized methods are those in which the teacher and the pupils coöperate. (3) Laboratory methods are those that utilize direct expression by the pupil.

Individualized Methods.—The usual methods so classified are the lecture, the sermon, and the story. They are more or less vicarious, and lack the values of first hand pupil experience. Learning takes place through experience. Experience may be had through direct activity, through witnessing the activity of another person, or through hearing from another the experience of himself or of some other individual. The experience of hearing becomes educative only in so far as the facts related become associated in the mind of the hearer with some experience in his own life. This is the most remote process of learning but is not entirely lacking in value. For persons of wide contacts, and of long exposures to life, the best results often obtain from the use of these methods.

The Lecture Method.—The lecture or "telling" method is adapted to certain instructional situations. Experience advises a sparing use of the formal lecture for the early adolescent ages, though lecturing for short periods is often desirable, provided the pupils are getting what the teacher expects of them. Interest and attention may not always mean understanding and learning. To be effective the lecture must "stimulate activity, raise problems, and lead pupils to ask questions." Certain subjects depend more upon the lecture method than others. Languages depend upon telling. History, geography, manners and customs, require much illumination through the lecture and the story. The introduction of any subject, even of a project or unit of work, requires certain types of lecturing.

Success in the use of the lecture method will depend upon the ability of the lecturer to explore the experience centers of his hearers. Before he can claim effective speech he must discover responsive areas in which past experience approves and accepts the new. The lecturer seeks to arouse interest in new situations, or to impart new knowledge. The story teller, whose process is one of telling, seeks to illumine truth by dramatized lecturing. The preacher through his sermon seeks to inform his hearers of vital truth, and by reviving emotional experience under a new direction to lead to decision and action. These are the characteristic lecture forms. The teacher of religion often combines the three forms, imparting exegetically the truth of the lesson, telling a story for illustration, and using the homiletical art for securing decision.

The development of a sound lecturing technique is imperative, especially below the middle adolescent years. Experienced lecturers advise several practices: Think through your message and how you are to say it. Speak to your hearers and not at them. Start the lecture with a problem, and keep the class in a watchful state of mind. Allow pauses occasionally for pupils to think through the presentation. Visual aids help to hold attention, and fix truth. The lighter moods interspersed will lift the heavier periods. The summary should gather up the threads into a compact message.

The Story Method.—The story should not be rated as a separate method. It holds a dependent position. As an illustration of a truth, as an "appetizer," or to motivate, the story serves with tremendous effect. As a unit of instruction it lacks purpose.

The general rules for the selection of stories have been variously stated. The first requisite is adaptability. Since small children are more responsive to stories their needs should receive first attention. Primary pupils usually care for a narrative filled with mystery, a part of which may be produced in the telling. They also wish an element of fancy. They live in the world of make believe. Fancy stretches their imagination, and imagination later makes faith possible. They also delight in a story that will bear repetition. A second requisite is action, for younger children particularly. A third requisite is that the story should be permanently useful to the child. The universally known stories are more interesting and constitute a bond of social cohesion necessary for developing human understanding and sympathy. A fourth requisite is that the central figure of the story should embody positive moral or religious values. Negative virtues in the hero do not seem to produce positive effects. A fifth requisite is that the story should reflect the highest ideals in plot, and in literary form. An effort to "step down" exalted imagery to the level of the child is tragic.

The sources of story material are usually listed as tradition, heroics, and nature. Legends, fables, parables, and well known fairy tales have come from many quarters and many ages. They bear their message of the conflict of good with evil, of the quests of men for the good. Lowell's The Vision of Sir Launfal, Tennyson's Idylls of the King represent a very usable group of this type. The heroics are numerous. Stories of poor boys who achieved fame, of heroes of mission field and frontier, are full of human interest. History and current literature abound in such stories. No stories excel those of the heroic period of Israel. Nature stories are numerous and lend themselves admirably to religious instruction. Jesus undoubtedly found inspiration and spiritual insight through watching the sparrows and the lilies. Interpreters of the animals, the plants, the rocks, and the stars, have opened a treasure house of materials for the teacher of religion. The Bible contains materials taken from all of the experiences of life. Bible stories lend themselves admirably to narration, and can be used with abiding satisfaction. Denominational publishers should be consulted for suggestions as to books of Bible stories.

Suggestions for telling the story are better made in larger studies.

In general, however, the theory of story telling embodies these principles: (1) Know the pupil. The narrator and the pupil should understand each other for best results. Preparation for telling includes an advance fitting of all the narrative to the mind of the hearer, and an advance answering of all questions likely to arise. (2) Know the story. Failures are often due to the fact that the narrator does not know "where he is going." The story should be so well known that it becomes a part of the experience of the narrator. (3) Know good technique. A well modulated voice, a natural poise, an easy manner, suitable facial or other gestures, imitation and impersonation especially with children, avoidance of gaps, explanations and stops, are essential to good effect. (4) Know when the message is felt. It is only when the hearers feel the message of the story that the story teller has succeeded. If the story has been well chosen, and well told, it will teach its own moral.

Socialized or Group Methods.—Since method is the way of making the materials of instruction accomplish the desired end in guiding the experience of the learner, it is natural that the socialized processes should be more effective than the lecture method. In the latter the responsibility of each pupil is to the teacher, and not to the group. There is no group aim, no coöperative attitude, no pupil responsibility, no sense of ownership in the enterprise, and no group recognition of common problems. In bringing the learner to think, to plan and to coöperate, these experiences are important. Personal responsibility for progress and for the subject builds up within the pupil a permanent interest in the procedure. It develops initiative, skill in clear thinking, ability to use freedom profitably, consideration for others, and skill in coöperation.

The Recitation Method.—The traditional question and answer method is commonly practiced, coming next in use to the lecture method. It is largely an individual pupil-teacher performance, lacking in group stimulus. It aims at impressing the memory with subject matter, and is concerned only remotely with thinking and acting. It centers in reciting to the satisfaction of the teacher, or in substituting the teacher for the subject matter, or in a memoriter learning.

The values of the question have been universally recognized. The first and widest use that the question has been put to is that of testing knowledge. A second function is to develop correct habits of response. A third function is to arouse interests and to discover tastes. A fourth function is to interpret and evaluate facts. A fifth is to stimulate pupils to think, which is the most important function.

To this end there should be great care in asking questions, and great wisdom in interpreting the answers.

Admitting the abuse and misuse of the question and answer there is no method that is so frequently employed by even the best of teachers. It supplements the discussion, by correcting error in understanding, and emphasizes important points made. It follows the story, the drama, the lecture, the assignment, the project, making sure that the learning has been experienced.

The Discussion Method.—The socialized procedure in teaching has developed into two general types, often referred to as the formal type and the informal type. The formal plan organizes the class after the scheme of some adult organization, as mission board, denominational state convention, church session, directors' round table for gathering up group conclusions, and court "panel" for considering the fate of a given topic. The group operates under the leadership of representatives, with guidance of the teacher, and the entire group assumes responsibility for its work. The other type is the informal group. This plan involves no special organization. Discussion is encouraged, with the teacher accepting a less conspicuous position in the class. Common goals are prominent. The informal type is in reality the discussion or the seminar method of teaching.

The discussion method consists of free interchange of thought by members of a class upon some problem more or less common to the class. The instructor simply guides the discussion by making clear the problem, by keeping on the main issue and avoiding fruitless digressions, and by keeping participation by members of the class in proper balance. Instead of asking questions the teacher raises problems, and then stimulates the discussion. Pupils talk to the group rather than to the teacher. The ordinary courtesies of debate are observed, such as avoiding interruption of the speaker, respecting the time of others, and steering clear of the trivial. Success in discussion requires a certain amount of subject matter, a diversity of points of view, and a well distributed time allotment.

The teacher's technique in conducting the discussion follows Dewey's procedure in productive thinking, stated by Graves.[1] (1) "Our thinking always begins with the recognition of a difficulty demanding adjustment." (2) "Next we formulate an hypothesis, or make a guess as a tentative solution." (3) "The hypothesis is applied to further material, gathered from our experience or reading,

[1] *Administration of American Education*, p. 17 (Macmillan, 1932).

in order that we may decide whether it holds true also in these cases."
(4) "Take the precaution of testing an accepted hypothesis by a
further appeal to experience, to see whether it will hold good in
every instance." (5) "If this additional test proves satisfactory we
venture to make a generalization or definition." Harrison S. Elliott[2]
has taught discussion leaders to provide for four kinds of questions,
"the problem question to open the discussion, the solution question
to introduce the material that will throw light on the problem, the
conclusion question for the purpose of gathering up the loose ends
and bringing the discussion to a head, and the action question which
seeks to discover how the conclusion is to be carried into actual
practice." (Betts and Hawthorne, *Method in Teaching Religion*, p.
411, Abingdon, 1925.) The latest experiments in teaching techniques
establish the value of stating the problem at the beginning of every
important paragraph in writing, and of every topic in discussion.
Books on the discussion method are generally available, and will
supply technical information.

The Unit of Work Method.—A unit of work has been defined
as a series of valuable experiences bound together around some central theme which is of interest to the child. The unit of work plan is
based upon the principles, (1) that in the end learning must be
direct learning and not lesson learning; (2) that the child's interests,
his past experience, his present needs, determine what his school
activities will be; (3) that pupils can learn together better than
individually; (4) that a procedure involving experiencing at first
hand, plus discussion in the group, is the most effective learning;
(5) that in the process of adjustment to environment learning is
most effective when a complete adjustment has been secured. Education is not a divided experience. In the process of education each
adjustment is called a unit.

The curriculum is composed of materials of learning which help
the pupil to adjust himself properly to the wide range of contacts
that he must make in life. Certain situations will give the pupil the
adjustment sought. The situations are the units. The facts, the
activities, and the events make up the experience. What he does
about these constitutes the adjustment. To become a unit these facts
and activities must be related to each other with a view to a useful
adjustment to life, and must be mastered by the pupil with full
knowledge of the results to be obtained. The total of the units
regarded as necessary to meet the requirement of the objectives is

[2] *The Why and How of Group Discussion*, pp. 54-55 (Association Press).

the curriculum. The minimum curriculum requisite for adjustment to normal life will require a period of years.

The selection of a unit will begin with a search of an area of life for the comprehensive and significant aspects of its environment. By "comprehensive" is meant that such aspects of the environment as may be found will explain satisfactorily the demands of that environment. By "significant" is meant that the aspects selected will possess intrinsic importance and prove essential in the life of the adjusted individual. The unit is intended to produce modification in the personality. The unit selected should be worthy of making such a modification. Of all institutions the Christian church stands first in breadth of opportunity in the matter of selection of units. The Christian must be adjusted in the home, in the school, in society, in the Kingdom of God. A Christian home life and its radiations offer a vast field for exploration. The church in its worship, its literature, its history, its leaders, its ministries offers a field for study by intelligent Christians. The social environment, causes of social ills, delinquency, crime, and their correctives lead into the purposes of Jesus. These areas suggest the possibilities of units.

The techniques of the unit of learning consist of principles successfully employed by Reed:[3] (1) the organization of the facts into a meaningful pattern, (2) practice for the sake of improvement by means of repeated efforts to do better, (3) recognition of individual variations as to capacity, interest and needs, and (4) motivation growing out of a felt need, with a movement toward the satisfying object. The location of a unit of interest will mean the building of materials around it for interpretation and meaning. Practice brings facility and often comprehension. Individual differences are cared for in grading, promotion, individual case guidance, and special classes for creating opportunity for meeting individual needs. Motives for increasing the speed of learning are effective as a goal is definitely set and its attainment made desirable.

Advantages of the unit of work plan lie in the focusing of significant materials on important experience areas. It results in learning Bible truths, and human relations vitally. It safeguards the truth by requiring a mastery of the whole, rather than in parts. It makes more certain the retention of the materials of the lessons, and a carrying over of the precepts into a wider life. On the other hand it does not promise to solve all of the educational problems. Its purpose is to

[3] *Psychology and Teaching of Secondary School Subjects* (Prentice Hall, 1939).

develop understanding and not information. If information is the objective some other method should be used.

Laboratory or Experimental Methods.—In the laboratory plan the students learn from original sources, or from secondary ones where necessary. The object is to relive the part or period studied. The teacher gives direction to the activities through "laboratory manuals," or prepared written assignments. The assignments may cover collecting objects pertinent to the subject, scrap books, paper-pulp models, pageants and drama. The advantages of the method are the realistic approach, and the opportunity to create activity and purposeful effort on the part of the pupil. Experiments testing the value of the laboratory as compared with the daily recitation procedure in citizenship studies, as reported by Reed (*Psychology and Teachings of Secondary School Subjects*, p. 379f), show that laboratory procedures earned as much as twenty per cent more points than did the daily assignment plan.

The use of experimental processes is as valuable in moral and religious education as in other fields. In this field, however, it is a method of learning more than a method of discovery. It is a method of reinforcing data that are already available. It provides for the pupil the experience at first hand, and in this manner makes more vivid and more accurate the impression than would be true in reading or hearing the data. Experimentation becomes a method of observing, and a method of problem solving. Through these processes the individual does make discoveries in relationships that lie dormant in lectures or reading.

Practical observations on the experimental method show its values to lie in handling qualities, events, and relations, as well as things. Its essence consists in the spirit of investigation. Its purpose is to make vivid through sensuous data the meaning of events or relations in terms of general principles. Its expectation is the solution of a problem which has arisen in the class, and which is conducted parallel to the work of the class. Its results should become a basis for class discussion.

Manual Arts.—The church is discovering that manual activity is not simply "busy" work. Often handwork has been introduced to keep the children interested. The aim of handwork is far more than making things. The director seeks to get back of the object finished to the urges that produced it. Such a director will feel that he has failed if he seeks only to work off a child's surplus energy through the hands. His real purpose is to provide an opportunity for expressing concretely a truth already acquired, for the sake of enriching appreciation. Certain by-values lie in the development of neatness and accuracy. The cultivation of the habits of economy, orderliness and cleanliness are particularly valuable in manual arts in teaching religion.

The manual arts are used for purposes of illustration, and for construction. Drawing is a better vehicle for understanding than words. There is less demand on imagination where lines and colors are employed for concreteness. A single mark on the blackboard will symbolize a man far better than the word "man" alone. Posters provide for a vivid presentation of the subject under study, and train the makers in arranging advantageously the materials employed. Scrapbooks have educational value when they are made for a purpose, such as portraying the life of a missionary, or creating interest in a local welfare project. Arranging the Gospels in harmony form, or a pictorial life of Christ, are worthy uses of the scrapbook. Map-making fits into the geography ages of the Sunday school. For studying the contour of the Bible lands, or the changing borders of changing kingdoms, or the historical connections with important places it is valuable. Construction includes paper cutting, clay modeling, wood working, and sand-tables. Special books on these subjects are available.

Certain principles have been found valuable in governing the use of manual arts for religious development. (1) Of chief importance is that the teacher must know the psychological reasons for using handwork in teaching religion, else the activity is mere busy work, and a waste of time. (2) The manual work must be connected with the lesson being studied or the educational value is lost. (3) Grading of the activity is as important as grading the lesson material. (4) The best results come from a service motive, especially when that service is personal and challenging. Making things for a needy family in the community will greatly impress the lesson on "being a good neighbor." (5) The incidental learning, neatness and the like, must be carefully safeguarded, or the loss will offset the gain.

Dramatization.—Visual aids to teaching usually include pictures, and motion pictures, the latter possessing superior values to still pictures. Of yet greater value for learning than the motion picture, which is but a substitute for real drama, is drama itself. Dramatization is one of the most effective means for conveying a sense of reality to the pupil. It makes a strong visual and auditory appeal. In this way identification of the actor with the situation becomes a reality. The ultimate effect of the drama is a more vivid understanding of the episode. Through dramatization the pupil sees and lives the life of the period under study. The aim of dramatization has been stated by Mueller[4] to be "to make the past so real and vivid to the learner that he will sense it and relive it as if it were a part of the present."

The value of presenting religious truth in the form of drama is generally recognized. Much ritual in religious observances is the dramatic expression of an earlier faith. The more ancient Christian churches continue the use of the dramatic method of presenting truth. The interest of the church in dramatization is chiefly educational. The old miracle plays, and the Oberammergau Passion Play, were produced as acts of devotion, but modern uses are limited almost entirely to educational purposes. Truth is made vivid when so presented. Dramatization utilizes the urge to activity, imitation, and play. It has educational value in that it releases the individual from his environment, and through his imagination enables him to experience the feeling of new attitudes, ideas, and powers.

To obtain lasting educational value certain principles are to be observed. (1) Dramatization must be made an integral part of the educational work of the church. The effort on the part of an unskilled teacher to "give a play" for the purpose of bolstering up lagging interest is pointless. Betts and Hawthorne have observed that "only those forms of dramatics have educational value which call for spontaneous interpretation and action on the part of the players," and that "by studying and producing prepared materials these same values and still others are developed." (2) Every pupil must be included in the production in one capacity or another. The purpose is to develop the imagination, the emotions, and to provide an avenue for self-expression. Every pupil must have this opportunity to visualize the teaching and subject-matter. (3) The informal dramatization is of chief value. The stage setting and costumes are not necessary for an educational effect. The presence of an audience defeats the primary purpose. (4) Dramatization must be purposeful, else it becomes undesirable for church purposes. Its purpose is to "reveal to them moral and religious values in action." Betts and Hawthorne interpret its function to be to "crystallize principles of noble living, set up worthy ideals and character made real in great personalities."[5] (5) The materials of dramatization must be chosen

---

[4] *Teaching in Secondary Schools*, p. 228.
[5] Ibid., p. 354.

for their permanent value to the developing lives of the pupils. The content must be usable, positive in moral and religious values, and adapted to the needs and capacities of the pupils. (6) The class discussion following the play is the most important feature. Questions will arise that should open wide discussion.

The sources of materials for dramatization include the Bible, especially the narrative portions of the Old Testament, the expansion of the church through missions, mission fields, hymns and other great music, home life, industrial relations, international relations, neighborliness and the like. The leading publishers among the denominations will gladly furnish information as to the best available materials for the use of the teacher.

Visual Aids.—The value of pictures has been found to be so effective that some of the nation's most influential journals tell their story of social change in pictorial form. Pictures tell briefly the contents of many words, and the impression produced is more lasting. History told through pictures is far more vivid than when told through the printed page. Other subject-matter carries over better by this means for the reason that pictorial is less variable than written or spoken imagery. It has the further value of vividness, and of greater permanence of retention.

Visual aid is the suitable term for the service of concrete materials to instruction. The most satisfactory learning takes place when accurate imagery accompanies the verbal symbols. Only to the extent that the learner forms a clear picture of the character, the scene, or the process, does he really learn. Much learning is wasted because the abstract idea presented does not take definite form in the mind. Those who have little apperceptive background are severely handicapped under verbal instruction. Visual aids supply that lack as they show what the idea is like or how it operates. Real things are more interesting than verbal symbols. Next to studying the thing itself the best approach is through studying a picture or representation of the thing. Pictures, drawings, diagrams, and films will provide this approach.

Not all subjects can be presented visually. Nor does all visual instruction have equal value. Where the material is not well adapted to the instruction the effect may be undesirable. Where the explanatory message is lacking, or the picture or film poorly selected, the effect will be disappointing. Good thinking cannot be aided by confused images. New images cannot be well formed from those that have not been directly experienced.

Types of visual aids include films, slides, charts, maps, stereographic views, pictures, relics, diagrams, graphs, and sand tables. The type to be used will depend upon factors existing in the teaching situation. Geography will call for maps, globes, slides, and stereographic views. Where social conditions or customs are to be taught films, charts, pictures, field trips will be of value. Pictures are particularly helpful in teaching the life of Christ. Many prints of the great paintings are available in inexpensive form. Collections of these should be available, and properly filed for ready use. Slides also are easily secured and at small expense. The film slide has come into use, and has certain advantages over the glass slide. Motion pictures exert greater influence on the emotional side of education. They have a place, provided there is careful preparation before, and careful follow up work after, the showing of the film. Full information regarding these materials may be had from the denominational publishing houses.

Certain common procedures apply to the use of these various types of visual aids. (1) The use of any type of visual material should be for some definite teaching purpose. There should be a definite function for it to perform. The need for such usually arises from the lack of adequate conception of the person, or place, or event, and the aid should supply just enough of the concrete for that need. Where the pupil can visualize such background there is little need of visual materials. (2) Visual materials are appropriately used when the subject presented is beyond the experience of the child to imagine, or where an interest in a problem can be aroused quickly through vivid material. (3) Visual materials are especially helpful in reviews, summaries, or where the shortness of the period of instruction makes adequate oral presentation difficult. Such materials may be used with profit to illustrate or to impress the content of a lecture. (4) With the exception of the blackboard perhaps, experience dictates that careful preparation should be made for the use of these aids. Pupils should be told what to look for in the picture, and what they are to retain. They should find that the aid supplies the needed information. (5) Follow-up work is the best procedure where the visual aids consist of more than illustrations of points in the lesson. Where pictures or other aids make up a definite part of the teaching, there should follow a careful check-up to determine whether they have served their purpose.

CHAPTER XI

RELIGIOUS EDUCATIONAL ACTIVITIES

The responsibility of Christian churches for meeting the issues where human values are involved has led to the promotion of activities for the achievement of specific ends. Schools have been conducted to instruct men in the ways of righteousness. Evangelism has been utilized for enlisting individuals in the Kingdom of God. Worship has been encouraged for deepening in Christians a sense of fellowship and power from God. Stewardship has been fostered for training men in the habit of Christian living. Through these activities religious education seeks to achieve moral and spiritual results.

INSTRUCTION

Religious education and instruction are not identical. Religious education is essentially a moral and spiritual process which consists of the operation of all the influences that shape character and faith. Instruction is one of the means of religious education for intellectual, emotional and volitional training in the building of character and in the integration of Christian personality. Instruction is concerned primarily with the intellectual aspects of the process of helping persons master essential facts that cannot be left to chance.

Objectives of Instruction.—Since the preservation of these spiritual facts and their interpretation are central in the objectives of instruction, the tangible aims may be stated as the preservation of the spiritual heritage, the formation of character, and the commitment of the individual to the will of God. The first is the transmissive act of teaching the literature and ideals of Christianity; the second is the creative process of building character, and the third is the evangelical aim of conversion.

Transmitting Christian teaching is a humanitarian as well as a church objective. God made the world for love and for unselfishness. The social order will not run harmoniously except in the Christian way. Discord and destruction follow the tilting of society off the Christian center. The constitution and by-laws of a good society are embodied in the literature of Christianity. The Christian centuries have charged these writings impractical idealism, but have demonstrated the futility of ignoring their teachings. The Bible is the perfect pattern of life, the standard of human measurements and values, the story of God's conquest of the heart. Planting the Bible facts for fruitage both for today and after many days is a Christian purpose of instruction.

Creative character building is a more intricate process. Instruction in religion and character training are not synonymous. Instruction in religion is thought of as instruction in the Bible, the catechism, Christian ethics and philosophy. Instruction in character is thought of as the impartation of certain traits, such as honesty, truthfulness, and sobriety. The public school emphasis on character development centers largely in trait development. Religious education accepts responsibility for specific traits, but assumes further the task of organizing personality around Christian purposes. The reason for emphasis on specific character education in the Christian sense rests upon the fact that tests have shown a lack of essential correlation between Biblical information and phases of conduct. Thoroughgoing tests have revealed the fact that correlations between knowledge of right and wrong and the expected conduct are the result of the human equation in teaching more often than of subject matter. Hartshorne and May found that the relative influence of parent, public school teacher, and Sunday school teacher, in affecting character stands in this order, .545, .028, and .002 respectively. Such facts challenge religious educators to undertake purposive character education on the Christian basis.

The evangelistic objective surpasses in importance knowledge of the Bible and well ordered habits of conduct. When one hears great Christian leaders say, "I never saw the world until I saw Christ," the reason is clear. Instruction in religion encourages and aims at a public avowal of Christian faith and discipleship. Every church leader will confirm the fact that two persons, otherwise alike, will differ at the point of the possession of a great purpose. The dedication to a great cause, commitment to a program like the Kingdom of God, are secret keys to a different life. Conversion, commitment and dedication, become central in the teaching objective of Christian education.

Contents of Instruction.—What the church wishes to be in the lives of its members must first be put into the curriculum. The curriculum is in the main a complete cycle of subject matter and other content so arranged as to give to the pupil a correct approach and setting for instruction. It will consist of all the experiences that children have as they occur under the direction of the teacher.

The materials of the curriculum fall into three functional groups. The first group seeks to achieve solidarity of the group, and consists of confessions of faith, creeds, doctrines and church polity. Solidarity depends upon bringing about proper adjustments within the group. The second group seeks to provide Christian culture and enrichment, and cor.sists of a division covering knowledge about Christianity, another covering Christian teachings on human relations, a third on cultural aspects of our faith, and a fourth on source materials of our faith. Included under these divisions are the life of Christ; church history; missions; Christian social relations like race, industry, international, and personal; Christian biographies; Christian art and hymnology; history of the Hebrews and neighboring peoples; oriental life and literature. The third group seeks to transform potentially efficient persons into persons of effective Christian living and consists of inspirational literature and practical helps in personal development.

Guided experience is educational and is a part of the curriculum. Expressional activity in its psychological meaning is a term long used for the term "guided experience." Its underlying philosophy holds that knowledge unrelated to life experiences has never been learned. Biblical knowledge, for example, unapplied affects no conduct, but may remain as an ungerminated seed in the mind until some later experience gives it life. Knowing the process, current education seeks through guidance to carry the pattern of experience in the material over into real experience. Three areas of experience split knowledge up into attitude patterns, skill patterns, and appreciation patterns. The first may be called the "core" curriculum, and includes those common experiences which all pupils are to. have under the guidance of the teacher, without respect to individual differences. These are the basic learnings, such as respect for life and property, a right regard for the human body, the making of a living, and committing the life to the Christian Way. These are the attitudes of Christian culture. The second area may be called the skills curriculum, and includes experience in the use of tools of learning, and the development of techniques necessary for the achievement of the first group. The third area may be called the individual interest or appreciation area, and includes those experiences connected with the making of life choices. Chief among these choices will be the commitment to Christ and the decision as to a life work.

Method in Instruction.—Method is the way the materials and the setting are handled to bring about the educational aims. The best method as stated by the International Curriculum Guide Book is "that which efficiently brings about guidance of the learner's experience toward conduct centering in Christian ideals." This implies two principles in method; first, that all materials must be pupil directed; second, that effective learning grows out of specific life situations.

Pupil direction means that the Bible is taught for the sake of the child. Through it God is proclaiming his quest for that life. The method aims at the creation of a motive Godward, and Christian traits manward. Guidance of the learner's experience may be sought through the initiation of the learner into the experiences that the material used has preserved in its record. The manner of achieving this end belongs to methods.

"Specific life situations" means the experiencing of the lessons in the processes of living. S. Wirt Wiley (Relig. Ed., Vol. 26, p. 348) sums up the primary laws of learning in a direct manner: "(1) What we would learn we must practice. (2) We learn only that which we practice with some satisfaction. (3) Learning follows the direction set by intent." In applying these laws several facts are of value. In the practice of the character traits the teacher should use all constructive agencies of society to make contribution to the training. The home, camps and character organizations get the finest results. Group activity is a powerful determinant in behavior. Closely knit groups, like gangs, clubs, troups, provide and utilize activity, and offer opportunity for democratic and Christian expression. Program making by the group is more effective than the standardized programs made for the group. The reason for this is that this method calls out initiative, coöperation, produces natural situations, and better enables the individual to learn to make adjustments to new situations. It is of special importance that the individual experience a sense of social adjustment in association with others. In such situations the learner faces problems in Christian life and faith, and determines a course of conduct.

Specific methods of instruction fall into three main groups—individualized, socialized, and experimental or laboratory. The first type projects the experience of the individual through lecture or story and becomes educational when the speaker through imagination creates in the hearer an experience of his own. The second type seeks to discover or create experience through discussion, question, panel, or unit of work. It becomes educational as it secures intelligent reaction and like conduct. The third type seeks to discover laws and principles through the doing of things. Its educational value lies in the interest of discovery, and the personal habits of precision, careful thinking, suspended judgment, and respect for the opinions of others.

WORSHIP

Worship is not an opening exercise which permits any procedure observing fair decorum. It is not good-fellowship which requires only one test, that of good feeling and a spirit of brotherliness. It is not preparation for a specific lesson, which merely uses related hymns and scripture to introduce the lesson facts, and express a spiritual sentiment. Worship is spiritual reality. The hymns and prayers and scripture are to produce a feeling of the presence of God. The place becomes a sanctuary. In this atmosphere the lesson becomes the word of God.

The Purpose of Worship.—Historically worship reënacts a drama of man's ways and means of approaching God. Seeking the will of God, propitiating an unsympathetic God, expressing gratitude for favors, and endeavoring to discover any unity with God, called for prescribed forms approved of God. Christ's answer to inquiring disciples removed feasts and ceremonies for subjective worship. The hymns, and the sacred writings, and the prayers supplant the objective acts. The great liturgies Atkins (Resources for Living, p. 145) calls "the sifted devotions of the centuries." Their litanies "rehearse timeless perils and voice unescapable needs for deliverance."

Escape from reality is a major purpose of worship. Men are seeking a plain road away from the daily life to God. They are confused by the impotence of moral achievement. They are abashed by human pessimism. They are baffled by human problems. They seek for escape from the toils and cares of life. They cry out from a sense of sin. Worship offers the answer to the human hungers. "My feet had almost slipped until I went into the house of the Lord" (Ps. 73).

A sense of direction is an objective of worship. To get any meaning out of the world, and our particular part in it, we must inquire why we are here, and what purposes we express. We plummet the depths of life to discover that only through the worship of a Supreme Being can we understand the mystery of man. The only answer to our quest for direction lies in the purposes of God.

Socialization is an objective of worship within the meaning of the

Christian faith. Genuine worship is a school for mutual edification. "Forsake not the assembling of yourselves together" is more than a principle of congregation building. Churches that truly worship create and keep alive a beautiful spirit of fellowship. Fellowship in worship sets the spiritual pitch of brotherhood. Singing, praying and working together in a sacred union nourishes a corporate sense in a congregation.

Vitalization as an objective in worship is suggested in Paul's experience, "I can do all things through Christ which strengthened me." One hour spent in worship does something to the spiritually sensitive akin to lifting one from a street level to the top of a high building. It gives one vision and stirs a sense of power to achieve.

Communion is the highest objective of worship. Isaiah "saw the Lord, high and lifted up." His vision of God brought a confession of sinfulness. Confession brought fitness for service, and a commission to go in the Lord's name (Isaiah 6). That form or ceremony that does not eventuate in some sense of communion with God is a desecration.

The Content of Worship.—Worship is intended to be experienced. The media of worship, hymns, scripture and prayer, are used because they are effective in producing experience. They are most effective when they have been born in experience. Hymns of greatest power were so born. Scripture came from hearts and hands that God had inspired with a sense of His reality. Effective prayer is made by men who know that God is real. Offerings that are worshipful outwardly express an inward acceptance of God's Lordship over all of life. No worship is complete that fails through these media to effect spiritual experience.

Scripture reading that suits the hearer's imagination must first stir the reader. Selections for public reading must possess qualities generally regarded as essential for effective reading. The reader must identify himself in spirit with the spirit of the passage and must read it as nearly as possible as it was originally read o spoken. The passage came out of intense life and worshipful reading will return it to intense listeners.

Prayer is the most intimate part of worship. In prayer the human spirit comes closest to the spirit of God. Prayer opens the mind to new insight into the will of God. It confesses sin and failure. It voices praise. It utters petitions. It bridges the gap between earth and heaven. In prayer a man is not spiritual as distinguished from intellectual and physical, he is all there is of him. He is offering to God all there is to give.

Hymn singing is a vitalizing part of worship. Paul advised the church at Corinth to check their growing coldness by singing hymns and spiritual songs. Hymns create an atmosphere of spiritual reality. They arouse congregational interest in the common faith, and enhearten Christians in the midst of suffering and disappointment. They stir a passion for the Christian conquest against fear and iniquity. They teach men the staunch doctrines of faith more truly than through instruction. Worshippers sing the hymns of experience to reproduce a kindred faith.

The offering or giving as an act of worship has been neglected. The Corinthians thought of it as practical rather than spiritual. The tragedy of the churches is the travesty of cajoling church people into giving and presenting it as a duty rather than a spiritual exercise. Correct conceptions of stewardship will make the act of giving an act of worship. It is an act of consecration, and consecration is the final step in worship. "Here am I Lord, send me."

Method in Worship.—The problem in worship is to help people in their quest for God, and to work with God in approaching the individual. Certain processes have been found invaluable in establishing this contact. There must be spiritual motivation; there must be spiritual sensitiveness; there must be creative experience, as men are brought into a sense of communion with God. Method must find the way. Method must not only tell men to pray, but must tell them how to pray.

The technique employed in securing a sense of reality in worship seeks three experiences in the individual, release, union, and power. Release means consent or the shaking off of a theoretical will, a subduing of the mind into a channel of contemplation. No one can come into a mystical union with God who reserves his will for wandering or for criticism. This consent comes on at least two conditions, first, that the truth of the media for worship conforms to the truth of the worshipper's experience, and second, that the agent in worship shall be thoroughly sincere in his ministrations. The second experience is union or communion, which becomes so after release, provided the power of suggestion of the media and of the ministrant continues uninterruptedly to a climax. A third experience is power, which follows a sense of communion with the Divine. It is a sense of confidence or victory that comes to one who knows that the strength of God fills out his own strength. "I have seen the Lord," and "I can do all things through Him which strengtheneth me" express the sequence that inspires invincible power.

The order of worship follows Isaiah, sixth chapter. It should begin with contemplation of God. The second step is confession to God. One cannot see the holiness of God without discovering the sinfulness of his own soul. The third step is communion. With the barriers of self and of sin removed converse with God is easy. The fourth step is dedication or consecration. Isaiah at this stage offered himself. These four steps are evident in well ordered programs of worship.

The details of the program are of less importance than the order provided the vision and the response continue in an ascending movement. The dynamic program moves upward through vision and response, the former expressing God's holiness, or hatred of sin, or desire for fellowship, and the latter expressing man's praise in return, or his sorrow for sin, or his joy in fellowship. The matter of ritual or no ritual, of formality or informality in the order of service is secondary. Lacking spiritual creativeness either may be impotent, or possessing such either may be dynamic.

Certain other guiding principles have been found of value in the conduct of worship:

(1) The culture level of the group or congregation should determine the form or content of worship. Responses, for example, would help in one group and hinder in another. The selection of hymns and the order of service should be made on the basis of the tastes of the people.

(2) Familiarity with words, music, and order of service is essential to true worship. Strange or unusual elements hinder the release of will.

(3) Participation by the congregation is generally imperative. We experience modifications in our attitudes as we allow ourselves to behave.

(4) Preparation in advance is best for those taking part. Notice to a leader that he will be called on to pray enables even those who are "instant in season and out of season" to think of the needs of the worshippers and to put himself in the mood of worship.

(5) Unity in a service safeguards against confusion and failure in worship. It is helpful to select an objective for the service and to reveal that fact to the worshippers. Even a hymn announced as for those in sorrow or those facing great temptation becomes tremendously moving.

(6) Massing the worshippers for singing, for prayer, or for reading

is important. A scattered or divided group lacks unity and sensitivity.

(7) Dependence upon the spirit of God will create greater results than all else combined. "God moves in a mysterious way, His wonders to perform. He plants His feet upon the seas, And rides upon the storm."

Evangelism

Evangelism is the heart of the church. As popularly conceived it is often more of a theory than a necessity, perhaps a fetish more than a fact. Actually it is the core of the Christian faith and the most beautiful of Christian practices. Evangelism is a *purpose*. All teaching and guidance is toward a decision for Christ and the rule of Christ for character and conduct. It is a *spirit*. It is a spirit of continuing love to Christ, and wishing his love for others. Without being conscious of the set of the heart, it is governed daily by a passion for winning men to Christ. It is a *method*. The teacher, parent or minister simply needs some occasion or stimulus "to bring to a focus the impressions and crystallize the convictions" that yield consent.

The Objective or Purpose of Evangelism.—"There is a shallow evangelism," Dobbins observes (A Winning Witness, Baptist Sunday School Board, 1938, p. 12), "that would seek primarily to add numbers to the membership of a church. Then there is an evangelism that stirs the emotions and leads to outward profession, but fails to anchor to Christ and his church. Again, there is dry-eyed intellectual evangelism that presents a system of doctrine and a standard of morals, but lacks power to translate creed and ethic into life. More common is warm-hearted, sensible, doctrinally sound evangelism that is inadequate because it is confined to a brief season of revival, and is not sufficiently preceded and followed by enlistment in service and nurture of the implanted life. We need for our day a vital evangelism—the living testimony of convincing Christians that Christ is able to save and keep and make strong and useful and happy all who come to God through him." It is such an objective that the religious educator makes central in the program of the church. At least three phases of the purpose stand out as objectives in the program of evangelism.

First in the process of evangelism is implanting an understanding of the nature and purposes of God. "How shall they believe in him of whom they have not heard?" (Rom. 10:14). In light of God's nature sin, which is the root of our problems, stands revealed as uncleanness of life, as neglect of the source of thought and life, as dominant selfishness, as currently and ultimately spiritual death. All sin means suffering for God. In light of God's purposes the present day difficulties become channels of strength for turning difficulties into triumphs. Spiritually sensitive men discover a passion for teaching others the beauty and the joy of a life committed to Christ.

Second in the process of evangelism is the expectation of a decision by the individual to accept Christ as Savior. The aim of evangelism is not acquiring knowledge or opinion, but life. A spiritual awakening follows in the course of the "seasons of the soul." As such it is seldom experienced before full instinctive development has been attained, and its peak occurs in the period of maturing emotions. These conversion experiences differ with the mental experiences of the individual, depending upon the temperament of the individual, his childhood training, and the period of life. The church teacher or parent seeks to understand these conditions that he may secure a personal commitment of the life to God.

Third in the process of evangelism is the training to make Christ Lord in the life. This is the easiest and yet the most difficult; easy because there is a new and powerful motive for learning, and difficult because it must register in conduct and habit. Salvation cannot be a negative experience. It does not rest in belief or in going to church but in losing one's life in an absorbing cause. To forsake a pupil at conversion is to offer God a dwarfed life. Full evangelism follows through to the full grown stature.

The Content of Evangelism.—Evangelism is a spirit, an attitude, a passion. It consists of sharing our Christian convictions, of mastering the art of living, and of loving our neighbors with a Christlike devotion. Christian conviction is more than assent to a statement, it is a personal commitment to a person. Mastering the art of living is more than a good character, it is falling in love with God for life. Loving our neighbors is more than sharing in the goods of life, it is an unquenchable and ceaseless concern for the neighbor himself.

The Christian convictions to be shared are that life's deepest needs have an answer; that human weakness has available an adequate strength; that life has a meaning, and that when understood this faith will be desired by our fellow-men. The answer is that captives of sin may be set free; that the gospel is for those who lack will power to master life except through Christ their dynamic; that men need not perish since God has provided abundance of life. **Men** who know these things, and pass them on will hear men answering back, "That is what I want."

Mastering the art of living is a Christian secret. The balanced life is Christ governed. Like the great flywheel of a factory that runs perfectly when on center, the Christian life runs smoothly and powerfully with Christ as center. It is when men regard the Christ as secondary that disaster ensues. Evangelism puts Christ in whom "all things hold together," at the heart of its message but its mission is not over until it has brought men to attain unto "the measure of the stature of the fulness of Christ."

Loving one's neighbors is evangelism. One of the strong proofs of the continuing life and presence of Christ is the Christlike life of his followers. When his disciples love one another they proclaim a living Lord. Loving one's neighbors is more than sentiment, it is a transforming force. It is a ceaseless concern for the neighbor that strengthens his weakness, rebukes his oppressors, protects him from his unsuspecting worst self, and interprets to him his highest values. Jesus commanded this love, and commended its accomplishments. "Inasmuch as ye have done it unto one of the least of these my brethren ye have done it unto me" (Matt. 25:40). A social gospel does not run ahead of a personal gospel, but it must follow after. Evangelism begins first as a brotherhood of religion, but its evangel spreads to include a religion of brotherhood.

The Method of Evangelism.—Method is the way the pupil learns the subject matter and not the way the teacher teaches it. That principle of instruction is applicable to evangelism. Method of evangelism then is the way the individual comes to accept Christ, and not the way some think he should accept him. The vital consideration is that the full evangelistic message shall be proclaimed, and that men shall be changed by what takes place in their lives.

The educational approach to evangelism seems to oppose revival evangelism to educational evangelism. On the contrary the whole of the program of the church has the evangelistic aim. Any apparent difference is in emphasis, educational evangelism emphasizing method, while revival evangelism emphasizes results. Educational evangelism and revival evangelism must recognize a mutual task. "There is no Christian education that leaves evangelism out," is Dobbins' way of declaring them inseparable (Ibid, p. 114, A Winning Witness, Baptist Sunday School Board, 1938, p. 114). "It is foolish," he continues, "to put evangelism over against Christian education as if they were opposites. Evangelism is the end, Christian education is the means.—As well try to separate the seed from the soil and expect a crop as to separate evangelism from Christian education and expect a gospel harvest. Where Christian education has done its work well evangelism is made easier and its results more permanent."

The continuous ministery of evangelism seeks in every way to win men to Christ. In the spirit of Paul who would be all things to all men that he might win some, the program of evangelism would use all spiritual methods with all men that it might win some. It would promote mass evangelism for the wider reaches of Christian influence, seasons of revival for the church school, units on evangelism for the class, and personal evangelism for individuals. One purpose runs through them all.

Mass Evangelism.—Within the community mass evangelism would arrest and enlist the attention of the indifferent. Through advertising, bulletin boards, and posters the church would appeal to the worth of religion; to a consciousness of personal needs; to a desire to be a better parent and citizen. One church carries this message on a highway bulletin board, "It costs much to follow Christ, but it costs more not to follow him." In this way, and by the confidence churchmen inspire in the unchurched, by their unselfish community service, as well as by individual appeals to the Christian decision, pastor and people prepare for a season of intensive ingathering.

Seasons of Revival.—Within the church seasons of revival will occur periodically as "decision" days, "win one" campaigns, as may be fitting. The pastor and the teacher have been doing the work of the evangelist. When the spirit of the Christ moves strongly in the hearts of the teachers and the pupils a season of revival will be set apart for the ingathering. The later childhood and earlier adolescent years will be particularly responsive to this method.

Units of Evangelism.—Within the class units on evangelism may produce finest results among middle and later adolescents. The unit consists of a series of worthwhile experiences brought together around some interest. The principles of the unit stress direct learning rather than lesson learning, activities determined by present needs, the superiority of learning together rather than individually, the value of first hand experience followed by group discussion, and the securing of a complete adjustment to the environment. Jesus' experience with the woman at the well (John 4) can become the basis of a unit on evangelism. Its ending is significant, "And many of the Samaritans believed on him for the saying of the woman . . . and many more believed because of his own words" (John 4:39, 41). This method should prove most effective with the unchurched within the group.

Personal Evangelism.—Personal evangelism is the method of Andrew who "first findeth his own brother Simon, and saith unto him, We have found the Messiah" (John 1:41). Underlying all methods is the man to man approach. Within the Church there should be a select group to whom this service is committed as a special interest. No method will avail apart from an evangelistic passion.

STEWARDSHIP

Great religious programs can never be realized until churchmen develop some greatness in their own souls. To this end the churches stress the training of men in the habit of Christian living. Training in church membership, leadership training, are but phases of the larger activity which the church fosters as stewardship.

Stewardship has meant to many the securing of money rather than the meaning and use of money. Church officials too often have looked at the pledge rather than at the pledger. Church offerings too often have been forced collections, sometimes accompanied with ribald buffoonery and the implication, "We need the money." Canvassers for church expenses have measured their success by the total money raised. Church societies have been judged and praised by the money they can produce. Little concern seems to be felt for the growth of each member in the grace of giving.

The new stewardship emphasis goes deeper than the legalistic accounting to God in Malachi and the motive of "proving God." Stewardship was made by Christ a spiritual principle. Living beneath a stewardship life is poverty of spirit. Stewardship is a way of life that finds its deepest meaning in "the potentialities of human personality." "I came that ye might have life and have it more abundantly." A steward is a new type of person.

Objectives of Stewardship.—While stewardship of time, of influence, of talents, and of possessions are specific practice areas for individual development, the real issue in stewardship lies in the relation of the individual to the material things of life. The work of religious education must come vitally to grips with the Christian's relationship to material things.

Practical objectives have been stated by Irwin G. Paulsen[1] as follows:

(1) "To develop such standards and ideals as will lead persons to material things, especially money, not for its own sake, but for the spiritual goods of life they make possible." How should a Christian live?

(2) "To develop a recognition and understanding of money as a form of power, the Christian administration of which is a sacred trust and obligation." Is my power to earn a sacred trust?

(3) "To foster the development of such an attitude toward life as will determine habits of earning, spending, saving, and giving solely on the principle of the sacredness of human personality." What is the guide to the use of money?

(4) "To develop a disposition to acquire money, and an understanding of methods by which it may be procured, in ways that do not harm but possibly enrich the life of one's fellows." What is my major motive in my vocation?

(5) "To foster in persons the disposition to spend money for the development of Christian personality in one's self, in those for whom one is immediately responsible through filial ties and in all members of God's family." Am I free to spend my money as I like?

(6) "To develop the disposition to share in the building of a Christian social order through the support of such institutions as have this for their purpose." When I give money am I giving a part of myself?

(7) "To foster an appreciation and importance of setting apart for specific religious purposes a stated portion of income, to do it systematically and administer it intelligently." What portion of my income shall I give away?

(8) "To develop a growing understanding and appreciation of what constitutes an adequate Christian motive in giving." Why is it a Christian's duty to give?

Content of Stewardship.—The motives of stewardship appear to be a trustee recognition of God's ownership, a duty to support the Kingdom of God, a sharing for the sake of human personality, and a corrective for spiritual poverty. The first emphasizes God's right to exact a portion as man's debt for the use of materials with which he makes a living. The second emphasizes the human regard for a proportionate part in maintaining a corporate organization working to establish the Kingdom of God. The third emphasizes the love born of Christ which prompts the relief of human suffering and want. The fourth emphasizes the value to the individual of sharing as a counteractive of covetousness, through which man comes into self-identification with the needs of the world and with the purposes of God.

Tithing with all of its values may not do more than pay a debt

[1] *It Is to Share,* pp. 24-28 (Methodist Book Concern, Cincinnati, 1931).

without recognizing all that is implied in God's ownership. The motive for tithing may be merely a profit motive, against which the church is educating. The motive for generous giving of substance and of self is the love of God. This motive causes men to suffer in the face of human suffering because it causes God to suffer. Depravity causes them to agonize, and covetousness causes them to grieve because they cause God agony and grief. In this spirit tithing may be stewardship and not legalism.

Supporting the work of the church with our money is stewardship. Failing this spirit we make ourselves beggars for Christ and thus dishonor him. Selling things "for the church" destroys self-respect and beggars Christ. A disproportionate budget between the local church and others dishonors stewardship. The building of character in its expanding interests is the object of proportionate giving for church support. System in the Christian life, an understanding of the objects of support and the reason for supporting them, broaden the Christian horizon. That is stewardship.

Sharing our possessions because of the worth of human personality is stewardship. Christ went to the cross to give the fullest and the richest life to every man. When we see that Christians must share this purpose with him the worth of human life becomes spiritual. We spend money for things we value. The tragedy of the church is the poverty of the budget for those without a chance, and the generosity of the budget for selfish interests. Christians will share when they care, and they will care when they see human life through the eyes of Jesus. This will be stewardship.

Full and complete Christian living is stewardship. So long as the main drive in the life of a man is economic he cannot experience the full spirit of Christ. "My business is serving the Lord," said a successful shoe manufacturer, "I make shoes for a living." He knew its meaning. Paulsen (*Ibid.*, p. 20) sums up this truth pungently, "know one's attitude toward the meaning and use of money, you need not be told about his manner of life." He explains that "until money, economic power, property, things, are regarded solely in the light of the worth of human personality and administered for the upbuilding of the life of the individual and society, we are not and cannot be Christlike."

Method of Stewardship.—Stewardship is brought about through building attitudes, ideals, and habits of life. The main concern is what the gift does to the Christian. That is a matter of diligent training. Along with educational practice three methods have been suggested by Christian workers—participation in program making, group discussion, and worshipful giving.

Participation in program making becomes a motive in Christian living when it is related to a life need, or comes within the range of individual experience. Lack of concern about the financial support of the church occurs when the member does not know where the money goes or how it is spent. Educational method in training in steward-ship suggests that the individual support objects within his interest, that he be given full knowledge of what the object is and why it is supported, and that he might be given some part in making out the budget occasionally for sake of developing loyalty to the obligations that have no glamor. By this method the budget grows, but better still the individual increases in the spirit of liberality as his knowl-edge of need widens.

Group discussion shares ideas and experiences. Facts gleaned by one member will stimulate the thinking and purpose of others. For young people and adults a series of discussion in the pulpit or at the round table on the philosophy and activities of stewardship will be helpful. Investigations of local community, church or mission needs, followed by discussions of the findings would stimulate the budget and the member.

Worshipful giving brings the experience of meeting human needs into the purposes of God. To pray about an object of stewardship enables us to see it from God's point of view. It may reveal in us a Christian in caricature. What the offering does for us is far more important than what it is used for. Training to give to God, with full knowledge of the human need relieved, will make for "abundant life on the Christian basis."

CHAPTER XII

LEADERSHIP

However needful it may be to select efficient personnel for the rank and file of any organization it is far more needful to place excellent men and women in positions of high·authority. An efficient executive can produce good results from the work of mediocre associates, but an incompetent executive will nullify the ability of the best of men. Objectives and curriculum may be ever so good but they fail to achieve their ends in the hands of a leader who has no skill in translating them into human faith and conduct.

The strategic importance of leadership is most evident when a change of officers occurs in an organization. A triennial turnover of 400,000 teachers in one large denomination, for example, contains serious implications. Every department suffers in function and spirit. Every removal from leadership means that "production" suffers until a successor is found. Time is lost in securing a successor. Efficiency in other workers is reduced by the extra load. Loss results in the time consumed in training a new man. Lacking experience or being incompetent the new man fails in production results. The new worker is an experiment and if he proves totally unfit for the place, may thus force a repetition of the whole process. Change and inefficiency are injurious to the Kingdom of God.

LEADERSHIP DEFINED

Ask three persons for a definition of leadership and there may be three different answers. One associates leadership with power. He has discovered in himself unusual capacity for imposing his will upon others and prides himself upon his ability to bend the wills of his fellows. Another associates leadership with position. He has discovered his ability to govern men by his control over their economic status, by his social or industrial position, or by other connections. He finds satisfaction in using his advantage for securing desired ends. Still another identifies leadership with ability to inspire men. He finds within himself a conviction as to some course in life and knows the way to its achievement. He discovers that the earnestness of his faith in the value of the venture arouses in others a similar passion.

When great crises confront men and heroic action is the way out, true leadership becomes the privilege of men who can inspire a movement.

A leader is one who has an answer to the problems of human need. He is able to show people how they are benefited by a specific course, and convinces them that they want that end. His integrity and ability to perform elicit their allegiance. Leadership consists of putting into operation a plan for the solution of a problem, and that through inspiring the group who must undertake and achieve the specific objective. Ordway Tead[1] defines leadership as "the activity of influencing people to cooperate toward some goal which they come to find desirable." Leadership is interested in how people can be brought to work together for a common end effectively and happily. Such a leader is not only interested in the result, but also in the process by which the result is attained.

The latter conception of leadership prevails in the work of the church. The intimacy of the relationship in a church, the delicacy of the process of education in morals and religion, and the voluntary nature of the service makes it imperative that the leader understand this meaning of leadership. The selection, training and support of every leader in the church field presupposes this conception of his task.

NATURE OF LEADERSHIP

There is a difference between an executive and a leader. The executive may be successful as a producer or organizer but a failure as a leader. Organizations need an executive who can plan and define policies and procedures, who can organize the activities of others, and who can coördinate the efforts of a large number of workers. In more recent times it is being discovered that organizations need another phase of direction, that of stimulating and vitalizing the individuals who make up the organization. Human energies can be combined in ways which create personal harmony in working together, and which can be tuned up to develop multiplied power in production. The attainment of this result is the function of leadership.

Experience justifies the leader type of executive. In spite of the method of elevation to leadership, whether by democratic selection, selection by those in power, or by individual energy and self-reliance, permanence in leading will depend upon the recognition of the human element in the process. The leader must be accepted before he can

[1] *Art of Leadership*, p. 20, McGraw-Hill Book Company, 1935.

lead effectively. He must inspire confidence in himself and in the direction of his efforts. He must recognize his dependence upon those who are led, which is the word of Jesus who taught men that those who would lead must be servants of all. The leadership of the general is seen when the trenches win the war. The leadership of teachers of youth is seen when boys and girls grow into strong Christian men and women.

This type of leadership is particularly important in religion and its educational processes. Unfortunately untrained men sometimes come into executive positions, and in their lack of training for leadership resort to domination or to subterfuge. They assume that the end justifies the means and do not hesitate to use any method necessary to obtain their ends. In so doing they destroy personality and suffer other results that come from broken laws. When the appeal is made to fear, hate, anger, greed, suspicion, the personality is integrated outside the circle drawn by Jesus who made love central. The real leader, however, stands out in front and calls the crowd to follow in a noble cause. To achieve moral ends the desires and the motives of the followers must be aroused, directed and released. It is the challenge to do something believed important which the good leader brings.

Among the objectives of education for religious leadership, as set forth by the International Council of Religious Education, the following essential skills may be named as requiring the leader type of executive: (1) "The Christian leader should be skilful in interpreting the contributions of the past in their bearing upon the present needs of humanity." (2) "The effective Christian leader should know how to arouse creative purposing in those with whom he shares in fellowship." (3) "The Christian leader is willing and able to lead his disciples to actual participation in finishing the unfinished task of the Kingdom." (4) "The Christian leader is skilful in helping others to discover, from their common experience together, meanings which have 'drive' for their lives." (International Journal of Religious Education, May 1935, pp. 8, 40.)

THE ART OF LEADERSHIP

The task of influencing others requires consummate skill in creating desires, in stirring motives, and in guiding action. There is an art in bringing people to work together. It has been called "the fine art of living together." There is an art in producing generated power. There is an art in making people want to do, and doing because they love the task. There is an art in building an *esprit de corps* in a church group whose intellectual, economic and social levels are wide. Like other arts leadership in religion has well established techniques which are available for the Christian leaders.

There is no excuse for church leaders to stumble over barriers when the problem is merely one of applying the rules of an art. A few of the accepted rules may be of help.

The leader must win the confidence of his followers. This means confidence in his character, his honesty of purpose, his sincerity of life, his knowledge of the task, and his ability to achieve. Lack of confidence in him at any point destroys his usefulness as a leader, particularly of one in church activities.

The leader must convince the followers that his objectives are reasonable and attainable. The leader achieves "only as he is in a situation where those he leads can achieve." A hopeless quest arouses no enthusiasm.

The leader will seek to arouse from within impulses and efforts which the follower accepts as "self-creative self-expression." There is a human resource in a sense of unity of personality and performance in which men realize themselves. The proof of leadership is in the group of those who are led. The individual must discover that the leader has done something to him rather than for him. The leader is an inspirer of men.

The leader who would continue to lead must help a group "to get what it wants with the least friction and the most sense of unity and self-realization" (Tead 29). Aims have an appeal when they help people to attain something they deeply desire. The leader must know human nature. Everyone wishes to be somebody and objectives based on this motive will produce action. The self of each follower must be served in some way. The skill required to secure social action of a group will include sharing in control and sharing in results.

The leader should be a comrade, not a boss. The power of leadership is not the leader's alone. It is his power to line up others with him to get a project put through. Arrogance, pride of place or selfish grasping of power defeats the leader. Humility of spirit takes the helper into the task, as together they labor for a common end. All the things that have any meaning for life keep their inner secret for the shared vision. There is a penalty back of the law which we break at our peril. The resources for creative living are conditioned by,

and dependent upon, our right relations with others. The outstanding "lag" is in the region of human relationship.

The leader who is undaunted in inspiring faith in others should practice the presence of God. In every age the men who have led great religious movements have been mystics. They have had definite fellowship with God. They are convinced of God's leadership and of their part in His plans. Times have not changed.

The Selection of Leaders

It makes a tremendous difference in personality as to who associates with the child and gives him his social inheritance during the early years. If unworthy leaders are followed it is very likely that their followers will have the same characteristics. Good leaders will produce good fruit, evil leaders will produce bad fruit. Personality is formed early in life from the ideals present. The person who seems to the child to be strongest in every way is his ideal. Likewise the child's ideal is the person who develops in him the greatest admiration and affection. It is therefore of great concern that the leader meets certain personal qualifications.

The qualities expected in a leader in the church are those expected of leaders in other relations, plus the added quality of spiritual awareness. Old Testament heroes revealed definite traits of physical prowess, a strong sense of direction, a contagious enthusiasm, personal integrity and an unconquerable faith in their God. The New Testament leaders, Peter and Paul, were cast in the same heroic mould. Outstanding qualities essential in a church leader of the immature are physical attractiveness, intelligence, temperament, and character. The teacher's temperament and his character occupy the chief place.

Physical attractiveness is primary, though not indispensable. One person vitalizes another. Something happens to another when such a person enters his presence. A leader's energy passes over to his followers. Physical vitality is basic in getting work done. The effect of a strong or weak teacher's mood in a school room is instantaneous. Nervous disorders, irritability, weariness for example defeat the work of a teacher. Christians who have tried to impress their religiosity upon others by their long-faced attitudes have failed. Jesus advised those who fasted against acquiring a sad countenance. Good health, zest, affection, on the other hand, are immediately reflected in the behavior of the room. Their presence at the beginning of the day assures a happy day. Their absence torments teacher and child alike.

Intelligence is important, but not indispensable. Some of the finest results have been achieved by uneducated men who were sincere and possessed practical common sense. The selection of leaders must give attention to more than intelligence. The ultimate test of a teacher is the character development of the pupil. Many Sunday school workers have possessed personal and spiritual qualities which have overcome any lack of technical and professional preparation. This quality, however, is to be sought as important.

Temperament is of more importance than intelligence. An even disposition, a sympathetic nature, an optimistic outlook, are requisites of successful leadership. One type of teacher exalts knowledge of the subject matter. The other type loves the child supremely. The old idea that a mastery of subject matter insures good teaching has been exploded. But it will ever be true that the teacher who loves the child and possesses these qualities will secure large spiritual results in spite of technique. Other things being equal, choose the man of heart.

Character stands above the other qualifications for leadership. Men of unethical character often appear more attractive than some who are ethically correct. Men of strong endowment and great energy often break the commandments and yet appear more attractive than some who keep all the commandments. Yet the stability of society depends upon moral integrity. There is much false thinking at this point. The gentler type is often strong in his resources of life, and most of the immoral are far from admirable. Character consists, not so much in external behavior, as in strength and unselfishness of life. Paul climaxes the demand of character, "be strong in the Lord, and in the power of His might" (Eph. 6:10). No character is complete that lacks a strong undergirding of faith in God.

Willingness to train is the final major demand. In general the ideal is a culture as broad as Christian truth, an attitude toward the social order that is thoroughly Christian, and a training that provides for adequate leadership. Training includes an understanding of religious objectives, a fair knowledge of the content of instruction, knowledge of human nature and the processes of learning, familiarity with the principles of administration, and the techniques involved. Since these needs will not be found ready made, it becomes a duty to train for the job. If one has a willingness to learn he will follow the outlines proposed for the training of lay and professional leaders.

The Training of Leaders

The fate of Christianity does not depend on the priesthood but on the laity. The genius of the Christian churches is the mobilization of vast armies of volunteer leaders. Professional leadership is necessarily limited by the prohibitive cost. Laymen must be depended upon for the bulk of leadership. The training of professional leaders will be cared for largely by the graduate universities and seminaries. The task of the churches is the provision for an adequate training of the associates in service, comparable to the work of the officers training camps in the American army during the World War.

H. G. Wells has well said that devices for making good teachers out of mediocre individuals will have to be multiplied. The churches have recognized this need and are supplying the devices. Three plans for training leaders are offered: the apprentice plan, the service or "shop" plan, and the collegiate plan.

The apprentice plan embraces a combination of study and practice. Study covers a period beginning preferably with entrance into the young people's department of the church. The need for maturity in the delicate process of education in religion makes it desirable to spend these later adolescent years in study, with occasional practice, rather than on assignment to teaching posts. Elective courses may be introduced in the department for prospective teachers. Such courses would include the history and objectives of the church, the source materials of our religion, the Bible, hymns, biographies of ancient and modern leaders. During the apprenticeship stage the individual will study, observe, help, and occasionally practice under supervision. The aim will be to keep a fair balance between technical mastery and the personal fitting of the individual for effective leadership. This method requires careful selection of apprentices and opportunities to practice. The promotion to assistant positions will come naturally and full responsibility will eventually arrive.

The teacher in service requires a distinct plan of training. The rapid development of knowledge of human nature and techniques in teaching makes a static policy tragic. Children are subjected to skillful learning processes in their grammar or high schools. The disparity in methods used by the two schools registers against their Sunday school teacher and against their church. Their loyalties become uneven. An unfavorable incidental learning has been harmful. To correct this situation definite planning must be done. State schools pursue such a course with great satisfaction. Churches are meeting with good results through their teacher training schools, institutes, conferences, assemblies, professional teachers' organizations, summer courses, local church surveys, visitations, self-rating scales, reading courses, and the use of departmental supervisors. The most difficult problem of the "shop" plan is that of reaching the "top leadership" of the church.

The collegiate plan rests on the fundamental assumption that modern churches wish to lift their leadership above mediocrity. Experience in public schools, agriculture, pharmacy, medicine and other areas of interest has established the value of college training for their leaders. Public school men have urged for two decades that Sunday school teachers "should have all the general scholarship and professional training required of public school teachers." The curriculum in the Christian college should definitely accept responsibility for preparing students for church leadership as well as for civic leadership, to teach in church schools as well as in public schools.

Advanced teacher training should be a definite feature of a Christian college. The cream of the church's potential leadership is in the colleges. Students are leadership conscious and responsive to college guidance. The college years provide time for unhurried and thorough courses. A certain degree of supervision is possible during the college years. The place of the teacher takes on a new dignity when the college handles the training. There is a broader training possible through wider contacts and varied observational privileges. Utilizing the college years in this way ties the student to his church purposes and returns him ready to lead. Churches look to the "new crop" of college students graduating into their communities to fill the teaching and leadership ranks of the churches and the community welfare agencies. The collegiate plan saves them disappointment.

THE DEMAND FOR TRAINED LEADERS

Churches like industry and government are awaking to the superiority of skilled workmen. In one of the larger Southern cities several of the strong churches are combing the city for men and women whose training qualifies them for their teaching positions. Replacing a teacher of a men's Bible class is as difficult as finding a pastor. Sunday school superintendents are as rare as church organists and strong churches will bring to bear all pressure possible for securing the congregational affiliation of a desirable prospect. City religious organizations seeking to offer parallel instruction to city school children are faced with the problem of enlisting qualified teachers. The wealthier churches that experimented with educational directors when untrained men only were available have abolished the directorship or found a man trained in a related field.

Why Does the Demand Exist?—Men are discovering that a properly trained leader secures better response and coöperation of fellow workers. A sense of unity of purpose in a common enterprise produces a community of action and a wholesome production. Even the Jerusalem church discovered that the laying down of dogmatic schedules for the control of their Gentile members was producing discord and disunion. The policy of conference and coöperation saved Christianity to Europe and the new world. This is supremely true in conducting a modern church.

The demand further arises out of the current philosophy that personality results are superior to the material output. Industry is magnifying the spirit of the worker, the human element, as the inescapable mark of a good business. Their vital problem is "how to make group activity a happy and satisfying experience for people." For such management only those skilled in the personalistic philosophy of leadership need apply. From industry the church is taking its cue as it recognizes in its objective the personal spiritual values to be sought in every organization within the church, in every class, and in every lesson. None but the trained leader can weave the pattern into the fabric.

A still further demand for trained leaders has arisen as a result of the effects of the use of large numbers of untrained workers. They lack basic knowledge of subject matter and correct ways of procedure. They have no experience in interpreting even their own faith and they certainly have no experience in aiding another to arrive at satisfying experiences. The scar left by such malpractice on a human personality is ineradicable. Whether it should be permitted is not the alternative. The fact remains that the teacher recruit must be used. The church lives under a moral obligation to develop them into more skillful leaders.

It is likewise true that the personal needs of the recruited leader demand a trained leadership. Young Christians may be made or marred in their initial effort in serving the Kingdom of God. A wise superintendent of a county high school confided to a friend that his heaviest duties concerned the adjustment and guidance of beginning teachers. Permitting defeats to occur or wrong teaching habits to be formed during the first weeks in the school room, would mean the fixation of inferiority complexes and in some cases the utter ruin of a teacher. The church can do no less for its recruits than offer the same encouragement, counsel and instruction that this superintendent gave daily to his staff. Love for the church, love for the people, love for guidance of youth in character and in faith, a more intense love for God, may be at stake in their initial effort in Christian service. There is a growing demand by churches for leaders whose training qualifies them for this exalted ministry.

Supplying the Demand.—Long time planning for leaders will begin with teaching men the spiritual value of their vocation. Any clash between one's vocation and his spiritual self-expression ends in a hollow, unreal, spiritual life. Through one's vocation there should be the fullest expression of his personality. The business or profession should be a means of helping fulfill God's purpose of creating a happier world.

Long time planning for leadership will impress upon Christian laymen the urgency of training for service. A frightful waste in Kingdom economy results from the fallacious reasoning of innumerable young people that any preparation for Christian leadership is only for ministers and missionaries. A young student hesitated to enter a college Bible class with scholarly aims on the ground that he did not need more than a general knowledge about the Bible, comparable to a cultured person's knowledge of Shakespeare. Since these youths plan to study medicine or law or business they think that spending a few hours in religious study is more than a waste of time. Sensing this waste the Latter Day Saints require of their young converts an interneship in Christian service. Christian churches are allowing their "acres of diamonds" to lie undiscovered and permit vast power to go unharnessed when they permit the impression to continue that only professional workers have need of training.

Training for lay leadership implies a two-fold obligation. The first is the obligation of the church to impress upon Christian youth the logic of placing the Kingdom of God first in one's life work. The other consists of teaching them. No medically minded youth should leave his church or his college without having settled the question that his practice of medicine is a ministry for Christ. Likewise the other professions and businesses should be so interpreted. The second objective of parent and pastor, and of college authorities, should be the completion of, or some achievement in, training for Christian leadership. Until the Christian colleges consciously accept this as a major function the work of Christianizing the world will go forward haltingly.

The church must revise its recruiting tactics. Efforts are usually limited to filling up the ranks of the salaried vocations in church organizations. The mission of the church does not preclude a call for dedication to Christian medicine or law. The traditional emphasis on the ministry or mission fields only has implied a release of church concern from the other vocations and possibly justified the impression that all other callings, professions and businesses belonged to the world, and should be conducted by the rules of the world. The test of a spiritual ministry in a church rests in the number of men and women who have carried out into their business life a conviction that their business is their witness to the reality of religion.

Vocational guidance is a church and college responsibility. Pastors should prepare themselves to advise youth in the selection of callings congenial to the Christian life. They need a ready knowledge of the general principles underlying the various professions and life callings. The rapid multiplication of vocations confuses youth and opens the way for a helpful ministry. The Christian college offers a major opportunity to pastor and professor. Pastors will be serving well when they encourage the young people from their churches to pursue training in religious education as a preparation for leadership. No student should be graduated from such a college who has not faced two decisions, namely, to make his vocation Christian, and to devote his service to the organized work of the church. Understanding the demands of the ministry and other Christian agencies he will know whether his best service can be directed through any of these channels.

Employing the Supply.—Remuneration is a determining factor in deciding one's life work. Many capable youths are willing to forego the social prestige afforded by more lucrative employment and undergo necessary training for the church if they know that a living wage can be had. Many graduates have trained for public school positions who wished to devote themselves to religious leadership because the church offers no employment while the state does. The number of "pay jobs" appears disconcertingly small. The church wishes trained leaders in every department but is unwilling to pay for any service beyond the pastorate. In view of this situation the church must realize the loss in leadership that it is suffering and enlarge the scope of its salaried positions. Under present institutional conditions this is right and necessary. The church must view such service as a ministry. Such a ministry is as truly related to the ultimate purpose of the church as is the preaching ministry. For such service the church and the individual must urge the necessity of adequate training. Less than adequacy will incur the reproach of every other human organization which has magnified a trained leadership.

The church job puzzles the youth. What is there to do within the church? Diverse types of service in religious organization may be classified as the ministry, missions, educational, promotional, secretarial, character forming, literary and social service.

The Ministry.—This service to which men traditionally have been called will continue its function of awakening the consciences of men. Young men of prophetic mind and passionate souls will find an uncrowded field. The broader the culture, and the deeper the scholarship the wider the opportunity for service.

The Mission Fields.—Since Jesus commissioned his disciples to cover the earth with his gospel there has never lacked either opportunity or resource for men and women who have capacity for interpreting one cult to another. Pauline capacities would be welcomed. To interpret Christ to pagan and non-evangelical life, to interpret Christ to internationalism, to interpret Christ to questing minds and hearts, places the foreign missionary in a strategic position. The channels of service are many: evangelism, teaching, medicine, social service, character building agencies, physical education, literature. The home fields open service to foreigners, negroes, underprivileged, unevangelized, frontiersmen, rural life, industrial life. "The harvest is white and the laborers are few."

Educational Ministry.—All education is technically a mission service. Educational directors and ministers of music are in demand by an increasingly large number of strong churches. Combinations of smaller churches form a "field" as in the ministry. Cities employ directors for denominations or for coöperating denominations. Colleges will continue to employ professors of Bible and religious education, with a staff of field workers as advisors and extension service men. Professorships in related fields are open to trained men in religion, and all Christian college professors should possess a background of such preparation. Denominations employ highly trained men and women for teaching and for student leadership positions in state and privately controlled colleges and universities.

Promotional Agencies.—These include denominational and other boards, field staffs, survey agencies, clinicians, financial canvassing. Most of the positions require highly technical skill.

Secretarial Work.—Secretarial work offers service opportunities to persons of administrative talents. Many boards and many churches employ executives of differing degrees of capacity. While widely different in type they are classified together for convenience.

Character Forming Agencies.—Character forming agencies employ vast numbers of more or less technically trained men and women. The Young Men's and the Young Women's Christian Associations, the Boy and the Girl Scouts, Sunday School Councils, employ a wide range of talents to care for their management, physical, educational, health, camping, community center, and foreign work. Specialized training is required for the important positions.

Literary Positions.—Editorial work in preparing lesson materials, denominational newspapers, the writing of books, open important positions to qualified individuals. Some of the literary work is produced in related professions, but there is a demand for permanent employment in certain departments.

Social Service.—Social service is a growing profession. Within and without the church there are influential and far reaching positions open to qualified persons. Welfare and uplift agencies, governmentally supervised work with underprivileged groups, relief workers, playground and recreational centers, employ large numbers of individuals, but favor the trained applicants.

Leadership lies at the base of the whole structure of a Christian society and of the Kingdom of God. Purposeful planning of the churches will include a program of recruiting which begins with the child and continues through the college. Scotch Presbyterians have helped predestination by holding constantly before their sons the ideal of the Christian ministry. The ideal of Christian service needs prominence in every household and in every church. The college is the harvesting floor. Jesus set the example as he struck conviction into their souls with his invitation, "Follow me, and I will make you fishers of men." Jesus pointed out the way as he trained with care the twelve, and at the end bade them, "Go ye into all the world—preach—teach—and lo I am with you." An intelligent passion in our churches for the reign of God among men will assure the needed leadership for tomorrow.

SELECTED BIBLIOGRAPHY
CHAPTER VII—PSYCHOLOGY

Corzine, J. L. *Looking at Learning*. Baptist Sunday School Board, 1934.
Powell, Wilfred E. *The Growth of Christian Personality*. Bethany Press, St. Louis, 1929.

McKown, Harry C. *Character Education*. McGraw-Hill Book Company, 1935.
Ligon, Ernest M. *Psychology of Christian Personality*. Macmillan, 1935.
Morgan, J. J. B. *Child Psychology*, Revised Edition. Farrar and Rinehart, Inc., 1934.

CHAPTER VIII—OBJECTIVES

Fiske, George W. *Purpose in Teaching Religion*. Abingdon Press, 1927.
Vieth, Paul H. *Objectives in Religious Education*. Harper and Brothers, 1930.
Betts and Hawthorne, *Methods in Teaching Religion*. Abingdon Press, 1925.
International Curriculum Guide, Books 1-3. International Council of Religious Education.

CHAPTER IX—CURRICULUM

Betts, George H. *The Curriculum of Religious Education*. Abingdon Press, 1921.
Bower, W. C. *The Curriculum of Religious Education*. Charles Scribner's Sons, 1927.
Caswell, Hollis L., and Campbell, Doake S. *Curriculum Development*. American Book Company, 1935.
Bobbitt, Franklin. *How to Make a Curriculum*. Houghton Mifflin Company, 1924.

CHAPTER X—METHODS

Betts and Hawthorne. *Methods in Teaching Religion*. Abingdon Press, 1925.
Elliott, Harrison S. *The Why and How of Group Discussion*. Association Press, 1923.
International Curriculum Guide. International Council of Religious Education.
Athearn, Clarence R., and Athearn, Laura A. *Discussing Religion Creatively*. Fleming H. Revell, 1939.
Morrison, H. C. *The Practice of Teaching in the Secondary School*. University of Chicago Press, 1931.

CHAPTER XI—ACTIVITIES

Sperry, W. L. *Reality in Worship*. Macmillan, 1935.
Powell, Marie Cole. *Guiding the Experience of Worship*. Printed for the Leadership Training Publishing Association by the Methodist Book Concern, 1935.
Maus, Cynthia P. *Christ and the Fine Arts*. Harper and Brothers, 1938.
Dobbins, G. S. *A Winning Witness*. Baptist Sunday School Board, 1938.
Paulsen, Irwin G. *It Is To Share*. Methodist Book Concern, Cincinnati, 1931.

CHAPTER XII—LEADERSHIP

Knapp, Forest L. *Leadership Education in the Church*. Abingdon Press, 1933.
Tead, Ordway. *The Art of Leadership*. McGraw-Hill Book Company, 1935.
Lincoln, Mildred E. *Teaching About Vocational Life*. International Textbook Company, 1937.
Watters, A. E. *Youth Makes the Choice*. Broadman Press, 1938.

Part III

Religious Education in the Church

CHAPTER XIII

THE SUNDAY SCHOOL (SUNDAY CHURCH SCHOOL)

Why the Sunday school? Is it worth while? What is it actually doing for character and life? Is being Sunday-school-minded an extreme form of credulity, or, worse, does it encourage the development of Scrooges? Is this Sunday school a social omnibus which transports prejudices—racial, religious, and personal? On the organizational side, is it the educational tail which is wagging the ecclesiastical dog? Further: should it have a more distinctive name generally? These and many other questions are being asked about this institution.

Recently the dean of a well-known theological school suggested that it might not be a bad idea for the parent to keep the child at home on Sunday morning and give him religious instruction, if neighboring Sunday schools do not provide meaningful religious activities.[1] Not long ago an outstanding evangelist publicly scored the Sunday school for interfering with the preaching services of the church and suggested that the day may come when local pastors will experiment with abolishing the Sunday school. The dean of a large Episcopal cathedral said to the writer a year or so ago, "Well, we are going to do away with our Sunday school for one year and see how it works."

So the Sunday school is criticized for not being important enough, on the one hand, and for being too important, on the other. What shall it do under these circumstances? The answer to this question will be found first of all in the answer to another question; namely, What does the Sunday school do? or rather, What is it capable of doing? Lastly, the answer may be sought partly in a frank appraisal

[1] Sperry, Willard L., *What You Owe Your Child,* pp. 128-139 (New York, Harper and Brothers, 1935).

of its limitations and its defects. This will be set forth at the end of the chapter.

THE TRUE FUNCTIONS OF THE SUNDAY SCHOOL

One of the advantages which looms large in Sunday school work, though often overlooked, is the opportunity provided for the individual to develop his sense of importance. There are four or more native human drives which are basic in the well-rounded life, and the urge to be important is one of these. In religious circles we have shouted so much about the need for self-effacement and humility that we have come dangerously close to repressing it. The urge to achieve, to be victorious, is quite necessary in the symmetrical and successful life. This is just another way of saying, in the field of Christianity, that the development of Christian selfhood—of happy and healthful personality—is basic with the church. We should never forget that Jesus grounds love for one's neighbor in a sound love for one's self.

Now the Sunday school through its class room procedures, its various expressional activities, and its official functions provides outlets and inlets, actual and potential, for a happy growth of the individual. The more officers, functions, and offices there are—provided they are both vital and properly correlated with the work of other agencies inside and outside the church—the better it is for those who make up its constituency. From this angle there is no such thing as baneful over-organization. A modern writer, with discerning insight, very happily speaks of this process as areation—an adequate exposure of the most surface in religion to the sunshine and fresh air of normal functioning.[2]

Next, the Sunday school helps the individual to achieve normal adulthood by way of creative functioning at the social level. Through democratic procedures, social inter-action goes on and numbers of people learn to work together. It may be in an instructional situation where guided group discussion proceeds. It may be on the tennis court where a number of young people meet, under the auspices of a class recreational committee, for regular exercise and fellowship. It may be in leadership situations of an organizational nature where attitudes of healthful domination and submission are at play. In other words, there are many opportunities, potential and actual,

[2] Douglass, H. Paul, in *Church and Community*, Oxford Conference book, article, "Church and Community in the United States," p. 251 (New York, Willett, Clark & Co., 1938).

which the Sunday school offers for the social development of individuals. And we should not regard these lightly, even though they may occasionally bring to the surface problems of acute maladjustment in the area of personal relations.

A third function of the Sunday school is that of character building. Now, we readily admit the pertinency of questions raised as to the ethical values of this institution in cases where improper management and poor character-conditioning prevail. But, in the absence of scientific surveys dealing with the total situation, it is not amiss to note the tools of morality that lie at hand and to point out the poentialities for ethical development. Also, the testimonies of many people to the effect that the Bible and the Sunday school have meant much in the shaping of their character may not be overlooked.

Roughly, the moral problems of human life may be grouped according to three stages of chronological development; that is, in terms of childhood, youthhood, and adulthood. Very broadly, there are certain persistent moral problems which every child, every adolescent, and every adult seems to face. For example, after allowing for some over-simplification in analysis, the three major problems with which youth is wrestling today are, when framed as questions, the following: What shall I do for my life's work? How shall I manage my sex life? What recreation shall I take up? Of course, many other vital problems stem out from these and take on rich colorings according to the landscape of particular situations, but the three major problems within this cycle are certainly crucial. Just here the *forte* of the Sunday school shows itself. By grading its constituency according to age and shaping its teaching tools and methods to fit chronological groups, as well as through providing buildings and equipment in terms of age needs, it is, to that extent, prepared to deal with the moral problems of these ages.

Grouping according to intellectual attainment, and not according to physical and emotional growth, as pertains in the public school, is not sufficient to take care of life's moral problems. However, ethical conditioning is much deeper than schemes for grouping people and details of buildings and equipment. It also lies beyond all current plans and theories of character education. Hence, a word about the highest function of the Sunday school is in order.

Lastly, and above all, this institution helps to build the right philosophy of life. By establishing right attitudes toward the total environment and by facilitating the individual's adjustment to the will of God, the Sunday school makes its most far reaching and profound contribution. Many people are unhappy today because they have no sense of direction in their living. There is no unity and harmony of activities. Banality blights their days. By giving direction to living and by generating an enthusiasm for life at its best, the Sunday school can be a blessing and a permanent hope.

As a sort of summary, then, we may say that the true functions of the Sunday school are of a psychological, sociological, ethical, and religious nature. We have said very little about organizational and promotional matters. We accept the dictum that "the Sunday school ought to grow," but our interest is in how it grows rather than in the mere fact of expansion. The levels of growth are quite significant and we may not ignore them with impunity.

Origin and Development of the Sunday School

One can realize more definitely the precise nature of the Sunday school today, if he sees how it has changed through the years, in keeping with changing social and individual needs. Such a study will throw into relief its true functions and make more specific what has just been said above.

The modern Sunday school as we know it is about a century and a half old. It started with Robert Raikes, of Gloucester, England, in 1780. He was a journalist who concerned himself with the deplorable conditions of the children in the pin industry of his town. From 9 a.m. to 5 p.m. on Sunday he held a school for them, in which the rudiments of education were taught, and this was called a Sunday school.

Raikes' school furnished the model for similar schools in England and Scotland, and even in America. In our own country considerable modification was made, in the light of conditions; but, in as much as illiteracy and low morals were rather common on this side of the Atlantic, too, Raikes' ideas prevailed here in general.

The second phase of development in the life of the Sunday school, as far as the United States is concerned, came not long after this. Immediately following the Revolutionary War public sentiment came to be so crystallized on the subject of the separation of church and state that all religious and moral instruction was taken out of the public school class rooms and put into the hands of the church. Now the church did not want the Sunday school at first, particularly on account of its lay leadership. But it was in dire need of an organization to do the job which the public school was relinquishing. Furthermore, the church saw that the Sunday school was going to succeed in spite of opposition. Consequently, there was every reason to adopt and utilize it. So the Sunday school became henceforth the religious educational agency of the church.

Also, as is to be expected, its program and activities changed. Catechisms and church doctrines now appeared in the curriculum. Consequently, the Sunday school became quite definitely a school of religion, and an agency whose policies were those of the church.

About 1830 a third change took place, though it was gradually coming for some time. This new development was characterized chiefly by the fact that the Bible was put at the center of the curriculum, as distinguished from catechisms, doctrines, and ecclesiastical emphases as such. The reason for this was that most Protestant churches came to see that the Bible is their chief authority on matters of faith and practice.

The fourth cycle of growth came when the shift was made from the material-centered curriculum to what is now known as the organized curriculum—with life needs and student interests at the center. This development began a little more than a quarter of a century after the 1830's, and was well on its way by the 1880's and 1890's. General improvement in secular education and vast social changes in society also came to be reflected in the life of the Sunday school. Interest in missions, evangelism, and community life were very noticeable. Even pronounced changes in internal structure appeared. For example, new members were added at the top, in the instance of adults and shut-ins, and the organization grew beyond the bounds of a children's agency. Today it is the one distinctive organization for all ages and all people in the local church, whether they belong to any denomination or not. And the growth of the Protestant churches is largely dependent upon its development, both as to breadth of interest and as to aggressiveness in contacts.

MODERN METHODS AND ACTIVITIES

It is well next, after what has been said, to examine the mechanics of the modern Sunday school. Such procedures as teaching, grading, worshiping, evangelizing, and character-conditioning come in here. However, for educational reasons they are customarily grouped under the broad divisions of instruction, worship, and activities.

Instruction: Learning Through Guidance.—Broadly speaking, the oldest and most prevalent procedure in Sunday school methodology is that of teaching. It is the one clear thing for which the institution exists and without which it would cease to exist today. But a further fact needs stressing also: the usefulness of the Sunday school at the present hour is more particularly grounded in the quality of the teaching than ever before. To be specific, educators are convinced these days that the once prevalent practice of formal and mechanical instruction must be relegated to the past, like old lace and pressed flowers. Guided learning and shared experience, with healthy growth for both guide and pupil, are necessary.

Very naturally, this means that instructors should have the best possible preparation in order to live with their pupils and guide their experiences. Accordingly, training schools of the highest character are called for. Furthermore, pupils have to be grouped according to age units, and life needs have to be met in the atmosphere of adequate buildings and equipment.

Then, too, the tools and materials which are used in the learning processes and in the meaningful situations must be scaled to fit the needs of the various age groups. Here is a perennial problem and one which is peculiarly acute at present. A single illustration will bear this out: the practice of printing a different lesson title for the different departments, though using the same passage of scripture for all ages, or even having a text discoursed upon by lesson writers for different ages, while not changing the text to suit the ages, belongs rather to the nineteenth century. Today, teachers themselves must be prepared to organize and use sources and vital experiences for maximum personal guidance. Also, pupils must be encouraged to participate in what is going on, and in an atmosphere of normal spontaneity.

At this juncture the old question always bobs up: What, then, should be taught? the Bible? church doctrines? denominational history? practical moral truths? Now, broadly speaking, the answer comes in the form of another question: Should the program be centered about subject-matter, as of old, or should it be student-centered and have the warm blood of life in it? If the last is what is really needed, and we most definitely think so, then we are up against a very difficult and complex problem; namely, that of constantly finding what pupil needs are and then setting about vigorously, persistently, and honestly to meet them. The Bible will have a big place here, and the teacher will certainly need to know how to use it to best advantage, of course. But, in the main, the reason we have done so little for pupils is not because the Bible or church doctrines have been forgotten. Such a criticism carries too simple an analysis. The real reason lies in the fact that few of us adults are qualified for the job of being good teachers or guides. We have too many prejudices, we are too limited in our equipment, and—worst of all—we, all too often, are suffering from inadequacy of personality. In short, we leaders stand in need of guidance ourselves.

Creative Worship.—Another consciously-chosen procedure or method of the Sunday school for personal self-direction and spiritual conditioning is worship. To be sure, this is not absolutely separate from instruction, inasmuch as guidance in class room activities ought to be carried on in an atmosphere of reverence. But it is treated separately for the sake of emphasis. Now, there are planned exercises and periods of worship labeled as such. These are structural forms of a program and tend to be regarded as the only worship moments in the Sunday school. This is a bad practice. Furthermore, where worship is formal and is largely confined to opening and closing periods, some Sunday school classes build up elaborate programs at these places and copy the church services. Special music, the taking of collection as in church, and even sermonettes at the instructional period are promoted. The result is that the members of such classes do not desire to attend preaching later because they have already got emotional satisfaction from the church service in replica at Sunday school.

This is just another illustration of the need to practice the new teaching procedures. May not the discovery of a new spiritual truth be an act of worship? And should not a moment of inspiration, in which one experiences a purging of life purposes, be divine? Such values as come from creative learning, may they not strike one's heart down before God? Furthermore, spontaneous worship and spontaneous prayer, such as are sometimes experienced in the Beginners' Department or in the Christian home, are eminently desirable. Opening and closing worship periods have their functions, of course, but real worship as Christ has taught us to practice it must not be forgotten.

Weekly Activities.—Next, we come to what is sometimes called "expressional activities," though such terminology is not precise, for there is a sense in which all activities are expressional. Furthermore, instruction and worship are themselves forms of activity. So the term is not meaningful, either way one takes it. However, it does have some value as applied by educators. The emphasis seems to be aggressive action as against passive impression.

But an illustration or so tells the story better. All efforts such as visiting sick people, sharing in recreational projects, helping the needy in a coöperative manner, and promoting extension work of a distinctively-religious nature (evangelism, for example) are classed as activities. Also, Vacation Bible School work and many week-day religious educational projects belong in this category.

Right here, therefore, is where the question arises as to a better name for the Sunday school. For the simple reason that there are program procedures which are worked out almost exclusively during the week, while there are others which are confined to Sunday, educators and churches are coming more and more to speak of the former as week-day religious education and the week-day church school, in contradistinction to what is promoted on Sunday. In this case, the term, "Sunday Church School," is reserved for the latter.

Supervisional Management.—Lastly, a word is in order about the manner in which instruction, worship, and activities should be managed. In the past our leaders have been occupied largely with the details of organization and promotion. These were the pioneer days of clearing the forests and opening up new territory for cultivation as spiritual soil. But the religious frontier has shifted now, and we must find a new direction for pioneering. We should settle down to the job of improving what we have—of doing something worthwhile for our constituency; hence the need for supervisional techniques. The pastor's cabinet for building a meaningful calendar of activities, the supervisor's schedule for improving instruction, correlational planning to knit the Sunday school with other institutions and to eliminate overlapping of activities, but, above all, an integrated curriculum are sorely needed in most places.

So far we have gone through a long period of "shadow boxing," and consequently have lost heavily in regard to these matters. But we are beginning to be realistic now and to see that it is necessary to "strengthen stakes" if we expect to "enlarge the place of" our "tent" and to "stretch forth the curtains of" our "habitations." The old enthusiasm for mere numbers is gone. It was an illusory goal, anyway, for we can never overtake the birth rate. Furthermore, where the church has made its membership identical with that of the state, more evils have been generated than have been overcome by it. Our business is to grow, we admit, but to grow through right motivation unto full-grown Christian character. However, tools, methods, and materials do have their functions, and they should always be properly positionized in the dynamic situations in which learning takes place.

IMPLEMENTAL GROWTH

Buildings and Equipment.—From the pioneer days of the one room "meeting house," which frequently served as a public school during the week and an auditorium for church services on Sunday, we have advanced to the age of the modern church with its separate educational plant. This growth is best understood in the light of changed ideas of teaching. Small class rooms to meet pupils' needs and furnishings in line with proper age groupings are now accepted as necessary. Even rural pastors are devising ways and means of reconstructing auditoriums so as to get separate walled-in class rooms. In some instances they are adding rooms from the outside or actually constructing a separate educational building.

But with all this expansion in buildings and equipment, many churches have suddenly realized that they have considered only the Sunday school in their plans. The consequence is that modifications are having to be made in order to care for the whole educational program of the church, particularly as related to the young people.

In other words, equipment needs must be seen in the light of all educational agencies and functions. This means, on the negative side, that no organization should be promoted as unrelated to the other organizations of the local church. We should like to go one step further, too, and say that the church in the totality of its building and educational activities may not overlook the community in which it is situated or the different communities in which its varied membership lives.

Literature and Teaching Materials.—One of the greatest changes which has come with changed teaching methods is to be seen in the field of literature and teaching tools. As a matter of fact, in some instances the advanced materials have been frowned upon, largely because the teachers have not been trained to use them. Here, obviously, change has put too great a strain on the leadership of the church. But educators have anticipated this. For example, they have created literature to fit all situations. There are the *new uniform* lessons, with the same text of scripture and the same "golden text" for all departments and ages of the Sunday school. Then, *closely graded* lessons are offered; with texts, subjects, golden texts, and lesson discussions graded closely to fit every age group. The lessons here are organized in units and are built around life's needs. However, we are now realizing that units are not sufficient as a final method for handling materials and situations. For one thing, they easily revert to the old subject-matter approach.

Lastly, there are the *group graded* lessons, and they are written to care for small Sunday schools which have only one or two classes to a department. A different lesson series is made up for each department, and yet the lessons are the same for all in the department. Emphasis is placed on life's needs, and the Bible is used creatively. Consequently, for the rank and file of Sunday schools the group graded lessons are quite satisfactory.

THE LIMITATIONS AND WEAKNESSES OF THE SUNDAY SCHOOL

Next, attention must be directed to another side of the Sunday school, if the whole picture is to be seen. When one frankly views this organization as definitely tied into highly-grouped modern life he becomes acutely aware of its limitations. For one thing, it gets the pupil, whether young or old, as a whole pupil, already highly conditioned by home, school, and play group. It does not get him simply for what he is religiously or what he can be. This makes the job of the Sunday school a very complex affair, if taken seriously; and few Sunday schools are prepared for so ramified a task.

Then, at best, the Sunday school has the pupil for about an hour a week or for only fifty-two hours a year. The chances are that the movies, for example, will take him through their paces more frequently than this. What can the Sunday school do with such odds against it? The only answer comes in terms of making the time spent in the Sunday school the most meaningful and challenging of any similar span in the life of the pupil—allowing, of course, for other religious agencies and activities. Can we honestly say the Sunday school has always done this?

But, there are more culpable weaknesses than these more or less necessary limitations. Broadly speaking, they may be grouped under two heads. First, tragic defects in *interpretation* exist, and rather generally. Secondly, colossal mistakes are constantly being perpetuated in *methodology*. By defects in interpretation we mean inadequate or wrong conceptions as to what the business of the Sunday school is. For instance, so many approaches tilt the scales of interpretation in favor of the institution instead of the individual—not consciously, but none the less tragically. The Sunday school in such instances becomes an end in itself, and its goals are defined in terms of organizational integrity or institutional growth. A complete roster of officers, teachers, and committees, along with a good statistical showing of people in attendance, becomes the *sumum bonum*. As if such functioning is not banal enough, now and then the robot is made to stretch itself, cover the community with a census, and take a few more people into its maw. Obviously, where affairs have taken this turn a general overhauling is needed. Let us not forget that the business of the Sunday school is to assist the individual toward well-rounded and successful Christian living.

The second area of rectifiable weaknesses is that of methodology. Frequently, procedures of organization and standardization go on without consideration for the local situation, and without reference either to other organizations in the church or in the community. Consequently, there is overlapping of function and duplication in curriculum, as well as doubling back in administrative duties.

Furthermore, we have not employed the instruments of tests and measurements sufficiently to see how we may proceed. For example, achievement tests, information tests, and attitude tests would serve to tell us more about the individuals of the Sunday school and to pave the way to better methods in helping them. Until we utilize such instruments we shall continue to work in the dark.

What of the Future?

In the main, three rather clear-cut conceptions prevail as to what may be expected of the Sunday school in the future. One is that of complacency, and runs something like this: Why raise any question about the outlook of the Sunday school, has it not succeeded in the past? The second view is characterized by mild cynicism and takes this form in thought: inasmuch as many representative leaders are absorbed with perpetuating what they have found and as they have found it, there is little chance of necessary changes being worked into the structure of the Sunday school. The third and most vital wing of thought sees reassuring signs of progress here and there. Experiments in drastic and creative administrative revisions are cited as tokens of hope. Also, in the churches where educational purposes and methods are understood shouts of rejoicing are heard.

The authors of this book entertain no serious doubt about the Sunday school, but they realize that the kind of structural form which the institution will have in the future is beyond human prediction, and may be of little moment—unless damage is done to individuals in personality and morality. On the other hand, they are definitely committed to a more vital and serviceable functioning of its activities, so that the fullest Christian life and the most well-rounded character may result for each one connected with it. What more could be desired?

CHAPTER XIV

YOUTH WORK IN THE LOCAL CHURCH—
THE BAPTIST TRAINING UNION

One of the most significant trends in social life today is the universal interest in youth. This interest is radically different from that which existed a century ago. For one thing it is much more self-conscious. There was a time when adulthood was considered the norm for all age cycles. Children were dressed like their elders and called "little men" and "little women." Adolescents were forced to be adults as early as possible, and maturity was brought on by early marriage and teen-age efforts to secure a livelihood.

Today the picture is totally different. Society is organized in such a manner that young people are forced to be adolescents long after the time for assuming adult responsibilities. Also, organized efforts are made to exploit youth. For example, commercialized recreation, in its more sordid expressions, is a constant offender here. Also, the high-pressure military machine is another. Furthermore, always and everywhere young people are told of their importance, encouraged to remain adolescents, and are more or less victimized by our society. So youth is having its flaming day, burning out and dying down to ashes in the intensity of its own vanity and helplessness.

But signs of hope are appearing here and there. First, education is awaking to its opportunities and is building a program of positive helpfulness for the youth of the land. Then, of late, the United States government has been trying to do its part in a number of constructive ways. Also, religion has not been unmindful of youth, particularly within its own bounds. However, there is much yet to be done. And to the possibilities of the future we shall address ourselves, especially from the point of view of religion. Accordingly, the remainder of this chapter will be concerned with historical development—to get a perspective—present-day organizational approaches, and social outlook.

ORIGIN AND GROWTH OF RELIGIOUS YOUTH WORK

Before 1800 there were no large-scale youth organizations in America, nor any concentrated efforts to utilize the youth power of the land. However, after this date numerous organizations sprang up which had some sort of program to appeal to young people. For example, there were singing schools which were composed almost entirely of adolescents, and were devoted largely to religious music. Also, temperance societies arose to draw within their circles a large youth group. Then, there was the senior class movement in the Sunday school which took in those above fourteen. In addition to this, various missionary and devotional societies now became prominent, and many young people joined them.[1]

The first Y. M. C. A. was established in England in 1844 and the Y. W. C. A. in 1855. Both of these organizations later took America by storm. However, distinctive religious organizations for young people as such (in the local church) trace their origin to the work of Dr. Theodore L. Cuyler, of Brooklyn, New York. He organized a young people's association in his church and used for a motto "young people for young people," a modification of the Y. M. C. A. motto. Young people of both sexes belonged to the association. Also, a pledge was adopted, a weekly devotional meeting was planned, and the society functioned through committees. Later, Dr. Francis E. Clark, of Portland, Maine, organized his Christian Endeavor Society, mostly after the work of Dr. Cuyler—which he saw in action. From this the Young People's Society of Christian Endeavor, embracing all denominations and having a national and an international reach, was born, in 1881.

The next cycle of growth was largely in terms of denominational organizations, with a plethora of religious differentiation. At this stage the denominational structures more or less displaced the interdenominational work. The Epworth League, of the Methodist Episcopal Church, was organized in 1889 at Cleveland. The Baptist Young People's Union of America came two years later, in 1891. Then followed in rapid succession the Young People's Christian Union, of the United Presbyterians; the Young People's Alliance, of the Evangelicals; and the Luther League of America, for the Lutherans.

The Baptist Young People's Union of the South followed the organization of the Baptist Young People's Union of America by a few years, and had the benefit of the successful experience of its sister organization in the North. It was launched at Atlanta in 1895, and was declared independent of all interdenominational connections. As a matter of fact, it functioned as a separate unit of work even in the South until experimentation had established it solidly in

[1] See Price, J. M., *Introduction to Religious Education*, ch. XVI (The Macmillan Company, New York, 1932).

the minds of the people.[2] By 1918 the Southern Baptist Convention felt sufficiently assured of its success to entrust it wholly to the Sunday School Board. The first distinctive young people's paper published for the B. Y. P. U. was the *Young People's Leader*. This, in turn, was supplanted by the *B. Y. P. U. Quarterly* in 1900. In 1907 the first study course was outlined by L. P. Leavell and was published under the title, *The B. Y. P. U. Manual*. In 1926 the monthly *B. Y. P. U. Magazine* appeared, under the editorship of J. E. Lambdin, and has since changed its title to *The Baptist Training Union Magazine*—in keeping with the name of the general organization.

DEVELOPMENT OF THE BAPTIST TRAINING UNION

Just here a few facts on the structural growth of the B. T. U. are important, as they show how this general organization came to be built up and how it differs from the work of the other denominations. At first the B. Y. P. U. was planned for young people of both sexes seventeen years of age and above. Then, the Intermediate Union was added to take care of those from 13-16, inclusive. Also, the *Intermediate Quarterly* was published as a program of work in 1908. By 1922 further expansion took place, and in keeping with the grading system of the more experienced Sunday school; with unions for Juniors (ages, 9-12), Intermediates (ages, 13-16), and Seniors (17 and above). A little later the Adult union was added, so that by 1932 it was incorporated into the general standard of excellence as required. This necessitated the placing of the Senior ages from 17 to about 30, and the Adult from about 31 and above. The Children's Story Hour has since been added to take care of those below the Junior age; and some churches west of the Mississippi have even gone so far as to grade these ages more closely into unions, after the manner of Sunday school grading. Thus we have now the completed general organization, the Baptist Training Union, and with a fully-graded system of unions, set up specifically to train and develop the entire membership of our Southern Baptist churches.

TYPES OF RELIGIOUS YOUTH WORK IN LOCAL CHURCHES OF VARIOUS DENOMINATIONS

Southern Presbyterians.—The Southern Presbyterians have what is known as the *unified* and *correlated* plans of procedure in

[2] See Price, Carpenter, Tibbs, *A Program of Religious Education*, p. 154 (Fleming H. Revell, New York, 1937).

the young people's work of their church. The unified plan provides for one group of officers to serve in what is called the Young People's Department.[3]

The department meets Sunday mornings as part of the church school, for instruction, which is the regular church school lesson. The department meets Sunday evening for a vesper service. The departments and classes will meet through the week as necessary for carrying out the through-the-week program.

Besides this so-called "ideal plan" there is the correlated plan, with the "group-unit," "committee unit," and the "Christian Endeavor" types. "The group correlated plan is for those churches which, because of size or peculiar condition, are not able to use the unified plan, but wish all their young people to be touched with a fourfold program each month. This plan is a good method of organization for those churches whose Sunday schools are not departmentalized. This organization may function at the church school hour, but this is not essential." In many Southern Presbyterian churches young people's work has settled down into a sort of forum procedure, with the chief features of the program scheduled for Sunday evening. There is much freedom and informality in the treatment of topics and in the shaping of the program.

Southern Methodists.—The Epworth League, which is the young people's organization of the Southern Methodists, is correlated with the work of the Sunday school. To carry this out there are two divisional meetings, and for only one department: the Sunday morning session consisting of instruction, and the Sunday evening session, which is devoted to expressional activities. In the latter case the application and utilization of what was learned at the morning session is emphasized.

This plan of organization is known as the Young People's Division of the church, and it calls for only one set of officers to carry out the work of both the morning and evening hours on Sunday. There is an adult counselor, or counselors, as necessity dictates, who sits with the young people in both sessions. A similar plan applies in the case of the Intermediates.

Northern Baptists.—The "Commission Plan" of organization for Senior young people prevails with Northern Baptists. Four commissions are provided for in addition to the cabinet; namely, the (1) "Devotional Life" commission, (2) "Fellowship" commission,

---

[3] *Kingdom Highways,* Introduction, p. 10 (The Presbyterian Committee of Publication, Richmond).

(3) "Stewardship" commission, and (4) "Service" commission. The "Cabinet" has charge of the organization and supervision. In working out the commission plan two types of "inter-group coöperation" are set up and are termed "different types of organization." These are the "Federation" and the "Council."

A *Federation* is formed when "two or more similar groups, such as two or more young people's societies" (we would say two or more "unions," as for example, the Intermediates and the Seniors), are correlated. (The plan of Southern Baptists provides for a *General Organization*, with a federation of four departments or unions— though not called a "federation"—in addition to a Story Hour. This is known as the Baptist Training Union.)

The second type of coöperation, under the commission plan, is the *Council*. It embodies "the relationship between organizations which are different in name and purpose, such as Sunday school classes, missionary organizations, and young people's societies."[4] This is in line with the organizational trends of the Methodists and Presbyterians above mentioned. Obviously it aims at the correlation and eventually the integration of the whole religious education program of the local church.

Southern Baptists.—Southern Baptists have what may be called the group-committee plan of organization for the individual units of the Baptist Training Union, including B. Y. P. U.'s and B. A. U.'s. When grouped together and under the general organization, which is a universal practice in the South, this set-up of coöperation and leadership is known as the B. T. U. The membership of each union, in turn, is divided into various groups and placed under group captains as leaders. Under this plan not over eight members are permitted in a group, in order to insure individual development and competitive interest.

Just here a word of caution is timely: the Baptist Training Union plan of today is *not* that of the former young people's society. It provides for the elected officers to be chairmen of committees in addition to serving as officers. Furthermore, a member of each group is selected to serve on each committee. Consequently, definite responsibility for the work of the several committees is secured in each group, and individual development is planned for every member of the Baptist Training Union. Also, the structure of the organization does not render its use impracticable in a church limited in numbers

---

[4] See *The Commission Plan Manuals*, five in all, of the American Baptist Publication Society, Philadelphia.

and leadership ability, as would be the case were the chairmen of committees elected in addition to the officers.

Finally, the Baptist Training Union is not the former young people's society in that it is not a loosely-organized unit of religious education, such as a prayer service; nor a hodge-podge conglomeration of various ages; nor an interdenominational service agency; nor a make-shift of totally different church organizations. It has a distinctive mission, appealing especially to Baptist youth—the B. A. U. to the contrary, notwithstanding—and running under adult supervision, which is not to be scorned. But this skirts the question of the distinctive aims and values of the Baptist Training Union, to which we may now devote our attention.

DEFINITE AIMS AND VALUES OF THE B. T. U.

The avowed purpose of the Baptist Training Union is that of "training in church membership," with all the implications attached. Usually this is interpreted as involving a well-rounded training for the entire membership of the local church, at least ideally. To such an end the organization is set up and the program of activities is laid out. Also, the printed curriculum calls for a discussion on the Bible, devotional life, doctrines, and missions for each month. Well-worked-out programs are provided in the quarterlies for the Juniors, Intermediates, Seniors, and Adults. Once a year, at least, a special study course is projected to round off leadership training to equip the general membership of the union in a more specialized manner. However, in every one of these plans a narrow aim may run "unless it is interpreted in the sense of training our people to be real Christians in the work of the world, and working earnestly to bring in the Kingdom of God . . . The church is not an end within itself. . . ."[5] However, we are told that "the aim of the Training Union is thus interpreted in all its literature."

But let us look at some broader *social values* which are more or less realized by the Baptist Training Union, and are suggested in the above quotations. For the sake of a fresh discussion we shall call them possibilities. First of all, there is the capstone value of *vitalized Christianity*, as over against moral legalism or mere credalism. Mrs. Franklin D. Roosevelt has raised the burning question in her own way, "Do our young people need religion?" She comments thus, in a national periodical, "Suppose these youngsters were to accept new values which tend to be more nearly akin to those preached by

[5] See Price, Carpenter, Tibbs, *A Program of Religious Education*, p. 156.

Christ Himself. What would happen if our young people only considered their own lives successful if they created success and well-being in their environment for everyone?" As far as the program of the local church is concerned—which is set up to realize this—our First Lady is rather critical. She remarks: "I am frank to say that I question if many of the churches to-day are giving the example of the type of simple spiritual belief which would make the young people of the nation feel that they are crusading for a spiritual ideal . . . Too many churches concern themselves with political and material situations, instead of realizing that their ultimate responsibility is in stimulating the basic loyalty of human beings to the beliefs which eventually will solve all the other questions."

Turning now from opinions about the church and its program, we may take a glance at the way youths themselves look at religion. The Maryland survey—which is a fair sampling of how the 20,000,000 young people of the United States between 16 and 24 think—shows that three-fourths of our young people regard themselves as members of churches, while 6 out of 7 attend services sometime during the year, and one half of them go to church once a week.[6] The report in the end generalizes rather hopefully: "For all its alleged decadence as a vital force, the church still retains a substantial measure of its original appeal."

The point we should emphasize just here is that, irrespective of whether the church's program for its youth is out-moded or whether young people still go to church, it ought to be accepted in the best Christian circles that vitalized Christianity is the chief value to be passed on by the church to its youth. And the B. T. U. must be committed to this great objective first of all.

In the next place, and as a sort of synonym for vitalized religion, the B. T. U. is an agency which should bring *full self-realization* to youth *in social service*. The motto, "We study that we may serve" is only high-sounding words if it is not actualized in service and in life. We have committees on fellowship and service, but what we need is a more adequate technique in this field. The B. T. U. is doing a great work in articulating and deepening right beliefs in youth; in teaching young people how to perform church offices; in helping to round off character-building; in providing opportunities for fellowship and social life; in affording outlets to talent in public speaking, music, and religious art; and in making some efforts to give guidance in choosing a vocation, developing leadership, and establishing a

[6] See Bell, Howard M., *Youth Tell Their Story*, chapter VI, American Council of Education (The U. S. Government Printing Office, 1938).

home. But what we have done so far, in comparison with what needs to be done, is only to get our sense of direction. We leaders need to look the facts in the face here, confess our sins, forget our foibles, scrap the frail structures of the past, and build largely.

Reverting again to the Maryland survey: scientific studies show that youth is seriously in need of vocational guidance, inasmuch as only a minority get it. Also, there is a woeful "lack of appropriate and adequate vocational training." Furthermore, "health education is needed, including social and personal hygiene." (Note the new emphasis on the latter.) "Leisure time is a social problem of real significance." And "the implications for citizenship in the attitudes of youth" are serious because so many young people are "indifferent to the ballot and other civic responsibilities and privileges." Finally, says the survey, there is "need for community planning for youth." At the present time "each agency works with no regard to the others."

Whatever we may think of such statements the fact remains that general education (the American Council of Education projected the Maryland survey)—both in the instance of the American Youth Commission and also in the case of the Progressive Education Association (their studies are now being completed)—and the United States Government are seriously attempting to get at the problems of youth and social living. Now, we already know what Communism and Fascism are doing for youth. Shall we be impervious to all these happenings? Do we not need a more creative and a more aggressive program?

LIMITATIONS OF THE B. T. U.

Before we go too far in bringing in services for the B. T. U. to take over let us note carefully that all public-serving institutions today are threatened with carrying an excess baggage of burdens thrust upon them by a society swollen with problems too great and complex for the traditional means of handling them. In other words, an individual agency can be forced to assume responsibilities which ought to be taken up elsewhere, and can to that extent depart from its distinctive purposes. Furthermore, vital energies will be dissipated, and the loss may be fatal. Therefore, it is well for the B. T. U. to canvass its limitations.

First of all, the Baptist Training Union, while doing its part to foster vocational guidance in the atmosphere of Christianity, nevertheless cannot be an employment agency. It cannot function, as our government is functioning, in affording the material "reaches" and personal power which are associated with the satisfaction of creature needs. The sooner the church admits that it is quite limited in exercising social control here, and wielding a potent influence, the clearer will be its vision, the humbler its pronouncements, and the more deft its spiritual efficiency.

Secondly, the B. T. U. is limited in its ability to satisfy recreational wants. All of the slack in recreation for youth cannot be caught up by the church. The task is too great, and the Baptist Training Union has neither the money nor the leadership to solve all community needs. However, it can do its share, and it may not repudiate all responsibility.

Thirdly, the B. T. U. cannot serve as a marriage agency for youth; nor can it solve all problems of courtship, love, and the family. Nevertheless, it can be informed in this field. It certainly has a responsibility to discharge towards the home, for example.

Lastly, the B. T. U. even in its strongest territory of creative contribution, that is, in religion, cannot shoulder all the burdens of young people's religious needs. The Sunday school must do its part, and the home must be brought along, too. In other words, somehow we must see a union of efforts for home, church, school, and community in all the matters above mentioned. But may the church not lead out in more coöperative, organic, and personality-building efforts? We are just entering the day of religious pioneering in this field.

The Social Outlook

The outlook of the Baptist Training Union for full Christian service in the society of today is in terms of individual units in towns, communities, and cities. Progress will come here and there, but not as a whole. Some unions will be samples of "social lag," and others will be great examples of Christian pioneering. But there is no reason to give up and join the defeatist chorus arising from some quarters, no matter what comes.

Our statistical growth has been steady, our curriculum is undergoing an overhauling, our leadership is learning more about sound techniques, and most of our people are forward-looking. In any event, the forces of evil are working too hard for the Baptist Training Union to slow up. Social movements may be baffling, and our procedures may be threadbare, but the vision is with us. Spiritual pioneers are needed, and let us neither disappoint our youth nor surrender them to defeat.

CHAPTER XV

THE WORK OF THE WOMEN: THE WOMAN'S MISSIONARY UNION

THE FRAMEWORK—CURRENT MORES

If one reads the New Testament with an eye for the part women played in the new movement of Christianity, he will find that their contribution was conditioned unconsciously by the position of women in New Testament community life. This is in line with the oft-stated dictum of theology that historical revelation is poured into the vessels of human instrumentation and—though eternal—is positionized in time and place. The finest illustrations of this are found in St. Paul's instructions to the women at Corinth, which we now interpret in the light of the peculiar Corinthian situation.

The same approach should be made to the place and work of women in present day Christianity. That is, the separate and supreme importance of women in church life, both as individuals and groups, must be understood in the light of current growth in the recognition of women's rights and the modern conception of their destiny. For example, as recently as 1885 the constitution of the Southern Baptist Convention was deliberately changed in order that the word "member" could be construed to mean only *brother*, and the two women messengers from Arkansas were thereby automatically eliminated from representation in the convention. In other words, until very recently there have been cultural handicaps lying like dead logs across the pathway of service, hindering the progress of women and compelling them to follow circuitous detours. Also, unfortunately toxic emotions have been impounded by these devious ways and have colored unconsciously the specialized meetings of women. As a matter of fact, sociologists look upon the phenomenal growth of women's groups as due in part to an unconscious reaction to the circumscription imposed by men. This is just another way of saying that the age-old struggle of the sexes is reflected in religion, though on the whole it is sublimated and may be vitally useful, flowing forth as a stream of idealized and enriched missionary work. However, with a few rural churches especially, where educational handicaps and cultural lag exist, the women's work jogs along slowly and must be promoted by the trained local pastor, if it makes any progress at all.

History and Growth

In the home of Mrs. Beeby Wallis, a widow, was organized the first "Missionary Society for the Propagation of the Gospel Among the Heathen." William Carey was sent out by this society to India in 1792. There were monthly concerts of prayer which grew up in this connection in both England and America, and they brought on a great spiritual revival.[1]

A missionary periodical was published, many of Carey's letters were printed, and newly awakened missionary interest bubbled over everywhere. Among these were the Wadmalaw and Edisto Female Mite Societies of Charleston, S. C., and the Hyco Female Cent Society of North Carolina. The chief objectives were prayer and giving, with a view to supporting mission work. However, the honor goes to Miss Mary Webb, a cripple, for organizing the *first woman's missionary* society of modern times. This was in 1800.

During the next two decades, however, the work expanded greatly. Phenomenal growth began with Luther Rice and the Judsons. In 1812 they went out to India under the Congregational Board, became Baptists, and gave our people a real vision. To Luther Rice, especially, goes the credit for this, for he came back to America to plead the cause of missions in person. Within eight months of his return to India was formed the famous *Triennial Convention*, through the thirty-three delegates who met at Philadelphia in May 1814. There were two boards, one to promote home missions and the other foreign missions. Adoniram Judson and Anne Haseltine Judson were accepted as missionaries, and India became one of the great fields for Baptists.

Growth of the Missionary Movement.—So rapidly were missionary societies growing now that by 1817, or the second Triennial Convention, there were reported 110 women's societies. By 1840, we are told, there were from one to fifteen units in each one of eleven out of the eighteen states in the Union.[2] In 1833 the Triennial Convention sent its first missionaries to China, John Lewis and Henrietta Hall Shuck. A sewing society of Beulah Church in Virginia aided

---

[1] Ragsdale, Elsie J., in an *Introduction to Religious Education* by J. M. Price (editor), p. 320 (The Macmillan Company, N. Y., 1932).
[2] *Op. cit.*, p. 321.

Shuck when he was a student in Richmond Seminary and outfitted him with clothes when he sailed for the field.

In 1860 an interdenominational organization for women was formed called the "Woman's Union Missionary Society." Mrs. Doremus of New York was the guiding spirit. In 1868 the Congregational women set up their own organization; the Methodist Episcopal followed in 1869; the Northern Presbyterians in 1870; and the Northern Baptists in 1871.

Also, in 1871 the Southern Baptists set up their organization (starting with the women of Baltimore)—though the inspiration for it was born at the Southern Baptist Convention which met in Baltimore in 1868. At that time Mrs. Anne Graves gathered the women together who were attending the convention and had them pray for Kingdom interests. Within five years organizations appeared in seven states because central committees were appointed for this purpose. By 1888 a complete organization was perfected in Richmond, Va.; and it had as officers a president, corresponding secretary and a treasurer.

The Organization and Work of the W. M. U.

A brief definition of the W. M. U. should precede a discussion of organization. "The Woman's Missionary Union is a graded system of organization for women and young people in a Baptist church, for the purpose of promoting world-wide missions."[3] The basic principles of Christian living color and suffuse its objectives. These are "Bible and Mission Study, prayer, and personal service, enlistment and soul winning, and Christian stewardship." The implication, of course, is that this definition is not arbitrary. It describes a religious educational unit which, in its structure and function, has arisen to satisfy a very definite need in church life. That is, like the Sunday School and the Baptist Training Union, the W. M. U. originated in response to a social and religious demand.

However, like other social institutions it has grown into *a hierarchy of organizational structure*. One may picture it in an outward and formal way as an ever-widening series of circles. Beginning with the local church—which has the primal and pre-eminently personal organization—a second circle may be drawn to represent the association; a third, the state—though there are usually districts within the state; and the fourth circle, the south-wide organization. Most manuals, however, list the south-wide organization first, due perhaps

[3] Bucy, Wilma Geneva, *The New How and Why of Woman's Missionary Union*, p. 31 (Baptist Sunday School Board, Nashville, 1934).

to its size and the further fact that promotional work begins at the top and works its way down to the local church. Then, too, the missionary Baptists are coöperative.

The most obvious reason, though, is the traditional one—which sociologists have explored for us[4]—namely, the tendency of all organizations to grow alike, beginning locally and expanding in an ever widening, as well as in a more or less impersonal way, until the state, the nation, and other nations are involved in a sort of "geographical hierarchy of administration."

Form of Organization in the Local Church

While it is not necessary to sketch in here the structure of organization in its totality, nevertheless a glance at the local unit is of value,[5] especially where the program is built up from the point of view of the local situation and not from the angle of an absolute or arbitrary standard.

First, there is the general organization embracing all the fully-organized women's work of the local church, graded down—as far as responsibility goes—through auxiliaries, and called specifically *W. M. U. Secondly,* the distinctive organization designed for all the women of the church over twenty-five years of age is the W. M. S. The Y. W. A. is the *next* organization, in the fully graded union, and it is composed of young women seventeen through twenty-five years of age. The Junior and Intermediate *G. A.'s* are made up of girls nine through twelve and thirteen through sixteen respectively. The Junior and Intermediate *R. A.'s* are composed of boys nine through twelve and thirteen through sixteen. The *Sunbeam Band* is the distinctive organization for children from three through eight years of age, both boys and girls.

At this juncture, however, it is exceedingly important to call attention to the absolute necessity for considering the type and condition of the local church as determining whether it is best to start out with the idea of setting up a fully-graded Union. Furthermore, the promotion of any religious educational unit, such as the W. M. U., ought to be planned with the whole educational program of the local church in mind; that is, in terms of coördination and unification of

---

[4] Tead, Ordway, *The Art of Leadership,* p. 7 (McGraw-Hill Book Company, N. Y., 1935).

[5] For a discussion of the association, state, and southwide organizations see Tibbs, A. E., "Organization of Woman's Missionary Union" in *A Program of Religious Education,* pp. 191-203 (Fleming H. Revell Co., N. Y., 1937).

religious activities so as to eliminate petty jealousies and useless duplication of efforts.

As to the officers of the Union, the situation again will be determinative—not some arbitrary "standard." In many cases a whole roster of officers is not only not needed but the local church does not have them. Where this is the situation, those which can be had will be elected, and the local Union should not feel one whit the worse for it. Of course, as the W. M. U. grows more officers may be added. In some small urban, community and rural churches a good wide-awake president and secretary-treasurer will be depended on almost entirely as the minimum staff.

No reasonable excuse exists for saying the church cannot have a W. M. U., or at least a W. M. S. If the women live long distances from each other and there is preaching only once or twice a month, successful work can be done by one or two leaders keeping the women busy through the mail, so that they are prepared when they do come together—if only once or twice a month. In this instance the "Royal Service" furnishes good programs—and at least one or more women take it. Parts are copied, and written suggestions are made by letter.

The authors of this book are constantly making the above approach and are laying stress on the *particular situation* as the final court of appeal in handling the structure of any church organization, because they are not interested in promotional and mechanical ideas as such. It seems much more sensible, for example, to have several A-1 standards for organizations, each an A-1 standard for a *characteristic local situation*; for there are and ever will be various types of churches —urban, rural, large, medium-sized, small, etc. Also there are peculiar local conditions which must be considered in every instance. Thus and only thus may personality and not machines be given pre-eminence.

The *duties of the officers* are not unlike those of other church organizations. The president plans for the monthly business meetings and presides over them. Also, she exercises supervision over all W. M. U. work of the local church; presides at the executive committee meeting; knows the duties of all officers; and supplies the necessary enthusiasm to give the work an optimistic and aggressive flavor. The first vice-president should understand the duties of the president and act in her absence; also, she is chairman of the enlistment committee. The second vice-president takes charge in the absence of the two officers above her. In addition she is chairman of the program committee and sets the pace in all program-building. The third vice-president officiates in the absence of the three officers above her. Also, she directs the young people's work of the W. M. U., leads in fostering the auxiliaries, and helps the counselors. The corresponding secretary writes the letters which are authorized by the society and publicizes the W. M. U. through the usual avenues of church bulletins, local papers, posters, etc. She is also chairman of the literature committee. The recording secretary sends out notices of meetings and keeps accurate minutes. She also sees to the promotion of the Standard of Excellence. The treasurer supervises and reports all receipts and disbursements of money. She may, in addition, be chairman of the stewardship committee, where the church and the local W. M. U. are small.

Qualifications of the Officers.—The qualifications of the officers have been much written about, often listed on the blackboard, and generally assumed to be carried about by the individual like a kit of tools—used, discarded, and supplemented at will. Generally speaking, the personal qualities and aptitudes, such as should characterize the various officers, are hard to describe since they are intangible traits and are enmeshed with situations. Furthermore, on the theoretical side at least, they belong in the realm of the psychology of leadership—about which we know so little—as well as in the field of social psychology.[6] All of this means that the local situation and the circumstantial training of the leader or leaders will color the official and executive functioning of the local W. M. U. Furthermore so many of us have damaged personalities, with quirks and kinks of one sort or another; consequently, all organizational units will have to get along the best way they can with such limited folks as we are. Much improvement, of course, will come with added responsibility, new opportunities to develop talent, and the hard knocks of experience. Here is where the W. M. U., as well as other organizations, makes a great contribution—though personality development is often overlooked in the mad scramble to build educational machines, and pile up imposing statistics for neat array in an annual yearbook.

ACTIVITIES

Objectives will be discussed in another connection; and much of W. M. U. work—as associated with the duties of the officers—has

---

[6] See R. T. LaPiere and Paul R. Farnsworth, *Social Psychology* (McGraw-Hill Co., N. Y., 1936); also Ordway Tead's *The Art of Leadership*.

already been taken up. So it remains here to consider the activities of the Union in general. *Mission Study* is a distinctive work, and has always been so with the women. Home and foreign missions, stewardship, Bible subjects, soul winning, and the like are studied. Also, these courses are graded for all ages and are promoted intensively. Furthermore, they are made up in units with rewards in seals or diplomas, and pyramided toward the acquisition of a standard.

Prayer.—Prayer is an important feature of the Union. A calendar of daily prayer is printed with the names of home and foreign missionaries to be kept in mind. Nine o'clock is the hour set for all loyal members to pray. Also, there are special weeks of prayer arranged in behalf of home missions (in March), state missions (in September), and foreign missions (in December). At this time an offering is taken in behalf of the particular work. Especially is great stress laid on the Christmas offering for foreign missions, and much money is raised.

Personal Service.—Personal service is a great field of activity promoted by the Union. Soul-winning, visiting the sick, helping the poor, fostering inter-racial coöperation, and sharing in mission Sunday schools and vacation schools are examples. Even here the work is graded in keeping with the age and capacity of the individual doing it. However, too much attention to credits has caused some Unions to seek recognition for things never intended by the term "personal service." This illustrates the need for eternal vigilance in order to keep out mechanical and non-personal motivation in church work.

Publication Projects.—These include such monthly magazines as "Royal Service," "World Comrades," and the "Window." The first is devoted to programs for women; the second, for junior and intermediate boys and girls; and the third, for young women. Also, tract and missionary material, leaflets, playlets, and pageants are promoted.

Finally, monthly programs—covering a wide range of missionary, educational, and denominational interests—*institutes and conferences,* and *graded missionary instruction,* promoted through the mother society and its auxiliaries, are outstanding activities. In all, therefore, the curriculum is a comprehensive and closely articulated system of work, incarnated in the local church and receiving its life blood from the efficient headquarters at 1111 Comer Bldg., Birmingham, Ala., where throbs the heart of the south-wide W. M. U. organization.

Objectives of the W. M. U.

As Ragsdale says, "The twofold *purpose* of the organization is to disseminate missionary information and stimulate the giving for missions among the women and young people of the church. It is seen from this that it is distinctively missionary and educational in its objectives." In other words, its sole reason for existence—granted that it is organic with a local Baptist church—is to promote the giving, sharing, and overflowing life in Christ both at home and abroad. So much for a generalized statement of purpose. Now we may ask: What are the particular goals?

If we follow the manuals we shall notice that a great deal of attention is given to such specific matters as:

1. Amount of increase desired in membership.
2. The manner in which reports are to be made.
3. Attitude toward denominational periodicals.
4. The solving of the absentee problem.
5. Promotion of similar (auxiliary) organizations.
6. Prayer, giving, personal service, and mission study.

Also, the formulas for handling these matters are neatly laid out in the official standard of excellence of the W. M. U. of the South. Furthermore, the usual form which it takes involves the following points:[7]

Standard of Excellence

Woman's Missionary Society, W. M. U. Auxiliary to S. B. C.

I. Meetings

Twelve meetings. . . . President, assisted by Program Committee.

II. Growth

Ten per cent increase. . . . First Vice-President and the Enlistment Committee.

III. Giving

Gifts according to state plan. . . . Treasurer, assisted by Stewardship Committee.

IV. Reports

Quarterly reports. . . . President, assisted by Recording Secretary, Treasurer, and Young People's Director.

[7] Standard same as Bucy's but arranged differently. See *The New How and Why of Woman's Missionary Union*, pp. 77, 78; also *Year Book*, p. 77, and *Manual of W. M. U. Methods*, pp. 48, 49.

V. Periodicals

Denominational periodicals. . . . Literature Chairman of Program Committee.

VI. Seasons of Prayer

Special prayer seasons. . . . President, assisted by Program Committee and Circle Chairman.

VII. Mission Study

Mission study classes. . . . Missionary Study Chairman assisted by Circle Chairman.

VIII. Personal Service

Organized personal service. . . . Personal Service Committee.

IX. Attendance

Fifty per cent attendance. . . . Enlistment Committee.

X. Subsidiary Societies

Societies organized and fostered. . . . Young People's Director.

As a caution against mechanical motivation we are given the following much-needed supervisional advice. "The Standard of Excellence is simply a measuring rod by which it should mark out its work and gauge its efficiency. It should never be regarded as an end in itself, but simply as a means to an end."

In the light of the principles of religious education, where adequate objectives are set up, certainly there needs to be some overhauling here in order to care for personality-building activities. See Chapter III in Part II of this book entitled, "Objectives in Religious Education," for a fuller discussion of the subject.

EVALUATION OF METHODS AND MATERIALS

At the outset it is well, in any reasonable résumé of religious organizational work, whatever its nature, to keep in mind two things: namely, the great work of the particular institution, where outstanding accomplishments are achieved, and also a critical analysis of the institution, for the sake of greater progress. This spirit lies in the background of what is said here.[8]

Methods.—Generally speaking, W. M. U. methods, as the scholar sees them, are largely promotional at present. The aim is to organize more societies and get more members. Other objectives certainly lie beneath the surface and are tacitly assumed; nevertheless,

---

[8] For a recognition of the accomplishments of W. M. U. see: Tibbs, A. E., "Organization of the Woman's Missionary Union," in *A Program of Religious Education*, p. 191.

organization looms large. The local church, the local situation, and the individual member should come in for more attention. Expansion of personality, feelings of satisfaction, proper motivation, right attitudes, and enrichment of Christian living need to be realized more definitely. It would not be a bad idea to articulate these formally in a list of objectives; and we need not fear that they will be incompatible with altruism and missionary endeavor.

Also, the small church, the rural church, and the poor church should receive more attention, commendation, and encouragement. The idea may not necessarily be a full-graded A-1 W. M. U. nor a large city church. Furthermore, suggestions for correlation and integration of organizations in terms of a unified and more harmonious program of local church activities should be accepted with more enthusiasm.

Materials.—There is a great need for biographical and inspirational books, though some new works are now coming from the press. So far we have a lamentable dearth of what may be called "trade hints," except those peddled around on platforms and at conferences by word of mouth. We should have more printed records of people's experiences—how they do the work here and how they do it there.

In the field of W. M. U. organization and supervision, at present two manuals are dominant. The one which was originally published in 1917 has been changed only slightly through three revisions, and it covers a period of almost a quarter of a century. The *Year Book* which gives the annual calendar of activities is commendable. There are five booklet manuals which describe the work among young people; and separate books are published on mission work. The *Woman's Missionary Union Annual Report* gives a record of the annual south-wide meeting. The monthly magazines, leaflets, prayer-season programs, etc., continue to come from the press. But there is room for creative and fresh materials, and a great need for original writers. The same condition, of course, exists with other church organizations among the Baptists of the South. Our hope is that the day will soon come when organization and mechanics will not sap all of our energies and absorb our creative talent. The change will appear, however, only when our objectives and our motivation have been reconstructed. We cannot think in low gear and run in high gear.

CHAPTER XVI

VACATION AND WEEK-DAY CHURCH SCHOOLS

The greatest progress in church school education during the last decade has come with the Vacation Bible School and with the Week-day Church School. Educators in the field of religion are particularly interested in this development because they see the educational work of the church being seriously maintained for the first time on a through-the-week basis. Also, they sense in these activities a widening and deepening of religion, wherein the church seeks more realistically than ever to assist the individual in becoming adjusted to his world through moral and spiritual orientation.

It is hoped that a new type of community citizenship, national loyalty, and world coöperation may result from this new canalizing of religion. Also, inasmuch as it is a new phase of the so-called youth movement and is spreading rapidly, it is attracting much attention. As ever, the test of its continued usefulness depends on the type of leadership and church support which religion can furnish. The two great dangers facing the movement are that it may either become too narrow or too broad. In the first instance it will result in reaching only a few people; in the second, it will become "watered down" and lose its appeal. At present, however, neither of these extremes is a serious threat, so we may go to work with hope and enthusiasm.

The Vacation School

General Survey.—The time of the school is, as the name suggests, confined to the vacation period when the public school is closed. Of course there are a few exceptions, such as pertain to mission work. Generally speaking, the Vacation Bible School of Southern Baptists is conducted by the local church at some time during the summer, when other schools are closed; and it lasts from two to four weeks, depending on the situation.

School membership is extended by the local Baptist church to the boys and girls of the community over five and under seventeen years of age. Also, provisions are now being made to care for those under five and over seventeen. In the former instance we have a slight parallel to the pre-school movement in secular education, but with distinct religious advantages. In the latter case, the church is definitely committed to more realistic adult education.

The church conducts the school after careful authorization in one of its regular conferences. It provides the teachers—usually through the Sunday School—furnishes the quarters, elects the principal, and buys the supplies. No fees are paid, and teachers are usually volunteers. Occasionally in mission centers, where an intensive program is promoted, and over a long time, financial assistance is sometimes necessary—especially if a few highly trained workers are brought in.

Books are not used by pupils, but are for teachers only, because the work is of a vacation nature and is rather informal. Also, home study is not required of pupils. The methods used correspond somewhat to those in vogue in the so-called organic schools—of course, with a religious setting.

The departments, as advocated by the Vacation Bible School Department of the Baptist Sunday School Board are five in number; namely, Nursery, Beginner, Primary, Junior, and Intermediate—corresponding to the grouping of the Baptist Sunday school. However, there are instances where it is not best to attempt all these divisions. On the other hand, adult education in the field of religion is coming in here, and we may soon see another grouping, where the local church can care for adults, also.[1]

The types of schools may be described under two broad divisions; viz., Vacation Bible School or Vacation Church School and the Summer Bible School. The Vacation Bible School meets daily for five days in the week from two to four weeks, and features expressional activities. The Summer Bible School has no handwork at all except map-making and notebooks. It arose in protest to what some regarded as too much emphasis, or else wrong emphasis, on handwork. Local types of vacation church schools are the community school, the interdenominational school, the denominational coöperative school, and the individual church school.

The origin of the Vacation Bible School may be traced back to the work of Dr. Howard Lee Jones, pastor of the Epiphany Baptist Church in New York City, in July 1898. Through the assistance of Mrs. W. A. Howes, Superintendent of the Primary Department of the Sunday school, a school was started which later bore fruit in the vacation school movement. Similar schools were conducted in 1899

---

[1] The new literature promoted by the department for young people and adults will have suggestions for adults, where the local church is interested in the work.

and in 1900. In 1901 five schools were promoted through the New York City Baptist Mission Society; in 1902, ten; and in 1903, seventeen. So the work soon passed from the experimental stage. In 1905 the Federation of Churches entered the field, through the influence of Dr. Boville, and the vacation school became interdenominational. The Presbyterians took up the work in 1910, the Northern Baptists in 1915, and the Southern Baptists in 1915. Most other denominations have also promoted their schools and even the Roman Catholics are now hard at work in the field.

Meeting Educational and Social Needs

The time demands a unified church program. The Vacation School is well adapted to such a need. It should be correlated with the Sunday school of the local church. In fact, the recommendation of the Sunday School Board since 1935 has been that the church vote in conference to make the Vacation Bible School a division of the Sunday school; so that now it has become a part of that organization, with permanent officers responsible for its promotion and operation every summer. When a church takes this action the pastor, the general superintendent of the Sunday school, and the departmental superintendents whose divisions are involved—in connection with others whom they wish to consult—are charged with selecting a time, securing a principal, and assisting him in the selection and training of a faculty. They should assist in promoting the school, coöperating during its existence, and helping after it closes to conserve its results. Thus they help to make the Sunday school and the church more efficient. The study course books for the Vacation Bible School teachers are now a part of the New Training Course for Sunday School Workers, and the movement is promoted by the state and local Sunday school leadership. Therefore when the movement for unification and integration becomes fully realized in the local church the vacation school will not lie without the bounds of possible coördination. A notch or two will have to be taken up in the educational belt, but her girth can stand it.

Social Needs.—Next, and perhaps more important, social needs enter into the definition and articulation of the Vacation Bible School. The emphasis of the "new" school, so-called, is a wholesome reaction and helps us to see what we are about—in becoming self-conscious about educational philosophy. But we also need to visualize our opportunities and leave room for the social situation to make its demands in shaping the school; in short, the community situation surrounding the particular local church. This our Southern Baptists have tried to do, and have realized no little success, but there is much yet to do.

There are upwards of 8,000,000 white boys and girls in the South over five and under seventeen years of age. About half of these, or 4,000,000, are not enrolled in a Sunday school and are not getting any religious instruction. If they are ever to know Christianity we shall have to go after them. Since they are not being enlisted through other church organizations, obviously some new organization such as the vacation school will have to reach them.

Furthermore, there are dangers which come to young people in vacation time. During one fourth of the year, approximately ninety days, children are turned loose and are allowed to shift for themselves —except as careful home supervision, vacation play schools or summer camps take them in charge; and only a small number come within this range. The result is juvenile delinquency, more traffic accidents, and waste of valuable human energies. The general hazards of vacation time are beginning to be realized, and the vacation school has grown up as an institution to eliminate such. This means that play life is now being viewed in the light of needed supervision. Purposeful guidance and creative experience through worship, discussion, music, drama, handwork, and directed play are necessary. They are no longer regarded as silly fads. Evil habits are now seen for what they are and hidden possibilities are regarded in their true light.

Finally, the church needs such a helper as exists in the vacation school. At its best the Sunday school has the pupil about sixty-five hours a year for distinctively religious instruction. The public school has him over eight hundred hours. Something ought to be done to correct this condition. Obviously, the Sunday school as it is organized at present, cannot meet the situation. It must have reinforcements. The V. B. S. will help materially. Furthermore, the pastor and the church at large, as well as the community, will receive benefits; the pastor in coming to know his young people better; the church, in receiving new summer vitality; and the community in seeing an influx of new idealism and a higher standard of morality.

Organizing and Financing the School

If the Vacation Bible School is to succeed, thorough preparation is absolutely essential. A last minute public announcement before the church, a hurriedly thrown-together faculty, and an unplanned program will botch the educational job. Over-simplifying of problems, and too careless a regard for the significance of the school also make for failure. Where an occasional church dreads promoting a second or a third school, the dissatisfaction can usually be traced to poor management in the organization of the first and second schools. Also, the focus of the disease will usually be found in one or more of the above-named evils.

Preliminary Steps.—Proper preliminary steps leading to organization are necessary. In initial cases usually the pastor has to take the initiative in making the church feel the need and value of a school, where it is church-promoted. He will not do this by springing the proposition on uninformed officers and deacons. Nor should he appoint a committee to begin with, because they may be ignorant of vacation schools generally and therefore may manifest indifference or even hostility. On the other hand, the pastor may begin by showing the church what happens to boys and girls during vacation time. Then he may explain at the proper time, the vacation school as an agency set up to minister to the spiritual, moral, physical, and group needs of children in a creative and happy way. Thus, interest will be aroused and the proper mind-set will be provided for the project. Only thereby may the pastor hope for the maximum of success.

Next, the one who is promoting the school will launch out into a campaign of more direct and deliberate publicity. The boys and girls will be contacted during the Sunday school hour; short speeches may be made before the various departments. After this the pastor should preach a sermon on vacation school work, though he will tactfully announce it beforehand as a special message which vitally concerns the interests of the home (leaving out the ponderous term, "Vacation Bible School"). By now, perhaps, church action may be secured. The last step in publicizing the school is advertising. County and city papers may be utilized for announcements. Short news sketches will be made all along concerning special features, picnics, enrollment items, etc. When the school is over a summary of the work should be given and a "commencement" featured. Bulletins, painted signs, posters, a mimeographed letter to parents, and special tags and buttons are also helpful. No matter how many times the school is held, advertising is good.

As a part of the advertising, though it will appear to be a joyous recreational outing, a parade is often promoted, on the Friday before the school opens on Monday. However, this usually takes place only after a general faculty meeting, a departmental faculty meeting (of an hour), and a registration session are held; in other words, after everything has been discussed in detail covering the first day in school, and after as many pupils as possible have been registered.

Next, the organizational structure of the Vacation Bible School should be constructed as far as possible in a non-mechanical and vital way, where organization is not an end in itself. As Blair suggests, it is "organization and administration which make for creative individual and group living."[2] That is, the needs of the pupil are to be properly considered and personnel guidance with proper spirit or class room procedure, is to be deliberately chosen. Personality and Christlike character are to come first.

The faculty will be made up of ten or twelve teachers and general officers usually, though the local situation and type of school promoted may demand some variations. Besides these workers there are the "helpers," made up largely of those who have not had experience in teaching. The pastor can serve profitably as principal of the school, or he may set aside a part of his time every day to tell the habit story or help with the boys' handwork. His presence and moral support are valuable. Getting someone else to run the school, going away for a revival, or taking a vacation deliberately to avoid being in the Vacation school shows limitations in training, interest, and vision. Of course, where there is a very large church, it may be well-nigh impossible for the pastor to be of great direct assistance.

The work of the principal is largely supervisional and administrative. His assistant may be a dependable high school boy, college student, or even older Intermediate. He takes over such tasks as icing water, running errands, and taking care of emergencies—which are sure to arise. There are four department superintendents where there are Beginner, Primary, Junior, and Intermediate departments; or three, where Intermediates are helpers. The assistant departmental superintendents are usually teachers in the departments. Not more than three teachers, including the departmental superintendent, are needed for a department, as a general thing. One teacher is used for story telling and dramatization. Another has charge of music. The third is responsible for the handwork. These three divisions of activities are arranged to insure coöperative, creative, and meaningful pupil-centered work. The helpers are assistants.

As to financing the Vacation Bible school, it may be said here that after the first school is held the others will largely pay for themselves; where handwork is sold at commencement, milk for the tiny

[2] Blair, W. Dyer, *The New Vacation Church School,* ch. vii (Harper and Brothers, New York, 1934).

tots is donated, and other items are given by interested parties. However, generally speaking, it is well for the church officially to assume responsibility for finances, as it does with the Sunday school. With careful economy, expenses can be easily met, and those in charge usually do not have to worry about this. Frequently, friends underwrite the finances for the first year or two. Parents also gladly make contributions when they see what is being done. It is not a bad idea to take up a collection at commencement. However, by no means should tuition be charged. In the North and East the faculty is frequently paid, but in the South this is not necessary. Our work is projected on a voluntary and sacrificial basis.

ACTIVITY UNITS IN THE PROGRAM (CURRICULUM)

This is not the place to go into detail concerning the materials and set up of the curriculum. The new departmental books published by the Baptist Sunday School Board at Nashville, and edited by Dr. Homer L. Grice, are the most recent, complete, and practical guides on the market.[3] They give the schedule by departments, the elements of the program, and practical helps for all procedures. Busy teachers will find almost everything they need in these books.

Generally speaking, there are eight important types of activities fostered by the V. B. S., and these vary according to departments, situations, pupils, etc. They are:

1. Creative Worship
2. Creative Music
3. Creative Story-telling
4. Creative Drama
5. Creative Handwork
6. Creative Art
7. Creative Discussion
8. Creative Play

While everything is planned and graded—in keeping with the latest methods in education and out of long years of experience on the part of experts—room is left for spontaneous activities and self-directed projects by the pupils. However, the extent and the nature of such activities are directly conditioned by the type of leaders and the kind of pupils which make up the particular school. In other

[3] Also see A. E. Tibbs on "Organization of Vacation Bible School" in *A Program of Religious Education*, where latest books are cited.

words, this means that the same storm clouds hover over the methods and processes of religious education as pertain in secular education, though they are not as highly charged with controversy nor as susceptible to change. Furthermore, in the South particularly, there is not as much uncertainty and inefficiency in religious education as perhaps elsewhere, though we have nothing to brag about. Certainly we do not have as much spontaneity, creative activity, and contagious good cheer, as we might have. But this is another story.

The Week-Day Church School

Facing a Tradition.—One of the finest traditions of American life is the separation of church and state. By keeping both the state and the church free from each other both administratively and financially we have preserved in America a distinctive form of government, and a new form of religion. This has meant virility of church life and independence of government. Our own peculiar Baptist position on this point received added emphasis at the Atlanta Baptist World Alliance and was warmly commended by a message from the President of the United States.[4]

Accordingly, when we learn through the office of Education of the United States Department of the Interior that there are classes for religious instruction conducted during school hours and that over 200 cities and towns in 35 states release their pupils from the public schools at regular school hours specifically to attend such classes, usually at some "center" or particular churches, we are likely to cite these cases as violating the spirit of our tradition. We may even say, "What will eventually become of the principle of separation of church and state?"

But these schools, to our surprise, do not abrogate the position of our forefathers, as we shall see upon more careful analysis. We owe it to Squires here that we are able to ascertain this fact. "In 1795 Governor Clinton established the public school system of New York State," says Squires. "In advising the state legislature during his campaign for the establishment of public schools, the governor said, 'Perhaps there is scarcely anything more worthy of our attention than the revival and encouragement of seminaries of learning, and nothing by which we can more satisfactorily express our gratitude

---

[4] The Congress was held in July, 1939, and had in attendance 60,000 people from 65 nations. In his significant letter President Roosevelt said, "The members of the great Baptist Commission have a peculiar heritage of devotion to the principle of religious freedom." (July 12, 1939.)

to the Supreme Being for His past favors, since purity and virtue are generally the offspring of an enlightened understanding.' "[5]

"The ordinance of 1787 for the government of the Northeast Territory, devoted section sixteen of every township to the maintenance of public schools . . . (and) it was stipulated . . . that 'religion, morality, and knowledge being necessary to good government and the happiness of mankind, schools and the means of education shall be forever encouraged. . . .

"As late as 1911 there stood in Hartford, Connecticut, a public school building across the front of which ran a motto in letters of gold which said, 'All thy children shall be taught of the Lord: and great shall be the peace of thy children.' "[6]

Two items in our Federal Constitution make provision for the separation of church and state. The Constitution itself contains one and the First Amendment the other. Article Six, Clause 3, latter part, reads, "No religious test shall ever be required as a qualification to any public office under the United States." The First Amendment contains these words, "Congress shall make no law respecting an establishment of religion, or prohibiting the free exercise thereof." Most of the State Constitutions also have similar provisions.[7] And some of the states have gone so far as to pass further laws or attach other provisions to their constitutions in order to have sufficient protection against sectarian educational influences.

The meaning of all this is that the framers of our laws meant only to declare that no particular religious sect should dominate the state. There was to be no established or state religion. They did not intend to rule out all religion and make public education non-religious or irreligious, as we have done—to our sorrow. As a matter of fact, all education in our forefather's day had a distinctly religious foundation, and people did not foresee the time when it would be completely secularized, as it is today. They certainly did not mean to stand for the dogma of absolute separation of church and state—with its future consequences of skepticism, agnosticism, and secularism—as some would have us think.

The truth is that we cannot have absolute separation of church

[5] Squires, W. A., *Educational Movements of To-day* (The Westminster Press, Philadelphia, 1930). The book is now out of print, but the arguments are sound.

[6] *Op. cit.*, pp. 8, 9.

[7] An exhaustive treatment of this subject by Dr. Carl Zollman, professor of law at Marquette University, will be found in *Studies in Religious Education* by Lotz and Crawford (editors), p. 403 (Cokesbury Press, Nashville, 1931).

and state in actual practice, anyway; and if we attempted it seriously the consequences would be dire. Are not our churches and church properties freed from taxation? How many millions of dollars this means! And do not our churches furnish chaplains for the Army and Navy? If no religion ever got into the state and state affairs, directly or even indirectly, what would happen to us?

Accordingly, the conclusion which seems clear is that the week-day church schools are in principle a further elaboration of the spirit of our forefathers in that negatively they do not violate the principle of separation of church and state because they do not set up any religious sect as dominant in the school system, and positively in that they definitely build a higher standard of morality and citizenship which furnishes a firm foundation for our laws and our government, municipal, state, and federal.

ORIGIN AND DEVELOPMENT OF WEEK-DAY SCHOOLS

Though there were some efforts here and there as early as 1909 which may be called beginnings, actually the first town taking up week-day religious schools on an extensive scale was Gary, Indiana, in the fall of 1914. Several churches coöperated and furnished teachers. They taught either in near-by churches or in specially constructed rooms. Pupils were free to take the work instead of art, music, or play activities. From these beginnings the movement has spread until today there are 35 states and over 200 cities participating. Furthermore, syllabuses are now promoted by the state departments of education to provide credit for high school work in religious education in several states. The states listed below allow high school credit for Bible study.[8] The star in each case indicates an official syllabus.

Alabama	*Maine	New York	*Texas
Arkansas	Maryland	North Carolina	*Utah
*Colorado	*Michigan	*North Dakota	*Virginia
Idaho	*Mississippi	Oklahoma	West Virginia
Illinois	Missouri	*Oregon	
*Iowa	*Montana	*South Dakota	
Kansas	Nebraska	Tennessee	

In some cases the state departments of education issue examination questions previous to granting credit to students. As to the courses in week-day religious education, a study of 600 schools

[8] Davis, Mary Dabney, "Week-Day Religious Instruction," p. 22 (United States Department of the Interior, Washington, 1933).

which reported on this item shows the nature of the course and the number of schools promoting it: Abingdon (272); the Bible (96); locally developed (65); varied (62); catechism (57); International Graded (14); Westminster (12); Scribners (9); Gary leaflets (7); Christian Nuture Series (7); Doran (2) International Group Graded (1).[9]

NEED FOR THE SCHOOLS

Need for the Schools.—Week-day church schools have come into existence in the last two decades because cities and towns have felt that public school education has needed more moral and spiritual ballast. They have followed in the tracks of the character education movement in the schools, and are the logical outcome of an ever-widening and more liberalized curriculum. In particular, juvenile delinquency and criminal acts among young people have created the demand for week-day church schools. Also, church people have become aroused and have welcomed any opportunity to help religiously. Furthermore, another reason the week-day schools have been received is that they are frankly religious in their aims and do not revert to secularism. In 1930 there were 40,755,591 people from 4 through 21 years of age in the United States. Not more than 15 or 16 million were enrolled in a Sunday school or its equivalent. This means that about 25 million young people in these age groups in America get no kind of religious instruction. The week-day church school, if it were fully used, could reach multitudes of these unenlisted and could minister to their religious needs to some extent.

Organization of the Schools.—The week-day church school is a school for religious instruction meeting during the week, and in coöperation with the public school. Pupils are released from classes in public school to go to church buildings and denominational "centers" for religious instruction. Or teachers of religion, in some instances, come to the public school buildings and teach public school pupils there, using the school's equipment and rooms. For Southern Baptists it has been suggested that the "free time" plan is the best, for here the church has to work out no schedule with the public school.

The steps in organizing the school will be in keeping with the local situation, though there are some things which have to be definite and

[9] Forsyth, N. F., *Week-Day Church Schools*, p. 38 (The Abingdon Press, New York, 1930).

rather fixed. Convictions should be aroused and suspicions allayed. The kind of program to be used must be thought out carefully and the approximate cost ascertained. However, one of the most perplexing of all problems is that of financing adequately and permanently the school. Usually three methods are employed; to inaugurate a drive for personal subscriptions; to use the community chest, or to write week-day religious education into the local church budget.

In order to care for the work sufficiently a committee of control must be formed. If the work is done in a denominational way, it should be definitely correlated with the Sunday school and the Vacation Bible school. A committee on religious education is therefore necessary. Where the work is done coöperatively one committee for the whole community will be appointed and each coöperating church will select delegates for the central committee. The committee must be small enough to be efficient.

There is much overhead work for this committee, with subcommittees, taking care of organization and administration. Such matters as arranging for teachers, setting up the curriculum of studies, caring for the budget, etc., are involved. In getting the classes under way it is wise not to attempt work for all ages and grades at first. A few grades should be taken up and handled successfully, and after this others added. Teachers and supervisors will also gain experience. The next great advance will be with the young people (18-23 years) and adults.

Generally speaking, the size of the classes will be regulated by the number of pupils electing the courses; and the elective principle should be kept inviolable in the field of religion. Under the influence of the public school the larger class of twenty-five or thirty is the norm, rather than the smaller class of the Sunday school.

Teachers will be secured mostly from colleges and seminaries and preferably from schools which devote due attention to week-day religious education. Emphasis is laid on leading pupils into fellowship with God and Christ, and establishing a Christian social order. Teachers with such a point of view should be chosen and should be full-time where at all possible.

Evaluation.—It is perhaps too early as yet to give a scientific evaluation of the week-day church school, but here and there hopeful results are reported. In the South Oklahoma, Texas, and Tennessee have successful projects going on. For a long time several cities in the north and east have kept up consistently their schools.

Week-day religious education institutionalized in separate classes may not be the ultimate solution to our problems of juvenile delinquency, crime waves among the young, and degeneracy in public morals—perhaps no one institution can do the job. But it is worth trying anyway.

CHAPTER XVII

SPECIALIZED MEN'S WORK (BAPTIST BROTHER-HOOD) AND TRAINING CLASSES (CHURCH SCHOOL OF MISSIONS)

THE BAPTIST BROTHERHOOD

The Present Situation.—Most of the early church work in America was unconsciously influenced by the patriarchal pattern of the home, as were our first laws. That is, the man had charge of all important matters and the woman came second in consideration. The modern democratic conception of the home, in which everyone is regarded as a personality of his own with the rights and privileges, had not yet arrived. Consequently, no one raised a question about man's place in the church. It was tacitly understood that he would manage the institution down to the smallest details and would see that his household discharged their religious duties by attending all services. In other words, as far as administrative and official functions were concerned the church was a man's institution. If there happened to be an equal number of women in the congregation, no one raised a question about the equalization of power, for numbers did not count in this matter of male supremacy, anyway. The upstart of all this was that there did not exist a need for a separate church organization ministering specially to men and catering to timid males who might have a feeling of inadequacy in the presence of efficient and articulate women. The men were managing everything already.

Today the situation is different. Many men do not attend church, and often frankly say that they leave religion for their wives. Also, in some quarters writers speak of religion as belonging to one of the creative, tender, and feminine arts—meaning, of course, to compliment it. On the side of the church, too, we find that much of the hard work, no little of finance raising, and the bulk of teaching, lies in the hands of the women. But this is not due to a preponderance of females in our population, as some think. In the northeastern states we are told that the distribution of population shows 99.9 men to every 100 women. In the western states are 107.7 men to every 100 women. In the north central states there are 104, and in the southern states 100.8 men to every 100 women. We must look elsewhere for the disaffection.

As to church membership among Baptist men 21 years and up, exact figures are not available. But an actual survey which E. P. Alldredge made of typical groups among 70 churches and four associations in the South shows that the distinctly rural association has *only 18.2 per cent men*, 21 years and up. "The churches in the town and country association showed *21.74 per cent* of the membership to be composed of men 21 years old and up. Whereas the most highly developed *urban association* showed *26.5 per cent* of its membership to be composed of men 21 years old and up."[1]

From 60 to 70 percent of these men belonging to the rural church were entirely unenlisted. The town and village church showed a somewhat similar though slightly improved situation, for only 62 per cent of their men were wholly enlisted. Now, there are over 4,000,000 Southern Baptists and over 800,000 men 21 years old and up. Two per cent, or 16,600 are in organized brotherhoods—(Southern Methodists have only 10,000 in the Wesley brotherhoods)—225,000 are in other forms of service. But 70.9 per cent or 558,400 men are wholly unenlisted in our Southern Baptist churches.[2]

The conclusion is, therefore, that something ought to be done in the churches to make religion more challenging to men. Unfortunately, we have blinked the situation so far. The Baptist Brotherhood of the South, however, proposes to arouse us and to offer a way out. Whether it will solve this knotty problem remains to be seen. Some doubt that segregation of men into special groups will suffice, and some want a different sort of program than now exists. Whatever improvement will come must start with church and denominational leadership and, furthermore, it will flow only through the new channel of a better unified and correlated set-up of religious education in the local church, we believe.

The Brotherhood in a Correlated Church Program.—The organization of men into a Brotherhood is the last step in setting up separate organizational units by the local Baptist church so far. If it be regarded as the final arc in rounding out the circle of religious educational work, then we can proceed to look backward or, rather, critically downward at the organizational machine with a view to tightening up its creaking wheels. Here is where correlation comes in.

[1] Alldredge, E P., *Southern Baptist Handbook,* p. 17 (Baptist Sunday School Board, Nashville, 1934).
[2] *Op. cit.,* p. 18.

The Brotherhood, in its historical development—being the latest unit to arrive—was forced to evaluate honestly the need for correlation. For one thing, it had to find a satisfactory time for meeting, and an extra night in the week was not always satisfactory. The result is that in many churches the Brotherhood meets on Sunday night one hour before preaching service.[3] The B. A. U. becomes, in this instance, an organization for women only; and to save an extra night at the church it correlates with the W. M. S., using the literature or the study book of the latter organization. Here the B. Y. P. U. preserves its distinctive (old) function and remains a young people's organization, which is not a bad idea.

When the organizations are correlated in this manner what should they be called? Some churches still use the term "B. T. U.," and others use separate terms to designate separate groups; viz., "B. T. U.," "Brotherhood," and "W. M. S." Still others employ the term, "B. M. U.," Baptist Missionary Union, to describe the differentiated and yet correlated groups looked at as a whole.[4]

The point is that we are becoming highly conscious of the creaking, loosely organized, and—to this extent—outmoded organizations in the local Baptist church; and we are willing to experiment on the elimination of overlapping, in the interest of conserving and utilizing precious human and spiritual energies. More of this point of view, however, will be found in Chapter XXIV, Part IV, entitled "Unification and Promotion." The authors of this book and of several previous books, as well as the members of the large Southwestern Religious Education Association, and the Southern Association for the Teachers of Bible and Religious Education, have disseminated this interpretation for several years now. Also, through our seminaries we are reaching our local churches.

The Organization and Work of the Brotherhood.—The Baptist Brotherhood has gathered suggestions for its organization from the structure of other successful church organizations—which is natural and wise. Taking its cue here, therefore, it has developed local, associational, district, state, and south-wide units. Also, the work of the Brotherhood, being modeled thus, is easy to understand, especially as to organizational set-up, grading, program, etc. Above all, its purpose is, *first*, to contact and to get the inactive men of the church; *secondly*, to develop them into more useful Christian stew-

[3] For example, in Louisiana. See Isom, D. R., *Baptist Brotherhood Manual*, pp. 38, 39 (Baptist Sunday School Board, Nashville, 1935).

[4] Some churches in Illinois observe this practice.

ards; and *thirdly*, to use the man-power of the church in service activities through the church and into the community. How this is done we shall see as we go along.

The *preliminary steps* in organizing a Brotherhood will vary somewhat from place to place; that is, the situation will have a lot to do with the work. However, right attitudes should be built up and the men must be convinced of its need. Here is where the pastor's enthusiasm and vision come in. Of course, he may be already heavily loaded with church responsibilities so that he will be limited in the amount of time he can devote to the organization, but his spirit and interest will go a long way, nevertheless. The deacons and officers of the church (where they are men) will be consulted and challenged. The W. M. S., though not wishing to be in men's meetings, can add its encouragement.

It is important to have a preliminary conference of a small group of men to plan the details of the first open meeting. This group acts as a sort of committee on arrangements. A nominating committee will be formed and a time discussed for regular meetings. Also, good program material will be collected. It is important, furthermore, to encourage the use of local men rather than to depend on some outside speaker.

Three men should be named on the nominating committee and these will select a *president*, a *program vice-president*, a *membership vice-president*, and a *secretary*, who will be officially elected by the group at large. Of course, it is understood that the new officers will be nominated on the basis of proper qualifications, willingness to serve, and desire to promote Brotherhood policies. It is best to contact these men before and tactfully ascertain their willingness to serve.

The success of the first regular meeting will usually depend on the initiation and work of one or two responsible persons. They will make proper announcements ahead of time, send out cards to each man of the church, and see that everyone is personally sold on the coming meeting. They may not think it wise to have a banquet at this initial gathering, but such matters will be determined by those in charge and according to the situation.

When the convocation is called some time should be devoted to deciding an hour for regular meetings. Weekly meetings are by far the best, but again the local situation will have to be considered. For the quarter or half-time churches such may not be possible. As a matter of fact, it may not be necessary to have a Brotherhood in some rare instances at all.

As for *programs*, "The Southern Baptist Brotherhood Quarterly," published under the editorship of our Brotherhood secretary at Memphis, Tennessee, will furnish a good guide, though much additional material or some modification will be called for—especially with advanced groups. An order of business such as the following may be agreed upon:

1. Prayer and Praise Service (10 minutes)
2. Business and Reports (5 or 10 minutes)
3. Review of Daily Bible Readings (5 minutes)
4. Discussion of Main Theme (35 minutes)
5. Recognition of Visitors (5 minutes)
6. Voluntary Remarks and Conclusion (5 minutes)

The work of the Brotherhood stems out from its organizational set-up and therefore embraces organizational functions, but these are only means to an end. Nevertheless, there is much personality development here and it should not be overlooked. The officers are pastor, president, program vice-president, membership vice-president, and secretary. As a general thing only one committee is necessary; namely, the executive. However, where the work warrants it a religious education, a community aid, and a Brotherhood service committee may be organized. The *president* is a sort of catalyzer for the whole organization, though it is a serious mistake to think that the "success of the whole organization hinges on the president." There are two sides to all leadership, the leader and the led. Each must discharge his own responsibilities. Leadership and leadership situations are likely to vary from place to place and from time to time. Accordingly, to hold up some arbitrary norm as a standard is to do violence to situations and to persons. The *program vice-president* should see that programs are inspirational, spiritual, and interesting. Though the "Brotherhood Quarterly" has fine discussions on missions, stewardship, temperance, tithing, the office of the deacon, doctrines, etc., it is necessary to bring in outside material and original work occasionally. The *membership vice-president* will build up membership by enlisting the unenlisted and will see that absentees are visited regularly. The *secretary* keeps accurate records and takes care of regular reports—weekly, to the Brotherhood; monthly, to the church; and quarterly, to the association.

The *executive committee* is made up of the officers of the Brotherhood, and it handles all matters referred to it. The *religious education committee* takes care of tithing and stewardship, the procuring of Bibles and tracts, creative interest in the denominational paper, building and library, and promoting study courses. The *community aid committee* wrestles with the problems of the sick and the needy, the unemployed, student and boys' work, and good citizenship. The *brotherhood service committee,* looks out for Brotherhood hospitality, publicity, and finances; in other words, all that pertains to the good of the Brotherhood—which is a large dish.

Below the top flight officers and committees the organization is broken down into *units* and *stewards.* Where there are fifteen members, for example, the group is divided into three "units," with five active members in each. The heads of these units are "chief stewards." This term is Biblical and unique. The chief steward works under the direction of the membership vice-president. Here we find the Brotherhood taking on the functions of other church organizations in its inner workings, though names are changed and a sort of esoteric flavor is invoked to appeal to men.

In conclusion, a quotation from D. R. Isom, in his article on "How the Brotherhoods Do Their Work," shows the emphasis on vital, personal, and dynamic features rather than the purely mechanical. He says, "What I conceive to be the work of the Brotherhood heads up in the individual man of the church; the type and volume of service rendered rests upon the spirit of that man."[5]

TRAINING CLASSES (CHURCH SCHOOL OF MISSIONS)

The authors of this text and numbers of educators, directors of religious education, and practical laymen who have dealt with the situation first-hand over a long period of time are strenuously advocating *one unified training school* and *one program of religious education* for the local church so as to eliminate competing and overlapping in training courses, and to conserve human energies and religious enthusiasm for a higher type of church work. Should this unified training school be realized, there will be the necessary units to take care of all the local work in all its necessary phases; but they will be properly tied together under one controlling leadership, making for agreement in dates and harmony in work. In the smaller churches, rotation from year to year of the separate units will take care of the situation, due to the type of leadership, resources, and constituency. In the larger churches a *continuous* training course, with less fanfare

[5] Alldredge, E. P., *Southern Baptist Handbook,* p. 19 (Baptist Sunday School Board, Nashville, 1934).

and high pressure, can be worked out according to the unit of work plan. Also, there will be the added feature of coördination and dovetailing so that each unit will supplement and conserve what the other does. In this way, the courses may be considerably simplified and the whole church can see what is being done, for there will be a hanging together about it all. The chief value is that the program will be local-church-centered rather than specifically organization-centered. There will be no reason for the local education committee any longer to feel that this or that outside organization is working from a distance to shape the local program—each in competition with the other.

In line with this plan we may proceed to discuss the Church School of Missions. That is, we do not see this training course as a separate, competing, and jealous church activity scrambling to monopolize the interest of Mr. Average Member. It ought to be one harmonizing and constructive unit of training, heading in the same direction and supplementing the others; not like a divorced digit on the clumsy hand of some unskilled laborer.

General Survey.—A church school of missions is not a school in the sense of lasting every day for five days in the week during most of the year. It is a school, however, in the sense of being deliberately educational. It has a planned program, carefully chosen texts, graded pupils, teachers, methods, and objectives. It is held in a church building and is pervaded with the atmosphere of religion and missions. Furthermore, it is intended to be a church-wide school, and not the child of one organization. To this extent it has an anomalous position among the other organizations of the church as presently constituted. But may it not be a prophecy of what will be done with the other units some day? If conducted once a year, the church school of missions should be promoted in such a way as to bring to a focus the missionary interest and world-vision which lie beneath the surface of every day life.

As to *objectives*, emphasis is placed on missionary motives and the desire to show true neighborliness both at home and abroad. In other words, the aim is to have everybody brought to the knowledge of Jesus as Saviour and Lord, and to keep within the "marching orders" of the "Great Commission." In line with this, certain very definite goals are named, and are frequently placed on posters in the class rooms.

Types of Schools.—Although the school which is held in the local church is the most usual variety, there are at least three types which may be promoted, according as the situation demands. This shows the elasticity of the institution. The three types are:

1. The Local Church
2. The Simultaneous Associational
3. The Unified Associational

The local church often has its own school without any relationship with the other churches, because of the local conditions. It may be held once a week for a number of weeks, usually six; or it may be conducted during one week. In this instance extensive study is carried on every evening. The latter plan has the benefit of bringing to a grand climax several weeks of thorough preparation and anticipation. Furthermore, the work is neither weakened through wide diffusion nor made superficial by a quick spasmodic effort. The other plan, though often what the situation demands, is sometimes plagued with lagging interest, for it is spotted with weeks of intermittent study. Of course, some knowledge is gained, but enthusiasm is lost.

The simultaneous associational kind of school is a grand associational-wide school, where each church in the association has its own school at the same time in which the other churches have theirs. While the same group of inspirational speakers can be used for all the churches on a rotating plan, and the work promoted by an associational committee, thus bringing unity and harmony to the activities; nevertheless, there is plenty of room for a variety of programs and procedures in each church. This type of missionary school is confined largely to live urban associations.

The unified associational school of missions is held only in one church. All the other Baptist churches of the association agree to meet with one church and have one program. Where transportation problems and weather conditions are bad, the local church in the totality of its membership is likely not to be adequately reached. Lesser motives can creep into church work and cripple seriously the missionary spirit.

In rural associations necessary modifications are applied to the simultaneous plan, but success can be secured. In fact, coöperative church life is more common in the country than in the city, in spite of intense individualism.

Organizing the Church School of Missions.—In setting up the school of missions it is well to be guided by the experience of other annual training schools, such as those of the Sunday school and the Baptist Training Union, for example. This will make for uniformity and for later correlation, besides insuring the success of the school. The pastor of the local church is the executive head, and much will depend on his missionary vision. However, it is fine for some other leader to preside at the meetings proper. The Sunday school superintendent or the president of the men's Brotherhood can do this. The pastor, of course, will be close to the management of things, and the church will depend on his wise counsel.

At first, interest should be aroused and simple preparatory plans made. To introduce one of the faculty ahead of time, or to show pictures from a mission field, or to advertise the titles of books through posters is good policy. This, of course, will come after the committee on ways and means has been appointed and has mapped out the program. The time for having the school—considering weather conditions, public school, etc.—will be determined. Teachers will be secured, using either local talent or teachers from a neighboring church. The rural pastor can teach the school, himself, if he has a woman to care for the children. Selected books and courses will be agreed upon, and usually with a view to carrying out some general theme. The latest book lists can be secured from the Home and Foreign Mission Boards, upon request. Where a general committee is appointed by the pastor to work at such details, a representative from the W. M. S., the Sunday school, the B. T. U., the men, and the church at large, is wise.

Fortunately, there are no external "standards" to distract missionary interest and there are no arbitrary organizational forms to import and yoke upon all churches alike, regardless of size or local situation.

Generally speaking, however, there should be grades and classes, teachers, and books. In the *small church* two good classes can make a successful school. Also, this will simplify the problem of books, teachers, and expense. One class may be conducted for the adults and one for the young people. Children can go with their parents or be taken care of by some interested and trained woman. Another arrangement is to place Primaries and Juniors together, and Intermediates and Young People, leaving the adults to themselves. This will make a three-department plan, and provide for three classes. Where Primaries and Juniors are separated, Intermediates and Young People are grouped together, and Adults kept separate, there will be four classes. A five-class grouping may follow the regular grading of the Southern Baptist Sunday School: Primaries, 6-8; Juniors, 9-12; Intermediates, 13-16; Young People, 17-24; Adults, above 24. The six department school will have Seniors, also.

As to a *schedule*, the class periods should be timed to the local situation, and in the light of whether there is to be a supper each evening—if the school is held at night. Below is a suggested program:

Program with Supper[6]

6:15 Supper
6:45 First Class Period
7:30 Assembly Class Reports
7:45 Second Class Period
8:30 Devotional and Address

Program without Supper

7:15 Devotional
7:30 First Class Period
8:30 Assembly, Reports and Address

Finally, in order to insure success for the school proper *supervisional* techniques must be employed. Everything should be planned ahead of time, and carefully. Very deliberately the meetings need to be made worshipful and prayerful. The right kind of faculty is necessary, and a thorough acquaintance with the books, plans, and methods of procedure, is prerequisite. Also, a thorough follow-up to see that results carry over into day by day living, is wise. The principal may even keep a notebook with a record of strong and weak features, books taught, expenses, etc. This will be a valuable aid in planning the next school. In short, great progress will be made through right supervision. Incidentally, educators expect the next great advances in religious education to be in the field of supervision.

A SELECTED BIBLIOGRAPHY FOR CLASS USE
THE SUNDAY SCHOOL

Armstrong, H. J., "Religious Education for Such a Time," *Int. Journal of Religious Education*, March, 1939.
Barnett, J. N., *A Church Using Its Sunday School*, The Baptist Sunday School Board, Nashville, 1937.
Bower, W. C., *The Educational Task of the Local Church*, Bethany Press, St. Louis, 1921.
Religious Education in the Modern Church, Bethany Press, St. Louis, 1929.
Bradley, E. F., *Teaching of Religion*, Longmans, Green, and Co., New York, 1938.

[6] See the pamphlet, "Church Schools of Missions and Catalog of Mission Study Literature," published by the Home and Foreign Mission Boards of the Southern Baptist Convention.

Brown, A. A., *A History of Religious Education in Modern Times*, The Abingdon Press, New York, 1923.

Burroughs, P. E., *Growing a Church*, The Baptist Sunday School Board, Nashville, 1927.

Conover, C. E., "Save Religious Education from Itself," *Christian Century*, July 13, 1938.

Denison, J. H., *The Enlargement of Personality*, Charles Scribner's Sons, New York, 1930.

Drummond, N. R., *Educational Function of the Church*, The Baptist Sunday School Board, Nashville, 1924.

Fiske, G. W., *Purpose in Teaching Religion*, The Abingdon Press, New York, 1927.

Flake, Arthur, *True Functions of the Sunday School*, The Baptist Sunday School Board, Nashville, 1930.

Harper, N. C., *Educational Work of the Church*, The Abingdon Press, New York, 1939.

Judd, C. H., *Education and Social Progress*, Harcourt, Brace, and Co., New York, 1934.

Lankard, F. G., *A History of the American Sunday School Curriculum*, The Abingdon Press, New York, 1927.

Lotz and Crawford, *Studies in Religious Education*, Cokesbury Press, Nashville, 1931.

Munro, H. C., *The Church as a School*, Bethany Press, St. Louis, 1929.

Peters, C. C., *Foundations of Educational Sociology*, Ch. xiii, The Macmillan Company, New York, 1935.

Shaver, E. L., "Whither Bound Religious Education," *Religious Education*, July, 1938.

Soares, T. G., *Religious Education*, The University of Chicago Press, Chicago, 1928.

Sperry, W. L., *What You Owe Your Child*, Harper and Brothers, New York, 1935.

Stout, J. E., *Organization and Administration of Religious Education*, The Abingdon Press, New York, 1922.

Vieth, P. H., *Improving Your Sunday School*, The Westminster Press, Philadelphia, 1930.

Watson, G. B., *Experimentation in Religious Education*, The Association Press, New York, 1927.

THE BAPTIST TRAINING UNION

Bell, Howard M., *Youth Tell Their Story*, United States Government Printing Office, Washington, 1938.

Boyd, Charles Arthur, *Young People at Work in Baptist Churches*, The Judson Press, Philadelphia, 1928.

Clark, F. E., *Christian Endeavor Manual*, United Society of Christian Endeavor, Boston, 1925.

Flake, Arthur, *Senior B. Y. P. U. Administration*, Third Edition, Baptist Sunday School Board, Nashville, 1934.

Harrell-Rogers-Hockett, *The Associational B. T. U. Manual*, Baptist Sunday School Board, Nashville, 1936.

Lambdin, Ina S., *The Junior B. Y. P. U. Manual; The Junior and Intermediate B. Y. P. U. Leaders' Manual*, Baptist Sunday School Board, Nashville, 1926.

Lambdin, J. E., *The B. A. U. Manual* and *The Baptist Training Union Manual*, Baptist Sunday School Board, Nashville, 1935.

Leavell, L. P., *Senior B. Y. P. U. Manual*, Baptist Sunday School Board, Nashville, 1934.

Lee, E. E., *Intermediate B. Y. P. U. Manual*, Baptist Sunday School Board, Nashville, 1934.

Mayer, Herbert Carlton, *The Church's Program for Young People*, The Century Company, New York, 1925.

Phelps, Edwin, *Pathfinder in Church Work with Young People*, The Judson Press, Philadelphia, 1928.

Preston, Mary Frances Johnson, *Christian Leadership*, Baptist Sunday School Board, Nashville, 1935.

Price, Carpenter, and Chapman (Editors), *Introduction to Religious Education*, Chapter XVI, The Macmillan Company, New York, 1932.

Program Resource Guide, American Baptist Publication Society, Philadelphia.

Stock, H. T., *Church Work with Young People*, Pilgrim Press, Boston, 1929.

The Commission Plan Manuals, American Baptist Publication Society, Philadelphia.

Price, Carpenter, Tibbs, *A Program of Religious Education*, Fleming H. Revell, New York, 1937.

THE WOMAN'S MISSIONARY UNION

Brown, Ina Corraine, *Training for World Fellowship*, ch. vii, Cokesbury Press, Nashville, 1929.

Bucy, Wilma Geneva, *The New Why and How of Woman's Missionary Union*, Baptist Sunday School Board, Nashville, 1934.

Diffendorfer, Ralph E., *Missionary Education in Home and School*, ch. I, The Abingdon Press, New York.

Gates, H. W., *Missionary Education in the Church*, The Pilgrim Press, Boston, 1928.

Heck, Fannie S., *In Royal Service*, Foreign Mission Board, Richmond, Va.

Loveland, Gilbert, *Training World Christians*, The Methodist Book Concern, New York, 1921.

Mallory, Kathleen, *Manual W. M. U. Methods*, Baptist Sunday School Board, Nashville.

Ragsdale, Elsie, "The Church—Its Missionary Organizations," ch. xvii, in *Introduction to Religious Education* by Price (ed.), The Macmillan Company, New York, 1932.

Tead, Ordway, *The Art of Leadership*, McGraw-Hill, New York, 1935.

Tibbs, A. E., "Organization of Woman's Missionary Union" and "Activities of Woman's Missionary Union," in *A Program of Religious Education* by Price-Carpenter-Tibbs, Fleming H. Revell, New York, 1937.

Warburton, Stacy R., *Making a Missionary Church*, The Judson Press, Philadelphia, 1924.

VACATION AND WEEK-DAY SCHOOLS

Armentrout, J. S., *Administering the Vacation Church School*, Westminster Press, Philadelphia, 1928.

Armstrong, H. J., "Religious Education for Such a Time," *Int. Journal of Religious Education*, March 1939.

Blair, W. Dyer, *The New Vacation Church School*, Harper and Brothers, New York, 1934.

Bower, W. C., *Religious Education in the Modern Church*, Bethany Press, St. Louis, 1929.

"British Conference on Religion in the Schools," *School and Society*, December 31, 1938.

Cather, Katherine, *Religious Education through Story-telling*, The Abingdon Press, New York, 1931.

Clausen, B. C., "Religious Education in the Public Schools," *National Education Association Journal*, January 28, 1939.

Conover, C. E., "Save Religious Education from Itself," *Christian Century*, July 13, 1938.

Cope, H. F., *The Week-day Church Schools*, The Abingdon Press, New York, 1930.

Davis, Mary Dabney, "Week-day Religious Instruction," Pamphlet No. 36, United States Department of the Interior, Office of Education, Washington, D. C.

Dimock, H. S., "Some Issues for Religious Education Raised by Recent Character Research," *Religious Education*, April 1938.

Getz, Elizabeth Moore, "Music and the Creative Expression through Music," *Building Character*, University of Chicago Press, Chicago, 1928.

Gove, F. S., *Religious Education on Public School Time*, Harvard Bulletins in Education, Harvard University, 1926.

Grice, Homer L., *Vacation Bible School Guide*, Baptist Sunday School Board, Nashville, 1926.

Hartley, Gertrude, *The Use of Objects in Religious Education*, Judson Press, Philadelphia, 1921.

Heaton, Kenneth L., *Character Building through Recreation*, University of Chicago Press, Chicago, 1931.

Lotz, P. H., *Current Week-day Religious Education*, The Abingdon Press, New York, 1925.

Lotz, P. H., and Crawford, L. W. (editors), *Studies in Religious Education*, chs. xii, xiii, Cokesbury Press, Nashville, 1931.

Price-Carpenter-Chapman, *Introduction to Religious Education*, ch. xviii, The Macmillan Company, New York, 1932.

"Religion in Schools, Eight Years Progress," *Times Ed. Supplement*, April 30, 1938.

Settle, M. C., *The Week-day Church School*, International Council of Religious Education, Chicago, 1930.

Shaver, E. L., "Whither Bound Religious Education," *Religious Education*, July 1938.

Shumate, Aurora M., and Grice, H. L., *Beginner—Book A*, Vacation Bible School Series, Broadman Press, Nashville, 1938.

Squires, W. A., *Educational Movements of Today*, The Westminster Press, Philadelphia, 1930.

Stewart, Willie Jean, *Primary—Book A*, Vacation Bible School Series, Broadman Press, 1938.

Junior—Book A, Broadman Press, 1938.

BROTHERHOOD AND TRAINING CLASSES

Alldredge, E. P., *Southern Baptist Handbook*, Baptist Sunday School Board, Nashville, 1934-1939.

Annual of Southern Baptist Convention, Broadman Press, Nashville, 1939.

"Church Schools of Missions and Catalog of Mission Study Literature," Home and Foreign Mission Boards of Southern Baptists, Richmond and Atlanta.

Gates, H. W., *Missionary Education in the Church*, The Pilgrim Press, Boston, 1938.

Henderson, J. T., *Brotherhood Organization; The Associational Brotherhood; Constitution and By-Laws for the Organization of a Brotherhood; Recognizing the Laymen;* Baptist Brotherhood of the South, Memphis, Tenn.

Munro, Harry C., *The Pastor and Religious Education*, The Abingdon Press, New York, 1930.

Isom, Dudley R., *Baptist Brotherhood Manual*, Baptist Sunday School Board, Nashville, 1935.

Soares, Theodore G., *Religious Education*, The University of Chicago Press, Chicago, 1928.

Warburton, Stacy R., *Making a Missionary Church*, The Judson Press, Philadelphia, 1924.

WORSHIP—MUSIC, DRAMA, AND ART

Alexander, Ryllis C., and Goslin, O. P., *Worship Through Drama*, Harper & Brothers, New York, 1930.

"A Symposium on Worship," *Religious Education*, October 1925.

Bailey, Albert E., *Gospel in Art*, The Pilgrim Press, Boston, 1916.
Use of Art in Religious Education, The Pilgrim Press, Boston, 1922.

Bailey, Henry Turner, *Twelve Great Paintings*, Loidlam Bros., New York, 1929.

Beard, Frederica, *Pictures in Religious Education*, George H. Doran Company, New York, 1920. (Out of print.)

Bonsall, Elizabeth H., *Famous Hymns with Stories and Pictures*, The American Baptist Publication Society, Philadelphia, 1923.

Dobbins, G. S., "Training in Worship," *Introduction to Religious Education*, ch. xi, The Macmillan Company, New York, 1932.

Duffus, R. L., *The American Renaissance of Art*, Alfred A. Knopf, Inc., New York, 1928.

Eastman, Fred, *Modern Religious Dramas*, Henry Holt Company, New York, 1928.

Hartshorne, Hugh, *A Manual for Training in Worship*, Charles Scribner's Sons, New York, 1915.
Stories for Worship and How to Follow Them Up, Charles Scribner's Sons, New York, 1921.

Ikenberry, Charles S., *Motives and Expression in Religious Education*, Charles H. Doran Company, New York, 1922.

Longford, W. W., *Music and Religion*, Kegan Paul, Trench, and Trubner, London.

Martin, A. W., *Worship in the Sunday School*, Cokesbury Press, Nashville, 1930.

Meredith, William V., *Pageantry and Dramatics in Religious Education*, Abingdon Press, New York, 1921.

Miller, Elizabeth, *Dramatization of Bible Stories*, the University of Chicago Press, Chicago, 1918 (Revised Edition).
Dramatization in the Church School, The University of Chicago Press, Chicago, 1923.

Overton, Grace Sloan, *Drama in Education*, Century Company, New York, 1926.

Parkhurst, Helen H., *Beauty*, Harcourt, Brace and Co., New York, 1930.

Pierce, Robert F. Y., *Blackboard Efficiency*, Fleming H. Revell Company, New York, 1922.

Pylant, Mrs. Agnes Durant, "Use of Art in Teaching," *Introduction to Religious Education*, ch. ix, Price, J. M. (editor), Macmillan Company, New York, 1932.

Reynolds, I. E., *The Ministry of Music*, Baptist Sunday School Board, Nashville, 1929.

Rex, Ruth Irwin, *We Worship*, The Century Company, New York, 1930.

Ross, G. A. Johnston, *Christian Worship and Its Future*, The Abingdon Press, New York, 1927.

Russell, Mary M., *How to Dramatize Bible Stories*, George H. Doran Company, New York, 1924.

Sellers, E. O., *How to Improve Church Music*, Fleming H. Revell Co., New York, 1928.

Seneker, J. S., "The Theory and Function of Worship in Religious Education," *Studies in Religious Education*, ch. iv, Lotz and Crawford (editors), Cokesbury Press, Nashville, 1931.

Shaver, E. L., and Stock, H. T., *Training Young People in Worship*, The Pilgrim Press, Boston, 1929.

Smith, H. A., *New Hymnal for American Youth,* Century Company, New York, 1930.

Sperry, Willard L., *Reality in Worship,* The Macmillan Company, New York, 1926.

Thomas, Edith L., *A First Book on Hymns and Worship,* The Abingdon Press, New York, 1922.

Tralle and Merrill, *Building for Religious Education,* The Century Company, New York, 1926.

Vogt, Von Ogden, *Art and Religion,* Yale University Press, New Haven, 1921.

Wallace, J. Sherman, *Worship in the Church School,* The Judson Press, Philadelphia, 1930.

Wieman, Henry N., *Methods of Private Religious Living,* The Macmillan Company, New York, 1922.

CHAPTER XVIII

SPECIALIZED EDUCATIONAL ACTIVITIES: WORSHIP —MUSIC, DRAMA, AND ART

As one traverses the field of this chapter he recognizes immediately that he is a religious traveler visiting the shrines of the ancient past and steeping himself in the lore of religious history. Also, he feels quite sure of his modernism and is likely to see the panorama through the eyes of science, philosophy, and present-day religion. Consequently, what he reports or proposes may appear to be anachronous, for a general mixture of past and present is sure to turn up in the saddle bags of his knowledge.

There has been worship from primeval times; and music, drama, and art have played a large part in it as far back as history goes. This is the skeletal framework of the anachronism. Furthermore, something of the *content* of that worship is also carried over into the present and is likely to persist in the future, hence we are only quasi-modern in religion, after all. In other words, art and not science is still our first love in religion, though we may don the rôle of a fickle suitor and woo both at various times—even to the point of proclaiming science our sole interest at one period.

What follows here, therefore, is done in the spirit of art; that is, it is highly selective, somewhat subjective as to standards, and carries its own *imprimatur*. The reader will reject what he wishes and will see what the eyes of his experience prepares him for. He should ask for nothing else. Frankly and unabashed, the writer has chosen to see his subject from the perspective of Christianity, and to reproduce it on the mental canvas with all the feeling-tones of his own individual experience, even though roughly he belongs within one of the many groups of Christianity.

THE NATURE AND FUNCTIONS OF WORSHIP

Christian worship means at its highest and best intelligent worship. Magic and superstition, personality-destroying practices, low motivation, and whatever makes religion a sham are beneath the dignity of intelligent Christian worship. On the positive side, worship is appreciating the presence of God and responding adequately to him, in terms of what Christ has articulated.

However, that there are differences of Christian outlook here no one will deny. One person is so constituted and habituated that he finds satisfaction in song, prayer, sermon, gift, and a modicum of architectural helps or ritual instrumentation. Another feels that the sermon is human intrusion, and enjoys the richness of color and music which are found in authorized forms and ceremonies. Nevertheless, in spite of the wide range in the manifestations of Christian worship, every one agrees that worship is primal with the Christian—it is the one thing without which he cannot live creatively.

As to *the functions of worship*, perhaps *comfort* should be mentioned first. Life is so constituted that disappointments, hardships, hazards, sickness, and sorrows are the lot of human race. Through worship the individual gains strength to meet these eventualities. With primitive peoples magical control of divinities is more important than the higher ethical values of Christianity. Consequently, comfort has little place. On the other hand, fear, appeasing the anger of capricious idols, and preoccupation with magical exercises, are focal. There are neither efforts to understand the dispensations of Providence nor ways and means to meet the tragic crises of life.

In the next place, worship brings added *strength* to the genuinely religious person. Where adjustment with reference to the stressful circumstances of living is achieved, and fellowship with God through Christ is realized, a new power is experienced. It may be in comfort, it may be in repentance, it may be in new insight into events. Irrespective of how it comes, the individual goes out of the sanctuary of worship into the busy world, and lives with zest and victory.

Thirdly, through worship the Christian sees life *synthetically* and *objectively*. One of the greatest functions of religion is to help the individual to piece together the fragmentary parts in the puzzle picture of living—to "see life steadily and see it whole." Also, it is quite an accomplishment to divest oneself of entangling emotions and to take an objective attitude toward the world.

Finally, to see life as a whole is, in the end, to have *fellowship with God* and be pleasing to him. This means worship at its highest and best. Whatever be one's definition of God, if he goes out into the universe in search of its final "togetherness," questing for the ultimate reality, and yearning for a meaning back of the fragments and banalities which spot the hours of routine, he will find the answer in communion with God.

Avenues to and Training in Worship

The chief avenue to worship has always been and is prayer, whether of the wild orgiastic sort of the primitive or the refined ethical type of the real Christian. Then, there are *symbolic ritual* or *ceremonies, song* and *music, meditation, contemplation, offerings, sermons,* and various kinds of *service activities,* all of which are manifestations of worship in varying degrees.

With Protestants, two trends are dominant; one characterized by ritual and symbol, and architecturally framed with the communion table at the center; the other vocalized in sermon, song, and prayer, and with the pulpit and the open Bible holding preeminence. The former is called the ritualistic service and the latter the evangelical. In the north and east and in Great Britain and Europe, as the writer has had occasion to observe, a combination of the two types is also not uncommon. In this instance architectural modifications are effected, with the pulpit only slightly raised above the communion table, and both at the eye-center of worship.

Generally speaking, it seems that the democratic free worship of evangelical Christian groups is moving more and more toward a beautifully satisfying service; in which shortened sermon, more elevating music, and a planned order and symmetry of worship are appreciated. Also, prayer, testimony, and conversion experiences, tend to comply with these new developments. Some people feel that such changes are packed with danger, but others are loud in praise of them. Psychologically, the desire for beauty of worship is a heart-hunger response due to the prevalence of strife, insecurity, and chaos in the external world. As such it cannot be lightly set aside.

As for *training in worship,* it needs no special pleading to convince modern Christians of its great *need*—nor is it incompatible with the spirit of genuine worship. Our emphases in Protestantism have been so pragmatic in the past that we have buried the worship *motif* in the heart of a statistical column or reduced it to an appendage in the financial report of the church. Now we are becoming more self-conscious about the matter and are beginning to admit that it is a lost art which stands in sore need of reviving.

Some agencies which have a definite responsibility for improving worship are *the religious school, the home, the Sunday school,* and the *Young People's Union.* Improvement must begin with top-flight leadership; and the seminary and denominational school—where leaders are trained—must take the initiative. All too often in the past these schools have been absorbed with mere knowledge-getting and fact-cramming. The time demands a different approach, where the curriculum will be reconstructed in such a manner as to allow for and encourage more worship, and where personality improvement —set in the atmosphere of religion—will be given more attention.

The Sunday school so far has been too much pervaded with the clatter of activities, the making of reports, and the stereotyping of religious expression—particularly in pious lectures and lesson talks— to give primacy to genuine worship. We have sought to offset this by having a special worship period and a departmental or class ser- monette designated to fill the aching void, but they are no substitute for a spontaneous worshipful atmosphere which should pervade the whole Sunday school hour.

The Young People's Union is one of the best institutions we have for teaching people how to worship, for it begins with the young and lends itself quite definitely to overt worshipful activities. What it needs is a better type of leadership and more adult leaders who will take the initiative in promoting genuine worship. However, this is a problem in supervision and must be traced back to the religious school for its ultimate solution.

Finally, though first in importance, is the Christian home as an institution for training in worship. We hear much these days about the need for reviving the "family altar" and "saying grace" at the dinner table. Such expressions of worship are exceedingly important, but it is far more important to promote these activities *in the right manner*. They ought to be high moments which symbolize and drama- tize the deep current of right attitudes and genuine Christianity which flows beneath the surface of living every hour of the day. Otherwise they are hollow forms which serve but to mock religion and drive boys and girls away from Christianity. Furthermore, there are other serious problems in family worship which must be solved before it can become effective. For example, it is well-nigh impossible to get the whole family together at the same time, whether at the dinner table or at bed time. Accordingly, modifications may have to be effected in the *form* of the "family altar." Also, we must remember that group worship is never a substitute for private individual wor- ship, even though it be at the family altar. Of course we are not arguing here against this institution, but we are pleading for a thorough over-hauling in the light of modern problems and in view of the demand for sincere religion.

THE MID-WEEK PRAYER SERVICE

Because of waning interest in the mid-week prayer service, due to a number of conditions—some local and some general—and in the face of its great importance the authors of this book have thought it wise to devote a special section to it. One approach is to trace the rise of the mid-week service historically and to show that the early Christians held prayer meetings *every* day. In this instance far less importance would be attached to a special day and time of worship spaced in the middle of the week. Such an interpretation would be in line with the view of many modern evangelicals that holy days and hours have a tendency to confine religion to special buildings and formal services.

Another approach is to accept the mid-week prayer service frankly as a modern institution, though redolent of the eighteenth and the nineteenth centuries; and see in it great possibilities for genuine worship. In this instance perhaps a good start would be to make a survey of the local situation and stage a panel discussion on some such subject as, What is Wrong with the Mid-Week Prayer Service? Then, the leader might gather materials on the content of prayer services in other churches and obtain valuable suggestions. Armed with this information he could set about establishing a real mid-week prayer service in his own church. Every one knows that too little time is now devoted to prayer, fellowship, and worship in modern life. Where a creative service is planned it is sure to meet with a hopeful response in most situations.

The opinion is ventured here that the average prayer service lacks previous preparation, is haphazard and meandering in its progress, and fails to challenge the general membership of the church. Perhaps this is why so few attend it, though we should like to think that peculiar local conditions constitute the chief handicap.

Some distinct advantages of the mid-week prayer service over the Sunday services are: informality; more personal fellowship in worship; opportunities for spontaneous expression of the soul in testimony, song, and prayer; occasions for Bible study; and greater evangelical opportunities—especially where the church leans toward formal worship on Sunday. In Great Britain and on the continent evangelical churches have utilized the mid-week service for great Bible study and periods of prayer. The local minister sees here the one big occasion to pour his rich experience into teaching and into training his membership in Bible study. Is it too much to hope that

American preachers may do the same? We have too little time in our studies already, and any added stimulus will be a great improvement. Furthermore, useless or pointless field calls are less likely to be expected of the minister if his congregation knows that he is compelled to spend many hours in Bible study in order to be prepared for more teaching services. On the creative side, the minister may even be inspired and encouraged to write a book or two in this connection.

USE OF MUSIC IN WORSHIP

Attitudes are all-important in worship, and stimulating the emotions is just as essential as enlightening the intellect. Hence music has always been and will continue to be a necessary part of worship. If any one has any doubts of this, he may recall readily how arguments and smooth oratory at one time or another failed to impress him, while a hymn was moving and creative in its influence. Just here, then, it is well to note the ways in which music may assist in establishing worship. Some of these are through the following manifestations:

1. Stimulation of the imagination and heightening of religious sensibility
2. Glorification of the commonplace and elevation of life through association with poetry and musical ideas
3. Creation of aspiration and summoning of the best within the individual
4. Recapitulation of gospel truths and creation of convictions and decisions through hymns and songs which carry messages of faith, repentance, salvation, and hope
5. Accessory values making for integration of life, release of energies, and harmony of living

The Protestant evangelical churches are emphasizing the ministry of music, perhaps more than ever, because they realize that the gospel is sent abroad on its wings. Also, a new appreciation of beauty in worship has added to the volume of this emphasis and has created a demand for the highest type of sacred song and musical accomplishment. Almost every theological seminary has definite training in music for ministers, and specialized courses leading to musical degrees are offered in many religious schools.[1]

The ministry of music is a new vocation with us, and many large

[1] The Southwestern Baptist Theological Seminary, at Fort Worth, has a three-year course beyond college leading to the B.S.M. degree. The Baptist Bible Institute, at New Orleans, also has a two-year course, and integrates it with religious education. In the North, music is offered in such schools as Union Theological Seminary (New York), Boston University, and the Westminster Choir School (Ithaca).

churches in the south, as well as in the north, have employed specially trained leaders to direct their music. In some instances these workers do nothing else but promote the musical program of the church, while in others they correlate their work with that of specialized religious education. Recently the Baptist Sunday School Board of the South employed a trained director to take charge of its department of music, and it seems that evangelical denominations, as well as individual churches, are becoming highly conscious on the subject. This is a giant stride toward a higher quality of music and a better type of worship.

Finally, *instrumental* music, *vocal* music, and *special-feature* music are the outstanding types of church music in vogue. The piano, the pipe organ, and string and wind instruments are rather generally employed. As to vocal forms, the gospel song, the hymn, and the anthem are most universally used. Song services, song-sermons, and cantatas also have their place.

If we may venture a prediction here, the church of the future will have a greater share in shaping the recreational program of the community and in raising the cultural standard of its environs through music, besides constructing its own worship programs. Consequently, it must be prepared for the enlarging opportunities of tomorrow.

EMPLOYING DRAMA

Today drama is coming to have a big place in religious educational work. Dramatizing the gospel through church ordinances, such as baptism, has been an ancient custom, though few have thought of the particular art involved because of the reality and the seriousness of the occasions. Also, the extremes to which the secularized stage has gone, and the reactions of the church in the past, have drawn attention away from drama, even from that which is largely vocal and unintentional.

But mystery and miracle plays are beginning to come back again, as in the Middle Ages, and educational dramatics is now being featured in church schools, especially of the vacation type, and in religious colleges and seminaries.

There are great *values* in religious drama both for the participants and for the audience. Those who take part in it directly find their interest spontaneously aroused. Also, imagination is awakened and developed. Perhaps the greatest benefit, however, comes from putting ideas into action. Religion can be left inarticulate and futile if it is not objectively actualized. The drama is one way to make religion vital, for it points out specifically the deed of kindness or the act of religious progress.[2]

For the audience, color, movement, and the spoken word—such as run through the drama—secure values which nothing else could. Generally speaking, the eye is more effective than the ear in acquiring knowledge, and religious drama utilizes this organ to the fullest. The spoken word, of course, is added, but the combination of the two is of greatest value. The sermon, for example, often fails because it is limited in its appeal.

The *types of drama* suitable for churches are dramatized Bible stories, the prepared play, shadow plays, tableaux, pantomimes, and clothespin-character plays.[3] Each one of these types has a technique of its own, but it can be learned through personal application and patience. The pity is that more churches do not use these materials to enrich and vitalize their programs.

ART AS A MEDIUM OF WORSHIP

The most tangible evidence of the influence of art on worship in the Protestant churches of America can be seen in the new type of church buildings which are being constructed. Not only is much attention being devoted to the styles of architecture, but also great labor is being employed to make the inner structure of churches artistically pleasing and religiously appropriate.

For two years now in the south Dr. P. E. Burroughs through the Department of Architecture of the Baptist Sunday School Board,[4] has assembled leading architects from the north and the south and has set up conferences on building churches. Many teachers from colleges and seminaries have also sat in these meetings and have shared in the discussions dealing with such topics as *trends in church architecture, types of buildings,* and *problems which must be faced.* Some religious schools have added courses on architecture,[5] and closer ties now bind architects and teachers together.

It is to be hoped that the day may soon come when the drab, often unpainted, and surely uninviting "meeting houses" which are a tradition in the country—and which constitute the majority of southern

---

[2] As a criticism of this point of view see Hartshorne, Hugh, *Character in Human Relations* (Charles Scribner's, New York, 1936).

[3] Pylant, Mrs. Agnes Durant, "Use of Arts in Teaching," ch. ix in *Introduction to Religious Education*, by Price (editor), Macmillan, New York, 1932.

[4] A recent book: Burroughs, P. E., *Let Us Build* (Broadman Press, Nashville, 1939). Helpful illustrations are used.

[5] *E.g.*, the Baptist Bible Institute at New Orleans.

churches—will give way to beautiful temples of God. When this time comes it will be an honor to Christianity and a challenge to thousands of communities—where new school buildings and modern roads have already gone. The urban churches have long kept pace with the times and made great strides in the direction of artistic buildings, as any one may see.

The next area where art has become a handmaid to worship in evangelical churches is in the specialized use of religious pictures, poster making and design work, modeling, chalk talks, moving pictures, film slides, stereoscopes, and handicrafts.[6] These materials have been developed on the crest of the wave of the new pedagogy, and are regarded as aids to objective teaching. Consequently, their use has been rather pragmatic and often amateurish. But there are signs here and there of a more professional and skillful employment of art.[7]

For a long time the Roman Catholic Church has used painting, sculpture, and architecture as material aids to worship; and it has done a prodigious amount of creative work in these fields, particularly in the past. The extravagances to which Catholicism went, however, caused the Protestants to outlaw art in general; and it has taken several centuries for evangelical denominations to get their balance. Of course, the use of art in religion is much older than the Roman Catholic Church. Even the ancient Hebrews had their battles with paganism in art; and they were the first Puritans.

SUMMARY OF VALUES

Worship is the finest expression of religion and the high water-mark of Christianity. It becomes particularly articulate and creative through music and the fine arts. The imagination of the Christian is awakened, implemented, and given direction through these media; and the harmony of body and soul is achieved. Consequently, the worshipper leaves the altar of vision and goes out into the world inspired and equipped to make society better. His power comes from above and his "directness" of approach to life's problems is born of inner harmony. The promise of victory is on his brow and he is of

[6] Pylant, Mrs. Agnes Durant, "Use of Arts in Teaching," ch. ix, *Introduction to Religious Education*, by J. M. Price (editor) (Macmillan, New York, 1932). Also see: Thomas, Edith L., "Music, Drama, and Art in Religious Education," ch. x, *Studies in Religious Education*, by Lotz and Crawford (editors) (Cokesbury Press, Nashville, 1931).

[7] *E.g.*, at Boston University, Union Theological Seminary, and Garret Bible Institute in the north; and at the Baptist Bible Institute and the Southwestern Baptist Theological Seminary in the south.

all men the most happy and the most fortunate. What greater tribute can be paid to Christian worship, with all its helps?

THE PULPIT

The term "pulpit" is used to designate a highly developed expression of educational activity in modern religion. However, it is none the less ancient. The preaching of Jesus was heavily laden with rich teaching. Didactic expressions dominated his sermons; and teachings concerning the kingdom of God and the destiny of man made up the content of his messages. In the Great Commission he commanded his followers to "go, instruct (Greek, *matheeteuo*) all the nations, baptizing . . . teaching . . . etc." (Matt. 28:18-20). Also, he was generally called "the Master," a term which is distinctly pedagogical.

The inner circle of Christ's leaders were very early known as disciples and teachers, as well as missionary preachers. Paul was quite self-conscious on the subject of teaching "his gospel," and he tells us that he was "appointed by God a teacher," as well as an apostle and preacher (Rom. 2:16; II Tim. 1:2). So the spread of Christianity from its beginning was effected through didactic preaching.

Today we have lost much of this emphasis, due to the influence of secular education, the press, and the radio—all purveyors of general information and culture. However, there is much spiritual ignorance in modern America, and this constitutes a need for didactic preaching.

Next, the pulpit is a great institution for religious education, whether the minister thinks much about it or not. Also, it has great possibilities for the future. The kind of teaching which the Sunday school pupil gets in the class room will never take the place of what he hears from the sermon, and experiences in the preaching service. For one thing it does not have the same atmosphere. Also, the teaching which is done by the preacher is likely to have a different "ring" and a different note of authority and urgency. The prophets of old were great teachers, as were the chief leaders in the romance of preaching—from the apologists to Savonrola, Spurgeon, and Brooks. If this note were sounded rather generally among our ministers instead of that which concerns the management of organizations and the details of clerical work, we should witness a new day for Christianity.

THE RADIO

On November 3rd, 1920, modern broadcasting was born. The Westinghouse Station at Pittsburgh broadcast the returns from the

Harding-Cox presidential election over KDKA. There were less than 400 listeners who composed this initial radio audience.[8] Today we have a potential listening public exceeding one hundred million persons in America alone. This means that the minister's audience has increased considerably. Also, added opportunities and new responsibilities have come.

W. J. Miller says, "The radio offers one of the great opportunities of the present day to present the claims of true religion and to make it applicable to every life. It should not take the place of the church and its services. It should not provide an easy way for men to secure religious instruction at the expense of attendance at divine worship. It should be the spreading of the blessings of the church to untold millions of people who would not otherwise be reached by the church."[9]

As to the manner in which the broadcast should be conducted, Miller says, in the same connection:

In religious broadcasting all selfish motives should be absolutely ruled out. Personal aggrandizement under the cloak of religion should have no place. The religious speaker should consider himself as a spokesman for God and should consider the opportunity offered to him as a special trust for which he must give an account to God. The truth of God as presented in the person of Christ our Lord must be presented in its purity. The "listener-in" has a right to expect this. He has the right to expect an authoritative gospel and not a merely speculative theory. He has the right to expect that which will be constructive, helpful, worshipful.

Details as to consideration for various types of audiences, kinds of programs, and the technique of broadcasting will be worked out by the religious announcer. There are good handbooks on the subject which may be secured from almost any public library.[10] Our interest here is in the *value* of the radio sermon and religious music. With the words of Stanley Marple we conclude:

The benefits accruing to organized religion generally, and to personal faith in particular, as a result of religious radio programs, are undoubtedly great. However, it is to be recognized that some programs are good, others better, and still others best. Broadcasting systems, in their personnel, have

---

[8] Hayes, J. S., and Gardner, H. J., *Both Sides of the Microphone*, p. 5 (J. B. Lippincott Company, New York, 1938).

[9] *Op. cit.*, p. 138, "Religion on the Air," Hayes and Gardner.

[10] *E.g.*, Burns, E. E., *A Study of First Principles for Schools* (D. Van Nostrand, New York, 1938); Haslett, A. W., *Radio Round the World* (The Cambridge University Press, Cambridge, 1934).

at once a task and an opportunity to make an effective and impressive appeal to religious sensibilities. . . .

I am convinced of the value of reading by radio the great biblical passages of the Old and New Testaments. But the reading demands preparation of material, and a rendering by voice quality and expression that is truly appealing. . . .

The value of sermons in their appeal by radio, will vary with the doctrinal background of each listener. For a general appeal, sometimes there is overmuch of theological teaching at the expense of practical Christian teaching. The present output of radio sermons would seem to be sufficient to satisfy all degrees of thought.

Probably the greatest response to phases of religious programs by air, is to be found in the multitude who enjoy the usual splendid chorus, and sometimes congregational singing. Of whatever creed, or lack of it, music speaks the universal language, and religious music is no exception. Therefore, we vote for continued, and even better, religious music, and the use of the great hymns of the centuries.[11]

VISUAL EDUCATION

Finally, the church may do well to secure the best visual aids possible in the promotion of educational activities. Public schools and public libraries have already added many new books and much equipment in this field. Good low-price projectors and still films can be had by almost any church. Films dealing with missions, the life of Christ, travel, the Bible, and hymns can be rented for as little as 50¢.[12] Also, moving pictures—some with "talkies"—are being promoted by many churches and educational institutions of higher learning.

The interest of the church in visual education is *religious, educational,* and *recreational.* Every minister and religious worker should have good books on the subject in his personal library, and should be well informed on the possibilities of the various forms of this new means of religious education. We are entering a new day in objective teaching, and the church without vision will fade out of the picture in modern religion like old lace and pressed flowers.

CONCLUSION

The pulpit, the radio, and visual education constitute powerful avenues for worship and for instruction in religion. They must be placed along with music, art, and religious drama as the chief in-

[11] *Ibid.,* pp. 140, 141, "The Value of the Radio Sermon."
[12] Upon request the Society for Visual Education, 327 South La Salle St., Chicago, Ill., will send catalogs of projectors, picturols, and film slides; also the Motion Picture Bureau of the National Council, Y. M. C. A., Chicago; or David C. Cook, Elgin, Ill., or the Baptist Sunday School Board, Nashville.

struments of modern religious education. One other added to this group will make the list complete; namely, the religious press—which will be taken up in another connection.

So far our leaders have been slow to utilize the material aids to religious education. The costs in equipment and personnel have largely retarded progress in the past. But the church of the future will regard all these implements as necessities, despite expenses, and they will no longer be looked upon as questionable innovations.

Part IV

Religious Education Beyond the Church

CHAPTER XIX

THE CHRISTIAN HOME

"Among all social institutions the family holds first place as a creator and guardian of human values. What the child shall become depends first of all on the kind of family responsible for his upbringing. The home is literally the nursery of humanity, the matrix of personality during the most impressionable years, and a continuing influence throughout life."[1]

Do you consider the above statement true to facts as you know them? Would you consider that there is over-emphasis or exaggeration in the statement at any point?

What are the main characteristics of homes as you know them— good influences, bad influences, advantages and disadvantages? What do homes mean, and what should they mean, to human life and civilization?

How would you distinguish between a home that is Christian, and one that is not Christian? What activities and practices have bearing on Christian education and development? What definite activities and programs can you suggest for the improvement of the home as a religious educational institution? How make the home more Christian, more wholesome and effective as a Christian institution?

If you would be an original thinker and student, try to answer the above questions before you read on. Let the class or group discuss the above questions before reading the rest of this chapter.

NATURE AND FUNCTION

Origin and Permanency.—*The home is man's oldest social group and institution.* The origin of the home is found in the experi-

[1] *The Purposes of Education in American Democracy,* Educational Policies Commissions, National Educational Association, pp. 3-4.

ences of Adam and Eve in the Garden of Eden. "Therefore shall a man leave his father and mother, and shall cleave unto his wife: and they shall be one flesh" (Gen. 2:24). This quotation from Genesis gives us the origin and nature of the home. The home and the family are fundamental to the life of human society and civilization. Jesus himself bases his teaching on the permanency of marriage, and against divorce, on the fundamental biological make-up of the human race— "Male and female made He them." Coupled with this, the idea of abiding love between one man and one woman, with the birth and rearing of children, makes the home basic and fundamental for the safety, security, and progress of the human race.

Function.—One of the strongest and most fundamental impulses of human nature, *love between one man and one woman, forms the foundation* for the home physically, psychologically, emotionally, and religiously. The home and family are basic and fundamental in human life. The procreation and perpetuation of the human race depend on the home. The home gives us a place to be born, to live, to be nurtured and to nurture, and therefore forms our most natural and vital human group. It is in the home where real living goes on, and a normal human being could hardly live at all without some kind of home.

If we look at the home *from the physical standpoint,* we see there the birth and growth of human life. Also it gives us the ideal social group, with loving and sharing among members of the family a central feature. Despite serious weaknesses and faults in many homes, the average human being finds in the home love and confidence, protection and security. *The basic economic needs* of human beings are found in and through the home: food, clothing, and shelter. People make a living together in the home. *Education goes on in every home* and all the time, and that of the most abiding and effective kind. Members of the family are teaching one another constantly by what they say and by what they do not say, by what they do and by what they do not do. The children inevitably learn from the parents, and the parents pass on to the children practically all that they have known and experienced in human living. Religion, or the lack of religion, is unavoidably passed on to the children. The home was the first school, and continues to be the most vital and real school in the lives of all of us.

Education and Religion Meet.—In this chapter we are to consider *the home from the standpoint of religious education.* Well, most certainly, education and religion meet in the home. The customs, habits, and traditions of each generation are passed on to the next

in large measure through the influences and teaching in the home.
In some ways the important question for us here is not how shall we
teach our children religion, but what shall we teach them; because
we teach them religion whether we consciously choose to do so or
not. However, we want to consider carefully the place and function
of the home in the religious education of people from the standpoint
of what the home is doing, and what perhaps it can do and ought to
do. In and through the home we carry on bad education as well as
good. By taking thought we can improve both the quality and the
content of our teaching.

ADVANTAGES OF THE HOME

What are some of the advantages in the home for the teaching of
religion and the development of character? The paragraphs above
help to answer this question and show us the power and prominence
of the home in human life and destiny, but we want to reemphasize
this and add yet another point.

Ideal Teaching Situation.—The family group gives us our
most ideal teaching situation. People teach and learn under the normal and natural conditions of living and making a living. The child
is born into the home and for several years is dependent upon his
parents and other members of the family circle for physical and
economic survival. He has the experience of loving and being loved
by members of this intimate circle, and quite early he learns close
coöperation and sharing in the struggle for existence. You have the
roots of religion in the experience of the child in being dependent on
his parents. This experience transferred to the larger universe, with
God as the supreme Creator and Preserver, gives him the foundation
for true religion. Also, he learns the basic social virtues of coöperation
and sharing. The best families give us the ideal society. The attitudes
and virtues developed in the good family, when transferred to the
larger world in which we live, become the qualities which we need for
building the best human civilization.

As we have indicated above, in the home we have education under
the most natural and normal conditions. If the parents and other
older members of the family have genuine Christian character, and a
good understanding of the fundamental Christian virtues and teachings, they have the best opportunity in the world to pass these on to
the younger generation. In the home you have much more than
formal instruction. There is a natural inclination to practice the basic

Christian virtues such as loving, sharing, and helping, virtues which are most vital in Christian living.

Most Important Institution in Character Building.—Germane and Germane, in their book *Character Education, A Program for the School and the Home*,[2] in answer to the question "Why is the home the most important institution in character building?" give us the following interesting and significant statements:

No other institution can do so much to shape human destiny for good as the home, for the following reasons:

1. The first five or six years of a child's life are the most impressionable. It is in these years that many of the primary emotionalized attitudes and reactions are formed for life.
2. These early years find the child almost entirely under the influence of the parents. Here are both a golden opportunity and a great obligation to lay a flawless, adamantine foundation for happy, progressive maturity.
3. Love for father and mother surpasses all other love. The child's confidence in his parents is unbounded. Their deeds, words, and emotional responses are imitated in ways that are startling.
4. Approximately 184,000 hours are lived between the age of infancy and legal maturity. But on an average only 7,000 of these hours are spent in school. Since child life is the most sensitive and plastic of all life and since it is lived for the most part either directly or indirectly within the home environment, the child cannot be other than a reflex of this home environment.
5. In a very significant sense parenthood is a second chance at childhood. Nature, in all her affluence, could scarcely have provided a plan more just in which adults could re-live their childhood as they wish it might have been lived. For if these parents, when children, were reared in an environment which fostered the learning of pernicious habits and unhealthy emotionalized attitudes, what an opportunity is afforded these same parents now to save their children from the same handicaps by setting up a wholesome environment. Thus each generation could be infinitely happier and richer than the preceding, if parents could but envisage the significance of their opportunities. Many parents fail to realize that their greatest opportunity for permanent happiness and for self-realization lies in the wisdom with which they nourish and cherish their re-created selves in the lives of their children. What achievements, what joys are comparable to those experienced by the parent who, in his own lifetime, sees the embodiment of all that he had wished for but somehow failed to be, growing stronger and sturdier in the children in his home?

The careful studies of educators and psychologists in recent years have shown unmistakably the primacy and vast importance of the home in character and religious education. For instance, the TENTH YEARBOOK of the Department of Superintendence of the National

[2] Part II, pp. 6-7 (Silver, Burdett and Co., 1929).

Education Association for 1932, entitled *Character Education*, has the following statement in regard to the family as an agency of character education:

The oldest of all agencies of character education is the family. Although it has been steadily surrendering educational functions to other institutions through the ages, and particularly during recent times, it remains today the most powerful of all influences affecting the moral growth of the child. In comparison the school is but a minor factor in the situation. Hartshorne and May[3] found a positive correlation of .545 between children and their parents in the case of moral knowledge. The potency of the family in this realm should cause no surprise. The child really lives in the home, whereas in the school he is commonly the passive recipient of adult ministrations and must feel himself dwelling for the time in an alien world. Moreover, the family has practically complete control over the child during the first six years of life. This fact alone is sufficient to make the family the most important of all our educational agencies. Also, father and mother and older brothers and sisters are largely responsible for the child during his out-of-school hours, which amount to approximately one-tenth of his total time and one-sixth of his waking hours. The parents, at least if they are well-to-do, may even choose the school which the child attends and determine the extension of educational opportunity beyond the age of compulsory schooling. Clearly the most momentous question with respect to the agencies of character education in the United States must pertain to the adequacy of the equipment of the family for the discharge of its heavy responsibilities.[4]

Equally True in Religious Education.—The above statements in regard to character education apply just as truly to religious education. A child's religion is rooted in the religious life of the family of which he is a dependent member. His ideas, habits, and desires concerning God and things religious are derived largely from the current spirit and practice of the home. And the father and mother should bring this spirit and practice to bear upon the lives of their children in ways not simply of unconscious influence, fundamental and unfailing as that is, but consciously through formal educational methods and directed experience. We want in every way possible to improve and make permanent the religious character of the home and give to all who are interested in it the best methods and plans for educating our children in religion. The rest of this chapter will be given to the more practical phases of just this matter of more and better religious education in and through the home.

---

[3] Hartshorne, Hugh; May, Mark A.; and others. "Testing the Knowledge of Right and Wrong." Monograph No. 1. Chicago: Religious Education Association, July 1927, pp. 43-45.
[4] *Tenth Yearbook*, p. 18.

Problems of the Home

Judge Irkham Scanlan, chief justice of the criminal court in Chicago, said some years ago, in addressing a branch of the Chicago Medical Society, that among the reasons for the increase in crime "the first is the passing of the old American home. The old American homestead, with its training in religion, was the finest and best factor in keeping down crime this country has ever known. As an institution it is fast falling into decay, with a resultant increase in crime."[5] Just what are the differences from the standpoint of religious education between the old home and the new?

The Old American Home.—Perhaps we exaggerate the differences between the religious influences of the old home and the new; for the halo of age is about the old home, and we like to think that it was almost ideal in its religious character and emphasis. But undoubtedly there were advantages in the home of the past. For one thing, the home of the past had fewer distractions, and the life and interests of parents and children were centered in the home. All the members of the family circle shared together in the duties and responsibilities of the home, and thus the children learned to live in a most wholesome way through actual living. They learned to do by doing. Fathers and mothers, if they were Christians, naturally taught their children what religion they knew, and actually guided them in the practice of it. They felt the responsibility for the spiritual development of their children, for one thing because there were no other agencies, such as the Sunday school and the public school, to which they could turn. The father was the priest of the family. He had the old fashioned family altar, reading the Scriptures daily, and praying with the family. Also he and his wife felt the responsibility for the discipline of the children, teaching and practicing the fundamental Christian virtues in connection with the task of living and working in the home and on the farm.

The Modern Home.—Now the situation in the modern home is usually quite different. Too often the home is not much more than a place to eat and sleep; the center for recreation, education, work and worship usually being in some institution outside of the home. Too, the distractions of the modern movies, newspapers, radio, and many other forms of amusement and entertainment take the time of the members of the family, and, to say the least, do not contribute

[5] *Minneapolis Journal*, March 4, 1922. Quoted in McKown, *Character Education*, p. 411.

directly to the spiritual and moral development of our young people. Even if the parents are anxious to stress religious training in the home, practically they find it difficult to do so. However, "Where there's a will, there's a way."

Constant Teaching, Good or Bad.—Parents, as a matter of course, teach their children all the religion that they really have and believe in. They teach every day by what they say and by what they do not say; by what they do and by what they do not do. In perhaps millions of homes there is not only not any positive teaching of the Bible and religion, but the moral and spiritual conditions are bad. Often there is lack of love and confidence between father and mother, and even between parents and children. There is even constant fussing and fighting where there ought to be genuine love and mutual sharing. Multitudes of homes are broken up by divorce, and that is a serious problem in America today; but, perhaps the greatest need and opportunity, from the standpoint of religious education, lies in the direction of the thousands of homes which never reach the divorce court but are in imminent danger because of the very low plane of living experienced in these homes. Indeed, the home has great influence in shaping character, and many times the influence is very bad instead of in keeping with the fundamental Christian virtues.

Ignorance and Poverty.—Ignorance and poverty are two of the greatest evils afflicting our American life and the American home. Ignorant parents, as well as wicked parents, make immense blunders in the training and nurture of their children. Poverty is a constant handicap. Millions of homes have difficulty in providing the minimum essentials of good health and education for their children because they cannot provide the means for medical attention, nourishing food, warm clothes, good books, music and art. These things are not luxuries but necessities. We must develop a public conscience on the matter of providing better living conditions as well as emphasizing the more formal side of religious instruction.

Positive Teaching of the Bible and Religion.—However, in the definite sense of religious education, we must give our main attention perhaps to the positive teaching of the Bible and religion in and through the home. The most serious problem from our standpoint in the modern day is that so few homes give definite attention to matters of character and religion. The rest of this chapter will attack more directly the problem of just this matter of stimulating interest in the practical living and teaching of religion in and through the home.

CHRISTIAN ACTIVITIES—MEETING THE SITUATION

In meeting the situation in the home from the standpoint of religious education, we naturally divide our discussion into the two main divisions of the informal and formal Christian activities. Both types of activities and emphasis are very important.

Informal Activities.—First, we take up the consideration of informal activities. *The very atmosphere of the home* is a matter of great importance. This may be intangible, but it is very real just the same. It comes through the genuine Christian character and living of all the members of the family. One cannot create the right Christian atmosphere merely by taking thought, but in a thousand different ways the right atmosphere is developed by our private devotions and thinking, by our reverence, our genuine love to God and man, and our practice of the fundamental Christian virtues in the "give and take" of daily living. The Christian mother praying for and with the infant of only a few days old makes a large contribution to the life of the child. In such a home the child breathes in and drinks in the Christian things of life long before he can understand them or is ready positively to yield his own life to Christ.

The child begins to learn the nature of religion through loving and being loved in the home. Here we find the roots of true religion. Later he learns that "God is love" and that the two great commandments are to love God supremely, and one's neighbor as himself. After all, love is the greatest thing in the world, and it is at the heart and center of the Christian religion.

Sharing in Christian living is an important phase of religious education in the home. This sharing finds expression in the actual work and duties of the home in practical ways, as well as in formal religious exercises like Bible study and prayer. We learn to do by doing, and true education comes through living. We not only want to teach our children the Bible, but we want to share with them in the practice of the fundamental Christian virtues in our daily work and play.

Among these informal activities we list *conversation in the family*. Ordinarily we are influenced more by informal conversation than we are influenced by formal lectures or preaching. Members of the family are constantly teaching and influencing one another by what they say and by what they do not say when it comes to spiritual matters. Parents, as well as the children, should be taught to make the ordinary conversation in the home wholesome and uplifting. References to the pastor, the Sunday school and church, our playmates and our neighbors, and what we say about human character and conduct should be in keeping with Christian ideas and teachings.

Underlying and running throughout these informal Christian activities must be listed the important matter of *personal example*. It is still true that what we do speaks so loudly that often our children cannot hear what we say. "Not everyone that saith unto me, Lord, Lord, shall enter into the kingdom of heaven; but he that doeth the will of my Father who is in heaven" (Matt. 7:21).

Formal Christian Activities.—We come, in the second place, to formal Christian activities in and through the home. Family worship is essential to the maintenance and propagation of religion. There is no substitute for it. Sunday school and church worship cannot take the place of it. It is not merely the forms of prayer or the words of the song we use. Primarily it is the internal attitude of reverence which displays itself when speaking of God, the Bible, the church, and sacred things. It is the attitude and spirit which members of the family show at all hours of the day in the work and play of life, and in crises which may come in the life of the home at times.

But there is an important place for formal and definite religious instruction and worship. We must have more than just silent influence however important that may be. Religion is "caught" but it is also "taught." Family worship expresses itself in three main forms: (1) grace at table; (2) the bedside prayers of the children; (3) general family prayers. Other formal activities would include Bible study and teaching in the home, coöperation with Sunday school and church, and sharing in and directing Christian service in the church and community.

(1) The regular custom of having *grace at table or prayer at meal time* is a natural and helpful one. Here we recognize God as the giver of all good things, including "our daily bread."

> "Come, be our guest, O Lord of good,
> And bless to us Thy gift of food."

Such prayers give a devotional and uplifting tone to the family circle at meal time. "They tend to hallow what should be hours of happiest fellowship, to clothe the routine of daily life with its true divinity, to lift the table-talk above the level of gossip and squabbling, and to bring God into the fellowship of the home."[6]

Usually the blessing may be asked by the father or mother. Often

[6] Weigle and Tweedy, *Training the Devotional Life*, p. 76 (Doubleday, Doran and Co., 1919).

it is wise to allow the children to do it in turn. Sometimes beautiful prayers will be repeated together by the whole family circle. In any case, the grace should be short, simple and sincere, and not stilted or over-pious. We give below two simple but beautiful prayers for meal time:

A CHILD'S "THANK YOU"

Thank You for the world so sweet,
Thank You for the food we eat,
Thank You for the birds that sing,
Thank You, God, for everything.
—Selected.

God is great and God is good
And we thank Him for this food;
By His hand must all be fed
Give us, Lord, our daily bread.

Heavenly Father, bless this food,
To Thy glory and our good.
—Translated from the German.

(2) *The bedside prayers of the children.* Even the tiny infant in a sense absorbs the spiritual atmosphere when the mother kneels and prays by its cradle; and the heavenly Father hears the prayer of the godly mother—"for I say unto you, that in heaven their angels do always behold the face of my Father who is in heaven" (Matt. 18:10).

Later the mother or father will have the child to repeat simple prayers, and gradually teach the child to form his own original prayers. Following this will come instruction in the meaning of prayer. The child can be saved from taking a rather mechanical view of prayer, expecting to get everything he asks for. He will learn that prayer is not merely asking for things, and that the ideal prayer breathes the sentiment, "Not my will, but Thine, be done."

(3) *General family prayers.* The old-time family altar may be gone, but its modern counterpart can and must be preserved. The father and mother will lead in this, but the children will participate as they get old enough. Just as in prayer at meal time, reading the Scripture, leading in prayer, and other parts of this service can be performed by different members of the family group. Some of this can be done reverently in concert. Various methods will be used. Sometimes the main part will be the reading of the Bible in a connected way through many books, with simple explanations for the children. At other times devotional books will be used as guides.

Many good books and manuals have been prepared in recent years by various publishers. *Open Windows,* published by the Southern Baptist Sunday School Board, is an illustration of an excellent publication along this line. The International Council of Religious Education has some manuals and guides for worship in the family, as well as a commission which is leading in the study of this matter, and in the help of families in this important function.

It is difficult to find a satisfactory time for family worship, but the earnest parent will find some time. Ten minutes just before or just after the evening meal will be found to be a very good time for many. Other times will suggest themselves according to the situation and needs of the family.

In addition to the more formal religious exercises of the home in the way of family worship, there will be a place in the best Christian homes for *teaching and guiding the child in the study of the Bible.* Graded Bible stories will be helpful for very young children, and various books and manuals will be used by older members of the family. The parents and older children will help the younger ones in the preparation of Sunday school lessons and other programs and services of the church in which the children participate. The home will coöperate with the church in all of its activities, and in turn the church will coöperate with and support the home in this vital matter of Christian nurture and guidance. This will involve, also, guidance in real Christian service in the school and community during the week. Our children must learn not only to worship, to study the Bible, and other matters of like nature, but they must learn to engage in the real tasks of Christian living and in building a Christian world.

Some Practical Suggestions

We list below some practical suggestions which have bearing on formal as well as informal Christian activities in the home. After all, the important thing is to be more practical and to do definite things toward the development of a Christian atmosphere in the home, and toward the positive guidance of our children in Christian living. All of these things involve also the Christian training and development of the parents.

Begin Early.—There is real point in the remark that the time to begin to train a child is a hundred years before it is born. There must be a real connection between the marvelous strength exhibited by Samson and the fact that his mother refused to drink wine or to eat anything unclean after his conception (Judges 13:3-4). The first-born of a happy young couple had just been delivered. The physician had picked up his hat to leave. "Shall we put out the light, doctor?" inquired the young father. "That depends on how you wish to train the baby," was the reply. "If you allow the light to burn tonight he will cry for it tomorrow night." Dr. George A. Gordon, for more than forty years pastor of the Old South Church, Boston, says in his autobiography that a child learns more during the first year of its life than in any ten years afterwards. There has been much and sad blundering at this point. The main tendencies of character and life are fixed during the first three or four years of babyhood, being absorbed from the atmosphere and picked up from the conversations and the actions of those about the child.

Don't Shift Responsibility.—It is clear that the Creator has charged those who bring children into the world with the responsibility of at least directing their "first steps" with as much care as possible. The nursery school, the Sunday school, the graded school, the Boy Scouts, the community clubs are all good, but they should be used only to supplement and reinforce the central point in all the child's life, the home. No parent can afford to turn over to any outside agency the task and the privilege which God has in the nature of the case committed to him.

Be Consistent.—One of the greatest shocks that a child can be called on to meet is when he first finds a parent speaking or acting insincerely or even carelessly; as, for example, giving the wrong age of the child on the train to avoid paying a fare, or having the maid report she is out when company comes.

Associate with the Children in the Daily Tasks of the Home.—Do it as early and as rapidly as possible. Of course they will break dishes, soil carpets, bruise their fingers, cut their toes, and bring trouble in a thousand other ways. It will be so much simpler and easier for mother and father to do the tasks themselves. But this is to rob the child of its birthright without even giving "a mess of pottage."

Give to Each Child a Definite Assignment.—For this make him responsible, and hold him to his responsibility without exception. The Jews of the Old Testament time were very careful in training their children. One of the Rabbis in the Talmud says, "He that has a trade, to what is he like? He is like a city that is fenced." Another Rabbi says, "He that fails to teach his son a trade has done the same thing as if he taught him to be a thief."

Democracy.—The home should be neither a monarchy nor a "duarchy." It should be a democracy in which each member shares according to his ability. And the "share" here should include all duties, privileges, responsibilities, cares, burdens, sorrows, joys, and all the rest. In this way each will come, by degrees, to know what life means in its deepest and most meaningful aspects.

Table Talk.—Three times a day the family gathers at the table. This period should never be a hurried one. Here is a great opportunity to talk over all sorts of things. With a little encouragement each one will be glad to bring in a worthwhile contribution. It should be understood by common consent rather than by formal agreement that nothing of an ugly or unpleasant nature will ever be alluded to at the table.

Have Stated and Special Seasons for Intimate Fellowship with the Children.—One family has what they call "The Golden Hour." This comes in the evening when the day's work is done and all can get together for reading a story, for learning the best poems, for singing hymns, for the cultivation of the best that our civilization has produced in so far as the parents have themselves been able to acquire this. Another mother through her life as a mother has had with her children what she calls "The Confidential Hour." With her this hour comes generally just before the bedtime prayer. Here the mother shares with her child all that she knows as the child develops and is able to comprehend. The child in turn tells the mother all that he knows—all of his thoughts, feelings, experiences of the day. It is understood that nothing said here is to be alluded to elsewhere, nor is anything said here to be used as a basis of condemnation. Here the mother is the true priest mediating the things of God. This is the true confessional. Here is the place to create attitudes toward things fundamental—God, home, sex, race, church, Bible, Sabbath—all the things that mean most in our life. Here character is born.

Make use of special occasions as they arise. Birthdays, holidays, Christmas, Easter; sickness, sorrow, death; special joys, perplexities; local, state and national elections; inauguration of a governor or a president; anniversaries, centennials, special trips are valuable. The home should make use of all such to teach the background and the meaning of each as it comes.

Nature.—What can be more fascinating than to study the stars, the planets, the birds, the flowers, the insects, the animals, the soil, the streams, and a thousand other objects of God's handiwork that either lie about our feet or stretch out before our eyes? Why not encourage the children to save their nickels and invest in a simple nature book rather than in chewing gum?

Music.—A Confucian canon says, "Music has its origin in heaven. Virtue is the strong stem of man's nature, and music is the blossoming of virtue. Music embraces what all can share equally. To go to the very root of our feelings is its province."[7] The Christian religion is peculiarly rich in its great hymns and tunes. A good hymn book—better, several copies of it—should be a part of the equipment of every home. The family should sing together. A very discerning man has said, "Let me write the hymns of a nation and you may let whomsoever you will write its philosophies."

Art.—It is quite easy these days to supply the walls with suitable pictures. The Perry Picture Company, Malden, Mass., will furnish a beautiful reproduction of almost any of the standard pictures for a few cents. Why allow commercial enterprises to use our homes and surroundings for advertising purposes when we can, for a mere pittance, keep before ourselves and our little ones character-building pictures, inspiring reproductions of great pieces of sculpture, and delicate suggestions in the form of tapestry.

Conclusion—Our Greatest Opportunity and Privilege

An adequate family program of religious education, with all that is involved in the way of church and community coöperation, will not only mean the Christian nurture of our children but will contribute to the training and enrichment of the lives of the parents as well. The parents have a chance to live over their youth again, and make good some of the failures of their lives in the blessing and development of their children. The blessing to parents in many cases will even be richer than that visited upon the children. And here is the point at which we perhaps make our richest contribution toward building a Christian civilization and the kingdom of God.

The fundamental Christian point of view and emphasis in the home, which makes up the ideal school and human society, transferred to the big world outside, will make the ideal world-society, "wherein dwelleth righteousness" and world brotherhood. After all, the supreme Christian task and challenge for us is to learn how to live together as human brothers in our heavenly Father's world. In love and sharing in the home we are learning how we should live together in the big society outside, and thus help to realize the abundant life for all.

[7] Quoted by Turnbull, Grace H., in *Tongues of Fire*, p. 138 (The Macmillan Company, New York, 1929).

CHAPTER XX

SOCIAL-RECREATIONAL AGENCIES

Play will influence life, either for good or bad. It is not only a possible but an inevitable factor in the formation of character. Character is not only tested by play, but it is largely made during play. The use or misuse of leisure time is both a test of civilization and a determinant of it.

The importance of play and recreational life in the development of the child is generally recognized. Froebel called play "the highest phase of child development." This was considered true because play is the "self-active representation of the inner." Luther H. Gulick, the American philosopher for the play movement, says: "If you want to know what a child is, study his play; if you want to affect what he will be, direct the form of his play." He suggests that man's long period of immaturity is given in order that the child might have ample time for play and thus get the preparation for the complex life of adulthood.

Joseph Lee, who has been for many years the president of the Playground and Recreational Association of America, has made a splendid statement of the place of play in child life. He says, "The thing that most needs to be understood about play is that it is not a luxury, but a necessity. It is not simply something that a child likes to have; it is something that he must have if he is ever to grow up. It is more than an essential part of his education; it is an essential law of his growth, of the process by which he becomes a man at all."

Recreation also has a place in adult life. It is being recognized that some form of recreation is not only natural to man but that it is necessary for man. The normal attitudes toward life and the proper relationships with others are impossible without some place for play and social life.

So play and social life have come to be recognized not as unimportant features in the life of children and young people, but as important features of all life; not as a sort of necessary evil, but as a necessary good; not as a thing to be condoned and put up with, but as a thing to be enthusiastically accepted and intelligently planned; not as something that contributes to a healthy bodily growth, but as an activity

that makes a decided contribution to the development of character
and the whole of life.

Increasing Importance of Social-Recreational Life

More Interest in, and Opportunity for, Recreation.—Modern athletics and commercialized amusements are attracting millions
of people, in fact nearly the whole population. People are interested in
social and recreational life. They give their time and their money for
those things which contribute to entertainment and amusement. There
is a deep-seated desire and need which is met by such activities. There
is nothing fundamentally wrong in this situation except that we have
too long left this important phase of life to commercialized amusements and worldly interests instead of capitalizing on it in the name
of religion by providing through our churches for a more wholesome
social-recreational life.

The shortening of the hours of labor and the freedom from labor
of many children has added to the hours for play. With the speeding
up of production by the machine, there had to be a shortening of the
hours of labor or overproduction and unemployment. The limit has
not been reached yet in the limitation of work time. Some economists
predict the three and four day week in the future. What will this
extra time be used for—to build or to destroy character?

Time is not the only thing conducive to play. For play to be
prominent in life there must be a relatively high standard of living.
There must be freedom from a constant fear of need and poverty.

There is More Need for Organized Recreation.—Specialization in modern industry has been carried to such an extreme that
there is little opportunity for the expression of idealism. Industrialism
"pays a premium on monotony." This monotony is an enemy of
idealism and endangers moral character.

All of this modern specialization means that work contributes less
to satisfactory living than in the past. Formerly the worker had the
joy of creation, when he completed the whole product; but now his
part is so small that he does not recognize the car or machine as his
creation.

Also, in big production there is little opportunity for close personal
relationship between employer and employee. There is not developed
a sense of oneness. The employee works to make a living and rarely
thinks of making a contribution to life. The employer thinks of those
working in his factory as so many machines, who are contributing

to the dividends of his plant. There is lacking a sense of moral responsibility.

There has also been a speeding up of all life. People live intensely. Such is not conducive to the most satisfactory life. Neither does it furnish the best basis for the building of intelligently directed character.

The increase in city population, a result of the industrial development, means a shifting of moral standards. Traditional moral ideals are less respected. There is not so much social pressure as in the country. There are few people who know and care what one does.

Modern Education Magnifies Play as a Method.—The trend of modern education is away from the transmissive to the creative idea of education. The formal recitation method has been supplanted by the fellowship of the teacher and pupil in a common search for truth. This has meant more freedom in the teacher-pupil relationship.

As a result, the problem-discussion, dramatization, and project methods of teaching have become more prominent. These represent the play and socialized method in education.

In addition there has been a new appreciation of the educational value of the playground and the athletic field. This is inevitable when the child is made the center of the educational process.

An Opportunity for Good or Bad.—This additional leisure time with the demand for more recreation and an increasing emphasis on the play method in modern education provides an opportunity for good or ill. Shall this added leisure time and increasing emphasis be used to build good or bad character?

Release from work means a curse to an individual or a civilization that has not learned how to use leisure time. This leisure time will in the future enrich or destroy civilization.[1]

RECREATION AND RIGHTEOUSNESS

Recreation may make a worthy contribution to the building of character if it has the right content and is properly supervised.

Health and Morality.—Play of the right kind contributes to health of body and mind. This is just as true of the adult as of the child.

A healthy body furnishes a better basis for moral living than a sickly body. Rousseau said: "The body must be vigorous to obey the soul. A feeble body weakens the mind." John Locke once said: "A

[1] For discussion of the dangers of increased leisure time, see Cutten, George B., *The Threat of Leisure* (Yale University Press, New Haven, 1926).

sound mind in a sound body is a short but full description of a happy state!" A healthy body and a healthy mind mean a better attitude toward life and toward other human beings. This makes health itself a moral responsibility.

The Playground and Crime.—Undirected play in a bad environment is a most powerful factor for evil. Thus the playground may develop criminal impulses and contribute to anti-social conduct.

But it has been proved that supervised playgrounds have meant a decrease in juvenile crime. In one district in St. Louis, juvenile delinquency was reduced 75 per cent in one year after the opening of a playground. Five months after the opening of a municipal recreation system in Passaic, New Jersey, the juvenile court was permanently closed. By providing play facilities for the newsboys of Milwaukee, the number sent to the reformatory was reduced from 70 to 3 within three years. Chicago has had a notable decrease in juvenile crime where playgrounds have been provided. One Chicago judge lately said: "It has been found in the city of Chicago, in every case where a study has been made, that juvenile crime has increased as the distance from the playground increases."

The Local Council of one large city in the United States has asked for the privilege of using scouting as a crime preventive. Troops of scouts are to be organized in the different crime centers of the city. The results will be watched with interest.

In one State Boys' School (reformatory) there were found to be about 85 per cent repeaters. Numerous programs had been tried, but nothing had helped the situation. The superintendent asked for the privilege of using the Scout Oath and Laws, and some of the program. In three years the repeaters had decreased 15 per cent.

In this same institution about 40 or 50 boys annually won the right to be paroled for the Christmas holidays. Usually about 10 or 15 violated the parole and the police had to bring them back. Since the scouting program was instituted not a single boy has violated his parole.

This wholesome influence of play is not due alone to the fact that the mind is kept busy and the individual is withdrawn from an evil environment. The influence of play is positive as well as negative. Lessons in democratic living are learned. Rules of the game are respected and this respect carries over into other relationships. A different attitude toward society is created. A sense of respectability and responsibility is built.

Play and Morale.—One is greatly influenced by one's loyalties. Loyalty may not be the chief virtue, but it should be numbered with the leading virtues.

Play, more than any other activity, builds group morale. One of the secrets to the success of the Scout Movement in the reform school mentioned above, is the fact that Boy Scouts have built a high sense of group unity and individual loyalty to the standards of Scouts. College loyalty is largely built around the inter-collegiate athletic contests.

The qualities developed in the team games have been well stated by Professor E. A. Ross: "The game fastens loyalty to one's fellows, to one's team, and to one's institution. It accustoms one to obey the captain, to accept without a murmur the decision of the recognized authority, and to work for the good of the whole rather than for self. It develops facility in concerted action and gives practice in quick, unreflecting adjustment of the intention and moves of others. In being required to abide by the rules of the game under circumstances which sorely try the temper, one acquires self-control. Sport, moreover, imposes the difficult ideal of a 'good sportsman,' who is just and magnanimous, who neither gloats in victory nor sulks in defeat."[2]

Games of simple organization and those activities ordinarily used in church life are also valuable in the development of loyalty. Church groups that frequently play together have a sense of oneness and spirit of friendliness not found in groups without these social activities.

PROGRAMS OF PROMOTION

With the increased demand and need for recreation and with the greater opportunity for participation there have come several attempts to care for the need. All of these attempts might be divided into: (1) commercialized amusements, and (2) socialized amusements.

Commercialized Amusements Unsafe.—Those providing commercialized amusements were the first to recognize the modern demand for increased recreation and have made millions of dollars by this discovery. These amusements have a tremendous grip on modern recreational life. Most of these are unsafe while some are positively harmful.

Motive wrong. One thing that makes all commercial amusements dangerous is the fact that they are dominated by the "profit motive." The main consideration is not the influence on life, but the money in

[2] *Principles of Sociology*, p. 616 (The Century Company, New York, 1920).

hand. Those who control the commercial amusements cannot be trusted to give the people what they need.

Participation lacking. For play to contribute much to the building of character, it must secure active participation. There is not much value physically, mentally, or morally, to watching someone perform, regardless of how skilled the performer be. But for amusements to furnish the greatest financial returns there must be a large number of spectators.

Aldous Huxley speaks of the "Vast organization that provides us with ready-made distractions—distractions that demand from pleasure seekers no personal participation and no intellectual effort of any sort. These effortless pleasures, these ready-made distractions that are the same for everyone over the face of the whole Western world, are surely a worse menace to our civilization than even the Germans were." Someone else has spoken of them as "vicarious exercises."

Destructive rather than constructive. While it cannot be truthfully said that all commercialized amusements are destructive morally, the accusation would to some extent be true. Most amusements, dominated by the desire for profit, are in the main unwholesome in their influence on the participants, spectators, and society in general. Gambling is prevalent, evil associates are common, evil thoughts are encouraged, the passions and desires unduly stimulated.

The commercial spirit is constantly encroaching into supposedly socialized fields. The commercial spirit is frequently found in the programs provided by industries and municipalities. There is also danger that the commercial spirit will dominate college athletics.[3] In the commercial spirit in college athletics some have recognized one of the major social conflicts—a conflict between business and education. The domination of college athletics by the professional spirit will mean the ultimate destruction of college athletics and will mean the loss of the fine character building values that come from intercollegiate athletic competition.

Recreation Activities under Municipal Auspices.—The paternalistic function of government has been emphasized more of late years. The responsibility of the government is recognized not only to protect, but to promote. Cities as the smallest, most compact unit of government, have given most attention to this phase of government. Public libraries and parks are provided. These serve a large con-

[3] For a discussion of this danger see Carnegie Foundation Report, Number 23, and Rogers, Frederick Rand, *The Future of Interscholastic Athletics*. Bureau of Publications, Teachers College, Columbia University, New York, 1929.

stituency and, in the main, are very helpful in their influence. A renewed emphasis on physical training as a feature of the public school curriculum has been given. But the major recreational program of municipalities is fostered by city recreation boards.

Under the inspiration and guidance of the Playground and Recreation Association of America[4] most of the large municipalities in the United States have provided for city supervision of playgrounds. Others have provided for swimming pools, athletic fields, golf courses, tennis courts, and field houses with provision for basketball, volleyball, and indoor baseball. This municipal program of play is the most extensive socialized program found at the present time.

Major Types of Church Recreation.—There are three or four major types of recreation promoted by the churches. (1) There are physical activities such as athletic games, swimming, playground activities, hiking, and so forth. (2) There are the more intellectual or mental types of activities such as the library and reading rooms, art exhibits and literary clubs. (3) There are creative activities such as dramatics, handwork, and the various uses of the project method in teaching. (4) There are social features such as banquets and teas, picnics and parties. These divisions are more or less arbitrary, but they are at least helpful and practical for descriptive purposes.[5]

While the churches will promote to some extent all of the above types of social and recreational activities, the major emphasis will be placed on the social and certain other educationally valuable agencies and activities such as the library and dramatics. Great hosts of our people, especially in rural and village communities, need a richer and more wholesome social and recreational life. When we learn to play together and have good fellowship together we learn to 'love one another. There are great moral and spiritual values in a good old-fashioned Sunday school picnic. We need to plan for more and better socials in the activities of the various groups and organizations of the church.

ADOLESCENT RECREATIONAL ORGANIZATIONS

There has grown up a group of organizations independent of institutional control that have provided for adolescent boys and girls. The three leading organizations are the Boy Scouts, Girl Scouts, and

[4] The name was changed in 1930 to National Recreational Association. The P. R. A. A. was organized in 1906.

[5] See Maston, T. B., *A Handbook for Church Recreation Leaders* (Baptist Sunday School Board, Nashville, 1937).

Camp Fire Girls. The Boy Scouts and the Camp Fire Girls foster pre-adolescent programs, the Cubs and the Blue Birds respectively.

A Guiding Principle.—The adolescent recreational organizations have been built on the theory that education comes by doing. There has been a minimum of instruction and a maximum of expression. The instruction has always been kept secondary to activity and often it is so mixed with expression that the boy or girl is unaware of its presence at all.

Character is not only tested by free expressional activities, but it is largely made by these activities. There is a place for formal instruction in the building of character, but it alone will never build character. Permanent impressions are never made without expression. The youth organizations magnify the informal in character education.

Religion Out-of-Doors.—All of the major recreational organizations for adolescent young people magnify the out-of-doors. The hike and the camp are regular features. All of these contacts with nature furnish a splendid source for religious impressions.

These organizations are not sectarian in their religious beliefs, but they are dominantly religious. The Camp Fire Girls give honors for church activities. The organization is characterized by a high idealism. The laws of the Camp Fire are:

> Seek beauty
> Give service
> Pursue knowledge
> Be trustworthy
> Hold on to health
> Glorify work
> Be happy.

The "Desire" of those attaining the various ranks of the Camp Fire Girls illustrates this high idealism. The Desire of the Fire Maker (the second rank) is as follows:

> As fuel is brought to the fire
> So I purpose to bring
> My strength
> My ambition
> My heart's desire
> My joy
> And my sorrow
> To the fire of humankind.
> For I will tend
> As my fathers tended
> And my father's fathers
> Since time began

The fire that is called
The love of man for man
The love of man for God.

Scouting, both for boys and girls, has a wholesome attitude toward religion.

(1) The Oath is:

On my honor I will do my best—
1. To do my duty to God and my country, and to obey the Scout Law.
2. To help other people at all times.
3. To keep myself physically strong, mentally awake and morally straight.

(2) The Scout Law also shows this same high moral and religious idealism, emphasizing that a scout is trustworthy, loyal, helpful, friendly, courteous, kind, obedient, cheerful, thrifty, brave, clean, and reverent.

(3) The constitution illustrates scouting's attitude toward religion. Article 3, Section 1 reads as follows: "The Boy Scouts of America maintain that no boy can grow into the best kind of citizenship without recognizing his obligation to God. In the first part of the Boy Scout's pledge the boy promises, 'On my honor I will do my best to do my duty to God and to my country, and to obey the Scout Law.'" The recognition of God as the ruling and leading power of the universe, and the grateful acknowledgment of His favors and blessings, is necessary to the best type of citizenship, and is a wholesome thing in the education of the growing boy. No matter what he may be—Catholic or Protestant or Jew—this fundamental need of good citizenship should be kept before him. The Boy Scouts of America therefore recognize the religious element in training the boy, but it is absolutely non-sectarian. Its policy is that the organization or institution with which the Boy Scout is connected shall give definite attention to his religious life.

Recently Chief Scout Executive James E. West in a letter to the President of the United States stated the attitude of the present leadership. He said: "At a recent conference of our Scout Executives at Estes Park, Colorado, where we spent eight days in analyzing conditions affecting the boy life in America, and planning our program for the next two years, I stated that after careful study of the whole situation, it was my conviction that the two things upon which we should place emphasis in our work for boys during the years to come were: first, to strengthen the influence of home in the life of the boy; and second, to see that all our scoutmasters and other leaders take full advantage of every opportunity to impress upon the boy the importance of religion in their daily lives."

Relation to the Church.—The Camp Fire Girls are usually organized with the home as a meeting place. Home Craft is the first of the seven crafts. However, frequently the organization is under the direct auspices of the church, and usually where the home is the meeting place the leadership and inspiration for the organization comes from the church.

Much of the program of the Camp Fire is in line with the program and purpose of the church. The fact that Camp Fire gives recognition to the formal activities of the church tends to dignify religious activities. Honor beads are given for such activities as attending religious services ten Sundays in three months, leading mission study classes three times, filling office of secretary or librarian for Sunday school one year, being an officer for one term of the Christian Endeavor, Epworth League, B. Y. P. U. or similar organization, read a chapter of the Bible or other religious literature every day for three months, know and sing eight standard hymns, help clean the silver three times, help provide and arrange flowers on pulpit or altar four times, and serve as leader of singing in church or Sunday school for three months.

The Girl Scouts[6] are not usually as closely related to the church as the Boy Scouts. However, as indicated above, their program is closely related to the purpose of the church.

The whole Boy Scout movement is closely related to the church. The vast majority of the troops are under the supervision and auspices of the church. In one Southern city, 56 of the 61 troops were fostered by churches. The national scout leaders and the majority of local leaders advocate church affiliation.

Ray O. Wyland, Director of the Department of Education of the Boy Scouts of America, in an address recently before a regional meeting set out the following advantages of the church as a home for the scout troop.

1. The church has a moral atmosphere which is wholesome for the boys.
2. The church can mobilize man-power worthy to set an example for the boys.
3. The men related to scouting in the church have long enduring patience and great determination. The majority of five, ten, and fifteen year veteran troops are church troops.

[6] The major part of the Girl Scout's program is the same as the Boy Scout's. For this reason little attention is given to Girl Scouts in this chapter.

4. Parents have confidence in the church and are willing to have their boys out until 9:00 o'clock at night under conditions provided by the church for the troop meetings.

5. The church completes the program of religious education in the life of the boy. Scouting is only a part of this program covering the entire life span of the individual.

In line with this policy of relating the program closely to the churches, the Boy Scout leaders have provided special literature for scouting under Catholic, Jewish, and Protestant auspices. This work has been done in coöperation with the leaders of these faiths.[7]

For Protestant churches there has been developed the Standard Church Troop. This improved program for churches was perfected by a committee of which Dr. Luther A. Weigle was chairman.

The main value in this standard troop program is that there will be a better "carry over" of religious ideals and ideas into the scouting program and a better application of scouting principles to the church contacts. All of this means a more completely integrated personality.

Social-Recreational Activities Under Church Auspices

With more attention given to children and young people and with a larger appreciation for the educational method, churches have come to give more place to play in their programs. In response to the demand of the young people practically all churches provide at least simple social activities. The programs range all the way from the simple activities to elaborate programs of physical, mental and social activities. Gymnasiums and swimming pools are provided, athletic teams are fostered, dramatic clubs are featured, and libraries are furnished.

Purpose of Church Play.—The ultimate goal in all the church's program of religious education is the development of Christ-like character. This does not mean mere faithfulness to the services and activities of the church, but the living of the Christ-life in everyday contacts.

While play is to add to the joy of life, the ultimate purpose of church play is a strengthening of Christian character. This is the only real justification of play under church auspices. It must culminate in good to those touched.

[7] Northern Baptists have developed a correlated program of the Royal Ambassadors and Boy Scouts. A pamphlet describing this plan may be secured from the Department of Missionary Education of the Northern Baptist Convention, 152 Madison Ave., New York City; or from Boy Scouts of America, 2 Park Avenue, New York City.

Contribution to the Church.—The church in this industrial age finds itself greatly handicapped in its character building program. With the complexity of modern life the church's influence on personal morality has been lessened. The church members' week-day tasks and contacts are so far separated from the Sunday activities that it is very difficult for the church's teachings to carry over into workaday relationships.

There is no realm where this lack of carry-over is any more noticeable than in the amusement field. Church members participate in large numbers in all the questionable amusements. This fact greatly handicaps the moral and spiritual development of the individual and the influence of the church. Much of the conflict that hinders the development of well-rounded integrated personalities is the clash of ideal and practice.

Recreational activities, well selected as to content, carefully supervised and properly motivated, will increase the church's influence for good over those touched. The play hunger will be satisfied and members will be won away from questionable amusements. This will make the Christian different and will give greater spiritual power individually and institutionally.

By mixing religion and play, religion will be made a more vital part of life. This will tend to make a religion a more dominant influence in life and will suggest a center for life's integration.

In addition to the more direct personal results play will tend to unify the group participating, build a spirit of friendliness and goodwill in the church and unit organizations, cultivate the democratic spirit, and stimulate group loyalty.

A Feature of the Educational Program.—If play is to be a vital factor in the building of character and is to make a worthy contribution to church life it must not be an attached activity. It must be made a feature of the established educational program. It must be thought of primarily as an educational method rather than as recreation.

This means that most of the leadership for church play will be the leadership of Sunday school and B. Y. P. U. and other established educational agencies. Officers and teachers will receive training along recreational lines as a feature of their preparation. This unity of leadership will mean a better carry-over. It will also contribute to a better direction of teaching and training. The close relationship of the play leader with the participant also gives an increased opportunity for wholesome influence.

Additional Principles.—There are other principles that should be followed in the promotion of church play. These will assure more satisfactory results.

Questionable amusements should be avoided. A good environment will not assure a good product. An incorporation of questionable amusements will hurt the church's influence.

Leadership is more important than equipment. If the right kind of leadership is not available, the activity will not be promoted. Native ability and training should be sought, but especially character.

The church's program should be one of participation. A minimum of attention should be given to spectators. There is little character development without active participation.

Persons and not programs should be the main consideration. The individual will be at the center of the program. Activities will not be promoted for their own sakes, but because of what they will do for individuals.

A balanced program should be promoted. Different types of activities should be provided and all ages should be reached.

The church's program of play should be adequately financed. If it is a part of the educational program and if it is a valuable character building activity, then its financial support by the church is as justifiable as the purchase of literature or equipment for Sunday school or young people's work. If any feature of the program cannot conscientiously be supported by the church, such a feature should not be fostered.

The program of play should be actively promoted. If play under church auspices has a contribution to make to the building of Christian character, then the play program should be actively promoted, just as is true with the Sunday school and other church organizations. Effort should be put forth to enlist the church members in active participation. This will be true because it is realized that the play program will make a worthy contribution to their lives.

An Appraisal of the Church's Program.—Most churches that have put on an extensive program of play have been disappointed in the results attained. This has been largely due to two or three things. Play has been considered primarily as a means of enlistment and enlargement. That should not be its main purpose. Often features have been provided without the proper leadership. Then there has been an attempt to duplicate the activities of the public schools and recreation boards. The church's program to succeed must be distinctive in emphasis, purpose and leadership.

The major emphasis in church recreation should continue to be on the simple social activities. These are more easily supervised, enlist more people, are already tied rather definitely on to the existing organizations. Whatever physical or other activities that may be provided will be secondary to the educational phases of church life.

CHAPTER XXI

RELIGION IN PUBLIC EDUCATION

CHARACTER EDUCATION IN ELEMENTARY AND SECONDARY SCHOOLS

The American Revolution brought into existence a new nation dedicated to liberty and with freedom uppermost in the minds of its leaders. There followed as a natural consequence the separation of church and state. Almost from the first the question as to the control of education constituted a serious problem. In a social order in which church and state are one it is a simple matter to teach religion to the youth, and to develop character in connection with the general educational program. With the separation of church and state and the establishing of state schools, there has been a growing tendency toward the separation of religion and education.

HISTORICAL TREND

Elimination of Religious Material from Texts.—With the separation of religion and education, it came to be regarded as an inevitable necessity to rewrite all texts and materials used in the state schools. The religious and ethical material of books like the New England Primer tended to be supplanted by stories, which, though more interesting and greatly improved pedagogically as texts for teaching reading, often contained little character-forming material. This was not only true of readers, but of all texts used. The old "Blue-back Speller" was a veritable manual of religious and character-building materials; Peter Parley's Geography was also a treatise on religion. Histories never failed to point to the hidden hand of Providence back of all human achievements. These religious and moral materials are not to be found now. The public school has sought to be non-religious, but often becomes irreligious.

Results upon Character.—There has been a growing uncertainty in the realm of religious convictions and ethical standards. Ethics is truly in a chaotic condition. As such it lacks its binding force in this twentieth century, which longs for the strange and the new. All phases of human conduct tend to be left to the thinking and the feelings of the individual as sole arbiter. Ethical anarchy threatens as a result and crime is the inevitable consequence of a state of ethical anarchy. In fact, the underworld threatens to set up its own "rules of honor," and, establishing its own law, to become respectable. Though the whole world is in a state of unrest, America is preeminently so. In all of our big cities, those who would be secure have often been compelled to purchase this security, not so much by the paying of taxes to guarantee for themselves police protection, as by the payment of bribes to leaders of gangs to prevent the attack of their henchmen. Life has actually become cheaper beneath the Stars and Stripes than in any other civilized country on the globe, there being more murders per thousand inhabitants here than in any other civilized country.

Inability of Home and Church to Meet Situation.—During the period just described the American home was undergoing a rather marked transformation. The lad formerly had worked side by side with his father in the field or in the small shop or place of business. With the coming of a rapidly developing industrialized type of life there came to be a tremendous migration from the isolated pioneer farm community and small town to that of the larger town or city. In the tasks of the city the father was no longer able to spend much time with his son. And as women have entered the business world the same transition has often come with the mother. So the home has been handicapped in character-building.

The church has probably never reached with its message of salvation and its challenge to high ideals more than a fourth of the youth of the land. Many of those attending its classes of instruction do so very irregularly. Those that do attend do not get much of the Bible and much of what they do get is not applied to moral problems. Thus it may be seen that the church cannot guarantee character, and that the character-forming ability of the home tends to decrease from year to year.

RECENT AWAKENING

Realizing the need for character education and the limitations of home and church there has been an awakening along this line on the part of the school within the last two decades. Especially has this been true since the World War with the enormous increase in crime that came in its wake. A long period of comparative silence has been broken. Numerous books on character education are rapidly coming from the press. Practically all magazines that enter the field of education are presenting articles on various phases of the subject. Everywhere educational leaders have turned their attention to the development of character.

Emphasis on Character.—In the bulletin, *Cardinal Principles of Secondary Education,* in which the Commission on the Reorganization of Secondary Education appointed by the National Education Association attempted to set forth the main objectives of education, *ethical character* was listed as one of the seven suggested. Bobbitt listed among the ten main aims of education, *religious activity.* One of the concomitants of religious activity was that of character, the assumption being that character was linked up with and vitally related to one's religious life. Charters, in defining the objectives of education, went a step further describing them in terms of *ideals* which are essentially spiritual and foundational in character. Thus he would view practically all education from the angle of character development. One of America's leading educators recently suggested that the one supreme problem of the next decade in education is that of character development.

The fourth objective of education as reported by the Commission on Reorganization of the Department of Superintendence of the National Education Association, meeting in Boston in 1928, was as follows: "To promote the development of an appreciation of the force of law and of love that is operating universally." And as an interpretation and emphasis on this objective, the following statement was adopted:

Man craves more than a knowledge of himself, of nature, and of organized society. He hungers and he thirsts after righteousness. Knowing his own imperfections, he feels that somewhere there is perfection. The great universe calls to his spirit, and unless he ignorantly or wilfully closes his ears, he hears the voice of God. . . . No greater task rests upon the secondary school than to help its pupils to find their God. How this is to be done is the greatest of problems. Of one thing only are we sure: we cannot solve this problem by ignoring it. There is no single way to apprehend Infinity. Each in his own way may draw near.

Demand for Scientific Study.—In view of all that has been said it would seem that a scientific study of how to form character is imperative. Most everywhere educators are interested, but there is a sense of a feeling of helplessness. The great question asked invariably is "how?" It must be admitted that we have a fairly good technique for teaching geography or mathematics but know entirely too little about how to form character. Much of our effort in this direction is wasted because of lack of aim or objective. Little is accomplished in any field without definite aims or goals.

While there is practically a common agreement with reference to some of the objectives or component factors of character, it must be admitted that this agreement is by no means universal.

Such a simple prohibition as "Thou shalt not lie" passed unchallenged yesterday. Under the influence of the relative theory of truth many are disturbed as to what truth is and as to whether it may not be ethical in some situations to falsify. Our conception of morals as *mores* or customs is an equally disturbing factor, especially in an age when it is popular to break with custom. In fact the answer with reference to the right and wrong of many situations would be given in various ways by various individuals. The first essential in character formation and the greatest need of this century is to determine what constitutes good or desirable character. After we have determined objectives we may then proceed to determine method. We tend to reverse the order in education too often. We must always know what we want in the way of an educational product before we can intelligently know how to produce that product.

A SUGGESTED PROGRAM

Thus far we have seen that the public school is considering seriously today its obligation to develop character. More and more it is attempting to work out an adequate program for character development. We think progress is being made in devising plans, but there is much yet to be done. Various methods and plans have been suggested and have been put into practice in various ways. No one plan, and perhaps all of them put together, will solve adequately this supremely important matter, but we thank God for any progress made and will press on in every way possible. In such a brief treatment as this we cannot hope to do more than stress certain main factors, but we venture to offer in conclusion, largely by way of synthesis, some suggestions that we hope will prove to be of practical value. The student should by all means read some of the latest and best books on character education and week-day religious education so as to understand better the needs and problems in this field.

Maintain a Religious Atmosphere.—As has just been suggested, the public school should not ignore religion. As a rule it has not done so. It has tended to remain an institution with a religious bias and a religious atmosphere. Religion can be instilled without sectarianism. The public school chapel is an outstanding example of this. It is a lamentable fact that the religious chapel service is being supplanted today in many instances by the non-religious assembly, which as a pep meeting for developing school spirit may have a place, but should not supplant the religious influence of the chapel program. The non-sectarian religious chapel service should not go. That it should be fairly conducted scarcely needs saying. Those of all religions should be welcomed there. As Max Muller well says, "There is no religion . . . which does not say do good, avoid evil." We even recommend admission of those who profess no religion at all to the chapel program, if they attempt honestly to inspire higher ideals and not to engage in sectarian propaganda.

Utilize the School Subjects.—All literature abounds in materials that inspire to nobler conceptions of living. In the Literature and Life series for high schools one of the main objectives given is that of character. More of character forming literature should be chosen. Literature is being taught in the more progressive schools from the viewpoint of appreciation and with character as a definite goal. Latin literature abounds in biographical sketches of great character building value. However, the usual Latin taught is a barren waste. Especially is this true of Caesar's *Gallic Wars*. The teacher interested in character may prophesy to the valley of mathematical dry bones and make them live. Mathematics may be so taught as to form habits of perseverance and accuracy. If related to life, budgeting and thrift may result. The social studies should not make their greatest contribution on the factual plane, but as means of inspiring attitudes and ideals. Their main goal is coming to be and should be the growth of personality or character. Many other subjects present excellent opportunities for character development.

Use Discipline.—Originally school discipline was maintained with three main objectives in view, *retribution, the good of the school,* and *the good of the pupil.* More and more wideawake educators are realizing that the supreme purpose of school discipline is the good of the individual. In other words the purpose of school control is to develop the individual who can control himself. Herein lies one of the advantages of student government. Whatever the form of government, this conception of discipline should become a universal aim of all school administrators and teachers.

Socialize the Individual.—Since "No man liveth to himself" every individual must be developed into a social being, who is able to live with his fellows and get along with them. But this is not enough. Moral responsibilities is not simply negative. It has a positive element. If progress is to be made, society must develop those personalities who will feel a responsibility for bettering the social order. In anything that approaches an ideal or Christian society there must be developed a keen sense of the brotherhood of man and a feeling that every individual is his brother's keeper. This is coming to be the primary objective of the social studies and of citizenship in its broadened sense as taught today.

Guide Personally.—Provision is being made for character guidance in an ever increasing number of schools. Deans of girls who guide developing womanhood through the dangerous maze of adolescence render an invaluable service and prevent many a shipwrecked life. Counselors of boys perform this same type of service. This type of service is being rapidly increased. In smaller institutions, and in fact in a measure in all schools, this service should be performed by the teacher. It would seem needless to add that this demands a teacher of a higher type than a mere hearer of lessons. It demands a teacher who lives what he teaches. The example of the teacher means much.

Coöperate with Church Schools.—We do not need a regular course with the Bible as a text in the public school. On the other hand, the utmost coöperation should be given the Sunday school, daily vacation Bible school, and week-day religious education program by public school administrators and teachers. Public school teachers should often teach in these schools. In the truest sense the entire religious educational program is outstandingly character forming in purpose, or should be. Any school or educational agency of the Christian religion misses the mark greatly if it fails to establish as a main goal the highest in Christian character. We too often err by contenting ourselves with cramming the head with Biblical facts with no definite purpose in mind. All Biblical facts, all religious teaching should be purposive. Certainly one of the supreme purposes should be the highest in Christian personality or character.

Religious Education in Relation to State Colleges

Beginnings.—It has been truthfully said that higher education in America is the "child of the church," since an overwhelming number of institutions of higher learning actually had their origin at the instigation of the churches. It is an historical fact that the impelling motive for the foundation of Harvard, William and Mary,

Yale, and King's College was the desire to provide religious education in its highest form. Consequently the curriculum of these first institutions showed a predominant emphasis upon Hebrew, Greek, Ethics, Philosophy, and Christian Evidences. Thus we see that America's first colleges, as well as her first grammar schools, were literally schools of religious education.

Secularization.—Schools, founded and fostered by churches, were destined soon to share the stage with an ever increasing number of schools founded and supported by the state. The establishment of the University of North Carolina in 1789 marked the opening of the significant era of state emphasis upon higher education. This does not mean, however, that there came a diminution in the work of the formerly established church schools, for indeed, as late as 1850 there were approximately 6,000 church-supported schools and colleges with an enrollment of more than 250,000 students. The churches continued to be the chief support of higher education until well past the period of the Civil War. Someone recently revealed the interesting discovery that in 1870 the total enrollment of all of the colleges and universities erected by the State was only about 6,000.[1]

Since the Civil War, however, the state supported schools and colleges have sprung up with almost magical profusion, so that today one finds forty-two state universities with an enrollment of approximately 125,000: even a larger number of teachers' colleges, professional schools, colleges for women, and the like. In the state and independent schools of the South today there are more than 127,000 students enrolled. In these centers of learning there has been a not unexpected divergence in curriculum and administrative emphasis from the strict religious emphasis of the early colleges. To these state school centers have gone Protestant students in ever increasing numbers, and today two-thirds of all the university students are members of Protestant churches, or more than are in the institutions which they themselves own and support.

Present Dangers.—President Faunce has pointed out the subtle danger of a policy of non-interest in religious education in the state schools on the part of churches in these words: "The Church may say, 'Education is no longer in our hands.' The State may say, 'On all religious matters we are silent.' Thus millions will grow up— yea, are actually growing up in America today—without any genuine religious training." The result of such a situation usually proves to

[1] "The Church and Its Students at Institutions of Higher Learning," from the *Presbyterian Yearbook*, 1930.

be indifference on the part of the student, which Dr. Alderman, President of the University of Virginia, describes as a stronger influence upon youths in college than skepticism or atheism.[2] There is danger, however, that with a secularized curriculum and with a materialistic emphasis in psychology, biology and elsewhere that worse than indifference will result with the student. Fraught with the keen consciousness of the fact that the state schools hold at least one half the dominant leadership of the nation, as well as of the churches, and that there is resident in the hearts of the great masses of these university students an interest in religion and religious education which cannot be stifled, various forces are now at work within our state schools to provide some form of religious education for the students of these schools.

STATE EFFORTS

On the state school campus of today there is a stronger emphasis upon religious training than there was in the proverbial "good-ole-days." This has come to be true because the administrations of the universities recognize that the absence of instruction in religion in schools which purport themselves to teach all the sciences is incongruous.

Through the Curriculum.—The state schools place their official emphasis on religious education through curricular activities. In a recent survey of eight representative state schools, including universities, women's colleges, teachers' colleges, and technical schools in five different Southern states, it was discovered that four of the eight schools offered Bible or religious education with academic credit. The University of South Carolina employs a regular professor for this work. There were only 281 students from the eight schools with a combined enrollment of 11,513 who were registered in these courses.

In some state schools of our country there are schools of religion and character education, as for example, the Universities of Oklahoma, Iowa, and Virginia. These schools of religion are on a par with the other schools.

In the overwhelming majority of our state schools, however, if there is any teaching of Bible or religious education at all, it is done either through one of the other departments, such as in various teachers' colleges, or by an organization approved by the university administration, such as the Y. M. C. A., local ministers' group, or

[2] Alderman, Dr. E. A., *Relations Between the Church and State Institutions of Higher Training.*

denominational foundation. In some Southern colleges of state control one or more of the local ministers or a denominational representative handle the Biblical instruction, for which university credit is given. In several instances the Y. M. C. A. or Y. W. C. A. secretaries teach the official Bible course for the university or college. In many instances the school authorities approve the teaching of the Bible courses but do not give academic credit. Thus in the matter of curriculum emphasis we find the state schools laying almost a minimum stress.

Through Religious Services.—In times past state schools had regular chapel services and sometimes maintained a chaplain, occasionally such is still found to be true. But for the most part in recent years there has been an almost complete abolition of the compulsory mass chapel services. An estimate based upon the survey of representative colleges indicates that not more than half of the state schools with the compulsory chapel services have more than one such service each week. Some state schools maintain full-time chaplains, while others depend exclusively upon the student pastors or upon the local ministers for chaplain services.

Thus we find that the need for religious instruction is amply met in neither the curriculum nor in the official services of the state school. The need must be met, if at all, therefore, by forces which, though they are not completely independent of the state schools are yet partially or completely supported by funds from without the University. Among these forces are the Y. M. C. A., Y. W. C. A., Bible chairs, denominational student workers, local churches, and a few minor forces. And let it not be thought that the state school administrators are antagonistic to these forces because they are not officially a part of the schools. Virtually all the heads of state schools endorse the student organizations, and well they might since without such organizations the religious education of state schools would be negligible. In looking into the students' religious work of the state schools, therefore, we should be mindful of the fact that they are the forces for religious education within these schools. If we approach the state school campus from this angle, we shall be obliged to place more than a casual mark of importance upon the leadership and work of these student forces.

INTERDENOMINATIONAL ACTIVITIES

For many decades one of the strongest forces at work in behalf of Christianity and religious education on the state school campus has been the Young Men's Christian Association and the Young

Women's Christian Association. Until the comparatively recent advent of the denominational student organizations, these Christian associations stood virtually alone in championing an organized religious program for the state school campus, and the work which these forces have done in creating and strengthening the religious life of college youth deserves more comment than this brief treatise permits. Though the denominational student organizations are meeting a need which the essential interdenominational nature of the Y. M. C. A. cannot meet, there will always be a sphere of great usefulness for the Christian Association on the state school campus.

The first Y. M. C. A. established on an American university campus was organized at the University of Virginia just past the middle of the nineteenth century. The early organizations functioned chiefly on the prayer meeting and student volunteer plan. From the beginning of its American collegiate career the Y. M. C. A. has set itself to tackle the problems of the state school in a sympathetic manner, and the triumphs of this challenging task are numerous. From the early simply organized Y. M. C. A. has proceeded an organization which today embraces many departments of work and which is cared for with superior equipment in well-constructed buildings and which is stabilized with large financial support.

The somewhat startlingly comprehensive program of activity and training directed by the Y. M. C. A. and Y. W. C. A. of the average state school includes practically all of the following activities: Devotional, Courses in Religious Education, Practice in Religious and Social Leadership, Personnel Guidance, Community Service, Church Coöperation, Extension and Deputation Work, Freshman Orientation, World Fellowship, Recreation and Reading Activities, Social Service, Inter-Racial Problems, Human Relations, Evangelism, Vocational Guidance, and General Problems. These activities are directed by members of the Y. M. C. A. cabinet, which is the executive force of the organization. The work is under the general supervision of a student secretary in most instances, there being eighteen such secretaries in state and independent universities in the Southern region now. Two Southwide secretaries conduct a close supervision of the activities of the local groups, while three state student secretaries are at present employed to direct the Y. M. C. A. work on the campuses of colleges in those three states. These state and Southwide secretaries plan excellent summer assemblies, retreats, and the like, in which they give a brief but intensive period of training in religion and Christian leadership to the group of student leaders from a large region. Pre-session retreats, state student gatherings, and weekly cabinet meetings aid the leaders of the Christian Association work in a systematic promotion of their work.

In addition to the Y. M. C. A. and Y. W. C. A. there have been a number of places, particularly in the North and East, where student pastors have been employed jointly by the denominations to look after the religious interest of the students. The Council of Church Boards of education has encouraged this but it has not spread widely.

But there is another phase of religious education which in the very nature of the case cannot be included in the program of the Y. M. C. A. and Y. W. C. A., that is, the training for leadership within the sphere of the student's own denomination. This phase of training, in addition to the deeper spiritual cultivation which naturally comes in a smaller and more unified group, is the distinct privilege of the various denominational student organizations.

DENOMINATIONAL WORK

The survey of eight representative state schools in the South referred to above revealed that approximately 83 per cent of the students in schools surveyed, are members of churches and for the most part members of Protestant churches. It is only logical, therefore, that the Protestant denominations should come to recognize their responsibility in the state school to the extent of promoting a definite program of religious education for the student members of their churches. This recognition was somewhat slow, however, and for decades the various churches left the full field of such endeavor to the interdenominational Y. M. C. A. Of course, churches for each denomination existed at the state school centers, but student programs were largely incidental in the work of such local churches.

The years since 1920 have seen a remarkable change in the situation, and today the chief Protestant churches have well-organized departments of student work, a chief part of whose work is the promotion of a program of religious education for their individual churches on the state school campuses. A brief survey of this will help the reader to understand and appreciate the indispensable impetus given to religious education by this means. Since the Southern Baptist Department of Student Work is one of the most fully developed of the various student forces, we shall consider it as characteristic in this discussion. The Methodist Church through its Wesley Foundation, and the Presbyterian Church through its Department of Christian Education are doing a similar, though not yet as extensive, work for the students of their respective denominations.

A Typical Program.—There are 60,000 Baptist students in Southern colleges other than Baptist-controlled schools.[3] There are approximately 40,000 Baptist students in the schools owned and controlled by Baptists. The Department of Southern Baptist Student Work recognizes its responsibility for the entire group of 100,000 Baptist students but particularly for those enrolled in schools of independent and state control. The work of this department began in 1922 under the supervision of Mr. Frank H. Leavell, who with two assistant secretaries, conducts full supervision of Baptist student work on virtually all state school campuses of the South. The two assistant secretaries stay constantly on the field with a minute program of visitation and advice, while Mr. Leavell directs a full program of correspondence, publicity, instruction, and the like.

The organization through which this department works is known as the Baptist Student Union—popularly, "The B. S. U." It is actually not an independent organization but rather a corporate name for the sum total of all Baptist student activities on a local campus. In this council sits a representative from each of the unit organizations, usually its president. A president and other officers are elected from a mass meeting of all Baptist students of the college. This elected group sits in council meeting once each week to plan the activities for the week ahead. Since representatives from all the unit organizations are participating, there is a perfectly correlated program with no overlapping. The unity of movement thus afforded is indispensable.

Special weeks and days suggested by the Department of Student Work are observed by each of the unit organizations of the campus. Some of these special weeks and days are join-the-church Sunday, sunrise Thanksgiving, student night at Christmas time, student evangelistic week, vocational emphasis week, missionary week, study course week, and similar emphasis on other weeks. This Department sends out detailed suggestions for the observation of these special occasions to the councils on local college campuses, and these councils adjust the official plans to local conditions.

Student Secretaries.—In many instances the work of the local campus is under the direction of skilled student secretaries, who lend a remarkable impetus to the religious life of the campus because

[3] This includes state schools, business colleges, graduate schools, private schools, and schools of other denominations.

of consecrated character and masterful preparation. There are thirty-five full-time Baptist student secretaries now in the South. In many instances a faculty member gives much of his time to the assistance of the student work. At present there are five Southern states with state student secretaries and seven part-time secretaries.

Along with the work of these secretaries should be mentioned the student conventions and conferences for leaders, which help so much to give inspiration and morale. Special retreats are held for leaders such as Montreat, Lake Junaluska, and Ridgecrest, N. C., for Presbyterians, Methodists and Baptists. State conventions and occasionally those for larger areas are held for leaders and other workers rendering invaluable aid to the denominational student work.

Material Equipment.—Since denominational student work in the colleges is comparatively new, the equipment in buildings and supplies is naturally much more limited than that of the Y. M. C. A. Splendid progress has been made, however, and on many state school campuses we find "Workshops," "Cottages," and similar arrangements for the promotion of student work. The support for the work of a local campus comes from the church, the state convention board, and from independent individual contributions.

Along with the equipment for student work there have been steps made to provide dormitories under Christian influences for the benefit of students. Instances of this are at the University of Missouri and the College of Industrial Arts in Texas. This is very important, especially in the light of the poor provisions by state schools and the inability to supervise adequately private boarding places.

Bible Chairs.—Along with student work, and in fact preceding it, has come the Bible chair provided by the denominations at the state centers. This was Jefferson's idea for the University of Virginia in 1822, when he suggested that the denominations "establish each for itself a professorship of their own tenets on the confines of the university—preserving, however, their independence." The Disciples did this as early as 1893 at the University of Michigan; Baptists through the Francis Wayland Foundation, and Methodists through the Wesley Foundation have done the same at a number of schools in the North, and various denominations have done such at the University of Texas, and elsewhere. It is a movement fraught with tremendous possibilities.

Other Forces.—Among the other forces which have helped greatly in the organized student work of the denominations are the local ministers and their churches. The original approach to a campus is made through the local minister and all subsequent work is done with his coöperation and approval. Many ministers have been virtually student secretaries. The local churches have thrown open both doors and hearts to the warm reception and assistance of the college and university students. The religious education program of the local church always includes departments of work for the students. These together with the intensive enlistment and supervision of the denominational student secretaries, student unions, and unit organizations have resulted in the enlistment of an ever-growing percentage of students in the state schools; B. S. U.'s reaching sixty per cent of Baptist constituency against forty-nine per cent enlisted by the Y. M. C. A. in the same field. Such a program will not only mean an immeasurable contribution to individual lives, but it will also bolster the denominational fiber with the strongest leadership it has ever had.

CHAPTER XXII

THE CHRISTIAN COLLEGE

Among the important agencies of religious education stands the denominational college. What its particular function is, how its work is related to the whole on-going program of the Christian movement, and how it is measuring up to its task are some of the questions which are being asked of the denominational school. The best way to begin to seek answers to these important questions is to study the historical development of these schools.

DEVELOPMENT

Early Christian Schools.—The Christian movement, quite early in its history, developed two types of schools. One of these was the *Catechumenal*, the purpose of which was to train or prepare novitiates for church membership. The second type was the *Catechetical*, the function of which was to train for church leadership. Among these early schools were two celebrated missionary training schools, that of Pantaenus, in Egypt, and the other on the island of Iona, on the coast of Scotland. The cathedral and monastic schools of the Middle Ages belonged to this latter type.

Beginning of Denominational Schools.—The denominational school proper is a child of the Reformation. This movement was quick to seize upon education as a means of perpetuating its religious principles. Luther urged the founding and maintenance of Christian schools throughout Germany. Calvinism also included a program of general education in its scheme of religious, political, and social reform. Hence, our Calvinistic forefathers, the Pilgrims, tell that as soon as they had settled safely in New England, "one of the first things we looked for and longed after was to advance learning." Accordingly, Harvard College was founded in 1636, to perpetuate their faith and provide for a trained ministry. The religious motive which led to its founding was back of the founding of every New England college which came into existence before the year 1800. Education in this early period was the servant of the church. The culture of the time was religion-centered and church-dominated.

Growth of Denominational Colleges.—Nine colleges were founded in the colonies during the colonial period. All but one of these were denominational. In the other the Bible was used as a text-book. Fifteen others were founded before the year 1800. Of the first 119 colleges in America, 104 were church-related institutions. Of the 246 in existence in the year 1860, but 17 were state institutions. Approximately 75 per cent of the higher institutions of learning in this country at the present time bear some relation to a denomination. Many of the existing independent institutions owe their origin to some denomination. One may thus get some idea of the strength of the religious motive in establishing and maintaining Christian schools in this country.

Beginning of State Schools.—About the middle of the eighteenth century, the theory began to be advanced by French thinkers that education was essentially a civil affair to promote the interests of society and the welfare of the state, rather than the interests and welfare of the church. These views had considerable influence in this country, where practical tendencies and the rise of the new national spirit were already leading many to feel that education should answer the needs of all the people rather than of groups or factions within the state. They thought that the kind of education given in the schools must ultimately influence the welfare of the state itself, and that it cannot, therefore, be regarded as a private matter.

One of the results of this feeling was the attempt to take over some of the denominational colleges and make of them state universities. King's College was taken over and the name changed to Columbia. Two other institutions were also taken over. The alumni of Dartmouth College, led by Daniel Webster, fought the matter through the courts, finally winning the decision in their favor from the Supreme Court of the United States. This decision saved the day for independent educational institutions and committed the country to a dual system of education—state and independent, or public and private. It also had the effect of stimulating the building of state universities, the University of Virginia being founded in the very year of the Dartmouth decision.

Founding of Baptist Colleges.—A wave of French infidelity swept over this country in the latter part of the eighteenth and the first of the nineteenth centuries. It brought religion to a low ebb and produced a lull in the founding of denominational colleges. After 1820 this activity was renewed. Among Baptists this was largely due to the influence of Luther Rice, who toured the country in the interests of the new Baptist Mission in Burma, where Adoniram Judson had begun his great work. Seeing, in his travels up and down the country, the educational destitution of the Baptist ministry, Rice became active for education as well as missions. At the first General Convention of Baptists ever held in America, afterwards called the First Triennial Convention, called to organize coöperative support of the new missionary enterprise, Richard Furman, of South Carolina, who had been elected president of the body, after the business of the meeting had been transacted, made an address in favor of education. He outlined a plan for a system of Baptist higher education which included a national university to be located in Washington which was to be fed by colleges founded in the various States. The state Baptist schools were slow in getting started, due partly to the fact that the institution which was founded in Washington absorbed all the funds that could be raised for higher education.

The Triennial Convention severed its connection with Columbian College in Washington in 1826. From that time begins the fruitful era in the founding of Baptist colleges. In 1800 there had been but one Baptist college in the entire country. By the end of the century there were 200 Baptist colleges. The number of students in these institutions increased during this period from 92 to 40,000. Endowments grew from $50,000 to about $44,000,000.

Other Denominational Schools.—Other denominations also became active in the founding of schools in this period. It is said that during the two decades from 1830 to 1850 more colleges were organized than had been established in the entire two hundred years previous, and that the rate of founding new colleges continued high up to the end of the century. By far the larger number of these institutions were denominational and looked upon their functions as largely religious.

The Effect of the Secularizing Tendency.—In the meantime many influences were combining to secularize state institutions of higher learning, particularly those in the East, causing them to eliminate religion entirely from their plans and activities. Religion was associated in the thought of the time with sectarianism, and therefore, could not be allowed where all faiths had to be educated together.

This tendency in state institutions caused many who were interested in higher education to fear grave dangers from a completely secularized culture and thus increased the zeal for the founding of denominational schools. Practically no settled policy was followed by many of the denominations in the founding of these institutions; hence a needless multiplicity of colleges resulted, many of them perishing within a few years for lack of adequate support and many others surviving only to eke out a precarious existence. This lack of system in the founding and locating of denominational schools has furnished one of the greatest impediments to denominational education. Great sums of money have been expended in starting new educational enterprises, doomed to failure from their inception. It would have been better if it had been spent in adequately strengthening existing institutions. As a result we have many small, weak, struggling schools, and but few strong ones.

This confusion and lack of wise policy of early years has latterly given way to greater prudence. Most of the denominations now have education boards to which are committed the policies and programs of the denomination in the educational field. There is now, also, an organization which undertakes the correlation of the policies of all the church boards.

Problems of the Denominational College.—Granted that Christian schools are still necessary, as most Christian leaders believe and the discussion further on seeks to show, they face yet other grave problems as to whether they can continue their existence. Many of them are finding it increasingly difficult to meet the *standards* which are set for them largely by the state universities. But to fail to attain and maintain standard rating means eventual elimination from the field of higher education.

One of the effects of the World War was to focus critical attention upon the colleges. A great many felt that there was something vastly wrong with education that the so-called enlightened nations of the world should be engaged in the ghastliest war of history. Sporadic complaints had been heard before of the influence of the colleges upon the faith and morals of students. During the war, with the common revulsion to everything German, it was held up to the people that German *rationalism* was rampant in the colleges. Immediately many became alarmed. A veritable wave of popular suspicion, directed against the colleges, swept over the country. Peculiarly, the denominational colleges suffered more from this than state institutions. Little to justify criticism was found in most of the denominational colleges, but great damage was done them in the loss of the confidence and support of large numbers of their constituency.

Some Tendencies Noted.—Competition with state institutions, criticism, and the demands of the church itself have produced some results with respect to these schools which are eminently worthwhile. There was a time when some of them sought salvation in imitating the state universities. This *secularizing* tendency among denominational colleges was quite strong not so very long ago. The influence of the Carnegie Foundation for the Advancement of Teaching helped in this direction.

There has been, more recently, a notable tendency in the *contrary* direction. This movement has been helped by such organizations as the Council of Church Boards of Education and other agencies within the denominations themselves. As a result the denominational colleges have been taking stock of themselves more closely. One effect of the secularizing tendency was to raise the jolting taunt—"Why have denominational schools paralleling state institutions, if there is to be no difference between them?" This question, and others, forced the attention of the colleges in upon themselves. Had they a distinctive mission in the field of higher education? Can there be a Christian type of education which meets the highest academic standards and at the same time answers the deepest needs of the Christian movement? If this is possible, then what are the essential characteristics of this distinctly Christian type of education?

DIFFERENTIATION

What makes a school Christian? A few years ago this question was put by the editor of *Christian Education* to a number of prominent men, including the secretaries of the various church boards of education. Their replies were quite interesting. These men said that what makes a school Christian is not the mere fact that it was founded by Christian people for Christian purposes; nor the mere fact of its attachment or relation to an ecclesiastical organization; nor any label; nor the theological position of the faculty; nor the fact that the Bible is read and prayer offered at the opening of the session each day; nor even the fact that the faculty are professing Christians. Some, or even all of these characteristics, may be true of an institution, but they do not in themselves make it a Christian school. Then what are the traits of a Christian school? Gleaning from their replies we note the following points. The Christian schools have:

A Christian objective, aim, purpose.
A Christian faculty and Christian teaching.
A Christian viewpoint.
A Christian spirit, atmosphere, life.
A Christian program.
A Christian product.

Whatever one thinks about some of the points made by these men, surely he would agree that a college, if it is really Christian, will itself have several of them.

A Christian Objective.—Some, perhaps, will say at once that the denominational school has always had a Christian objective. Nevertheless, there are those who ask, "Is it any different in its real objectives from many other schools which make no such lofty pretensions?" It must not rely upon the purpose of its founders, or upon its connections, or upon its label to be counted Christian. For what goals is it striving? The answer to this question will determine whether it is really Christian or not. If it does not itself have a clear-cut Christian purpose, it has no right to claim to be a Christian school. It must so relate itself to the whole program of the Christian movement that it fulfills a distinctively Christian mission.

Christian Teachers and Christian Teaching.—Another differentiation with respect to the Christian college is that it has Christian teachers and Christian teaching. Without a Christian faculty, it cannot be Christian. It cannot have a Christian atmosphere or spirit unless the lives of the teachers radiate it. Dr. Henry van Dyke, answering the question, "What makes a school Christian?" says, "Undoubtedly, it is the spirit of the teachers working with the scholars and helping them in all ways to think and feel and act according to Christ."[1]

The Christian teacher is the crucial factor in the process of Christian education. There are other factors, to be sure, but the teacher is the prime factor. It is more important to have Christian teachers than Christian textbooks, or Christian trustees. Students largely absorb the views and acquire the outlooks on life of their teachers. They unconsciously imitate them, especially if the teacher is a combination of splendid character and attractive personality. This is perfectly natural. It must have been partly in this way that Jesus incarnated himself in his disciples so that they became Christmen. Even Paul, after long spiritual fellowship with the risen Lord, could say, "It is no longer I that live, but Christ liveth in me." There is no contagion like that of a great personality.

Teachers and teaching must be Christian in the Christian school. This does not mean that theology is to be taught in every classroom, nor does it mean that there is such a thing as Christian chemistry or physics. There is, however, as one writer puts it, "a vast difference between a course in science under a professor who is able to think

[1] *Christian Education,* November, 1925, p. 26.

God's thoughts after Him, and a course in science under an atheist who has said in his heart that there is no God."[2]

Christian Worship.—Another differentiating characteristic of the Christian school is to be found in its chapel service. Vital Christian worship will be a part of the program of the Christian college.

Investigations made in recent years reveal that, in some quarters at least, college chapel is not what it once was. In some institutions it has lost all religious significance and is nothing more than a student assembly. In other schools, where the religious form is still retained, it does not function as an important factor in college life.

Some of the reasons given for this state of affairs are:

(1) Students object to compulsory religion.
(2) Chapel is not an expression of campus religion.
(3) Chapel is too much like church.
(4) Chapel talks are too often poorly prepared, and, therefore, are of little interest or value.
(5) The whole chapel service is so much boredom.

It would probably not be difficult to find students in most colleges who object to chapel. The remedy lies not in giving up the worship period, or in modifying or eliminating its distinctly religious character, but in making it more vital. If there are any points at which the Christian college differs from secular institutions, one of these ought to be its chapel.

The Christian school will use its chapel as a means of bearing *witness* to its claim and aspiration to be a Christian institution. In their service, it will be proclaiming its own faith and its own conception of what is highest and best. Furthermore, it will be seeking to impress its conceptions of the highest values upon its students in order that they may have a constant enrichment of their religious experience.

The Christian college will use its chapel as a means of *worship*. Dr. Robert E. Speer says of the Christian school, "The institution will meet regularly for worship and prayer."

As to the content of the service, there is considerable difference in various schools. In some, there is Bible reading, one or two songs, and prayer. The service lasts only fifteen or twenty minutes. No announcements are made and no itinerant speakers are allowed. In other schools, in addition to the above, the president or some designated member of the faculty makes a short talk on some religious topic. Some colleges arrange a yearly schedule of addresses by out-

[2] *Ibid.*, p. 31.

standing speakers. These addresses may not necessarily be on distinctly religious subjects, but on vital problems with Christian interpretations and applications. The idea is to present religion to the students as it comes to grips with the practical problems of life in order that they may thus learn to appreciate Christian values and see the Christian way more clearly.

The Christian college will also use its chapel as a means of promoting student *morale*. One of the reasons why chapel is retained in colleges where it has lost its religious significance is for promoting unity and morale. A recent writer claims that a religious program is better for this than a non-religious one.

Christian Activity.—In addition to the Christian objectives and atmosphere provided by the Christian college, there are a number of activities that are very definitely Christian. One of these is the student organization called in Southern Baptist schools the *Baptist Student Union*. It seeks to correlate and foster all phases of Christian life on the campus.

As integral parts of this general organization we have the *unit organizations* for the different groups of religious workers. One is the ministerial group, made up of the prospective or actual ministers with stated meetings for mutual counsel and inspiration. Another is the volunteer band, composed of those who are volunteers for home or foreign missions. Often there is a special workers' group for those planning for religious education, gospel music and other church work. Sometimes there is an organization for lay workers.

Along with these general and departmental organizations there are several very definite *service activities*. One of these is the annual revival meeting, which is a distinctive characteristic of the Christian college. In it most of the unconverted are won, indifferent ones reconsecrate their lives, and others surrender for Christian work. Along with this is the enlistment through the year of the students in the different phases of church work such as Sunday school classes, young people's activities, mission study groups and the like. Frequently a daily or weekly prayer meeting is carried on by the students. And a great deal of extension work is done at jails, homes for the poor, and other needy places.

SPECIFIC FUNCTIONS

"The Christian college is essentially an instrument of the Christian movement." It is its business to prepare young men and women to function effectively in this movement both in churches and in community life.

Training Christian Leaders.—There is desperate need today in every field of human activity for leaders whose outlooks, ideals, and purposes are emphatically Christian. But leadership of all kinds falls largely into the hands of the college trained men and women. This tendency will doubtless increase as the general level of culture continues to rise. Therefore, if Christianity is to have a voice that will be heard, an influence that will be felt in community, state, national, and international affairs, it must get it by supplying to all these important areas of human activity leaders of outstanding ability whose lives are actively motivated by Christian ideals.

Herein lies the work of the Christian college—to equip and send out young men and women who will become great Christian homemakers, Christian teachers, Christian club-workers, Christian doctors and lawyers, Christian public officials, and Christian leaders in the political, commercial, industrial, and occupational spheres. In this way the Christian dynamic will interpenetrate and become effective throughout the entire social order. The college which helps to this end is sharing definitely with the church in the movement for the coming of Christ's kingdom "on earth as it is in heaven."

Training Lay Leaders for the Christian Movement.—There are increasing opportunities today for those who wish to take up some form of religious work, other than the ministry, as a *vocation*. There is need for specialists in religious education who are equipped to teach in college, or to direct this work in the denomination or in the local church. Field workers, church secretaries and musicians are needed. Leaders are needed for camp work and other semi-religious movements. Vocational opportunities of a religious character are increasing and offer splendid fields of service to college men and women.

There is need for a far larger number of well-equipped *avocational workers* in the local churches. There are many minor places for religious leadership in the churches. They are minor, however, not in the sense of being unimportant. If they are filled with persons who lack needed training, the bad effects will show in the work of the entire church. The Sunday school boards of the various denominations have done a notable work in improving the quality of the Sunday school personnel. Local churches also undertake to train some of their leaders. The denominational colleges are equipped to render the churches valuable service at this point, by supplying them with trained leaders for all phases of their work.

Training Leaders of Christian Thought.—Since the various denominations in many cases cannot maintain more than one strong college each in any state and consequently the vast majority of our young people and future leaders must get their education in state or independent schools, the question often arises, why try to train any in such schools? Why not provide Bible chairs at state schools and free the denominations from the expense of keeping up colleges? Besides the facts already given there is another argument seemingly invincible.

In addition to filling the places mentioned there is the necessity of having a group of thinkers in our midst who will be recognized as specialists in their fields and be able to lead the thinking in their lines. In other words there is the necessity of having leaders of thought who can leaven the educational lump. Unless that is true the time will come when we will be at the mercy of a secularized educational system that will lead us in the direction of Germany. There is no way of estimating the influence of Christian thinkers in the fields of Bible, psychology, sociology, the physical sciences, and elsewhere. This is perhaps the Christian college's most indispensable sphere.

Training Ministerial and Missionary Workers.—Christian colleges were established originally for the primary purpose of training men for the ministry. In the colonial period, and for a long time thereafter, there was a shortage of ministers and especially of trained ministers. This was due to the fact that, with the rapid growth of population and its spread southward and westward, churches came into existence so rapidly that the demand for ministers far exceeded the supply and many men came into the ministry with little or no education.

The Charleston Baptist Association, the General Baptist Association of Virginia, and some others before there were colleges in their sections, developed plans for assisting worthy young men of limited means to prepare themselves for the ministry. They were to study in the homes of older pastors, under their guidance, using their books, while supported by funds raised by these associations. But such plans were unsatisfactory; so attention was turned toward the founding of colleges to train the ministers that were needed so badly. In this way they had the example of New England. Harvard had been founded primarily to train ministers, as the founders said, "dreading to leave an illiterate ministry to the churches when our present ministers shall lie in the dust." Yale and most of the early colleges were founded for the same purpose.

It is the distinctive function of the denominational college to help prepare young men for the kind of pastoral leadership which is required of them today. It shares this responsibility with the theological seminary and the graduate school. The college furnishes the broad cultural foundations while the other-named institutions furnish the needed specialization. The colleges also offer pre-theological courses in Bible, religion or Christianity, and religious education. The ministerial student will need some of these courses, but, if the college is truly Christian, the cumulative effect of the entire liberal arts course will be such as to give him valuable religious training and experience. Working through the fields of history, literature, philosophy, sociology, psychology and the natural sciences with teachers of deep religious convictions, he will be getting Christian points of view and Christian interpretations and evaluations in all the broad areas of human experience. In this way, he will come to know more of what Christianity really means than if he had a few courses in religion without this broader Christian education. He needs both, as a matter of fact, for the most important phase of the whole educational process comes when the student seeks to synthesize or integrate all of his particular learnings so as to get a true idea of the whole.

OUTLOOK AND NEEDS

What of the future of the denominational college? Is the denominational school passing? Will it be ground to pieces, as one writer puts it, between the "upper and nether millstones" of the public high schools and junior colleges, on the one hand, and the state universities, on the other? The denominational academy passed, practically, from the field of secondary education because of the development of the public high school. Will not the church college go the same way?

There are prophets who are and have been for some time predicting this very thing. About thirty years ago, the most outstanding educator in this country predicted that in twenty-five years seventy-five per cent of the small colleges would either have ceased to exist or would be transformed into other types of institutions. Since most of the small colleges were denominational institutions, it was a dire prophecy for them. At that time seventy-five per cent of the institutions reporting to the United States Bureau of Education from the South had less than one hundred and fifty students. Of course, we know that this prophecy missed the mark. There are a third more colleges today than there were in 1900, six times as many college students, and five dollars in college endowment now to one in 1900.

True, as Dr. Robert Kelly recently pointed out, some colleges have ceased to exist, but so have some churches, and some towns, and some banks and business houses. Many denominational colleges have, in the past century, passed out of existence because they were unwisely founded. Some now are merging with others and thus losing their separate existence. But all of this does not signify the passing of denominational colleges.

Values in Denominational Colleges.—President Edward Everett Rall offers the following reasons why the church-related colleges should be continued and not allowed to pass:[3]

(1) One-half or more of the college youth of the land are attending these institutions. The states are finding it difficult to find means to educate the other half. If there is to be higher education for a large number of our youth, the church must provide it.

(2) The church must maintain these schools if it is itself to survive, since they furnish about eight out of ten of the preachers.

(3) The church-related college can accomplish what no other type of higher educational institution can accomplish in respect to the teaching of religion.

(4) The church-related college can give a Christian interpretation in all departments, and thus help, as no other agency except the church itself, to make and keep our civilization Christian.

(5) The church-related college safeguards the Christian character and faith of its youth by placing the primary emphasis on these things.

(6) The church-related college is primarily a college of liberal arts, and it is to these institutions, more than to any other source, that we must look for the preservation of our precious heritage of Christian culture and all the finer and nobler things of life, and for preventing the over-emphasis of the material and economic aspects of education.

On the basis of these values, the statement of which has been much condensed here, he thinks the church-related college ought to survive. Whether it will survive is another question.

Present Needs.—One thing is certain. If these colleges are to survive, we must take care of them now. What are their needs? Upon what factors does their survival depend?

(1) Adequate *support*, financial and otherwise. Colleges cannot run without money, and few, if any, of these colleges have enough money to meet their bare necessities. Many of them are in a critical condition, financially. They must have more adequate support, if they are to survive.

[3] *Ibid.*, March, 1931, pp. 663-667

(2) A Christian educational *conscience* on the part of the church people.

(3) Wise educational *policies* on the part of denominations and their education boards.

(4) *Coöperation* among all the friends of Christian education.

(5) *Loyalty* to Christ on the part of the denominational colleges themselves.

This last point we would emphasize. Certainly the future of the denominational colleges depends upon it. If they become secularized, they are doomed. State institutions will supplant them. They must be true to their Christian mission if they would survive. "Upon this rock I will build my church, and the gates of Hades shall not prevail against it," Jesus said. That rock, we think, was confession of faith and loyalty to Christ. Our nation is built upon the belief that the best kind of government is a government "of the people, by the people, and for the people." Destroy that faith and our government will perish as a democracy. So the church-related college, as also the church, rests upon a faith. In that lies its security. Destroy that faith and it will perish. Of course, the large independent institutions will probably live. No college, according to a recent authority, that had a million dollars' endowment has ever died. But most schools do not have that much endowment. Furthermore, with the increasing financial demands which are falling upon the colleges, even those with a million or more endowment will probably find it hard to continue to function in the future in the face of advancing educational standards unless it has great resources in the shape of popular support. The greatest of all loyalties is Christian loyalty. We believe that it will outlast every other loyalty. Therefore, in loyalty to Christ lies the hope of the future of the church-related college. Since this is true every Christian college should put at the heart of all of its activities the splendid motto of MacMaster University, "In Him all things consist."

CHAPTER XXIII

RELIGIOUS LITERATURE

Influence.—The power of the printed page over the minds and actions of people is immense, and it was never greater than today. Books, papers, and magazines by the millions are being published every year, and these various publications are shaping the thoughts and actions of individuals and nations.

A large percentage of these books and papers are not of the highest type; in fact, many of them do more harm than good. We need to do all we can to save our people from the cheap and harmful types of books and papers, and at the same time we should try especially to encourage them in the reading and study of the very best literature to be found in the land. This applies especially to the importance of getting the best types of religious literature in the hands of our people. The volume of religious literature is immense, and this type of literature is of great value in giving religious information and guidance to our people.

Function.—The printed page has become one of our primary means for the communication of religious knowledge, and for the promotion of religion in almost every direction. The religious press has become one of the most important phases of religious education. This has not been true always. In the early Christian centuries, the church's chief medium of communication, both within its own circle and between itself and the world, was the spoken word. There was writing, of course; a great deal of it. But the oral word was the principal means of instruction, exhortation, and the propagation of the faith. Only a few people read; the multitudes heard public discourse. Even the Scriptures were learned in the main through hearing them read and discussed orally. Hence the importance of preaching and the public services of the church. Winfred Ernest Garrison says, "The practice of spoken discourse for the promotion of religion has neither ceased nor diminished. But with the introduction of printing, with the increase of literacy and of the habit of reading as well as the ability to read, and with the rise of journalism to the place of

304

primacy as the means of disseminating intelligence upon all kinds of subjects, the press has brought powerful reinforcement to the pulpit as an agency for the communication of religious knowledge."[1]

GENERAL VIEW OF RELIGIOUS PRESS

The réligious press is a mighty factor in the cause of religious or Christian education in particular. We look to this source for our curriculum materials, and a large percentage of all that is involved in study and teaching. No statistics are available to indicate just where in the billions the output of pages will stop. From gigantic presses of great publishing houses which operate day and night to the small machines of local shops there flow the constant "black and white" streams of Christian truth.

Kinds.—There are three kinds of "religious press," viz. denominational, interdenominational and non-denominational. These are largely supplemented by general commercial publishers whose fractional religious output is very considerable. Not all so-called religious publications are educational in the best sense, nor would we label general educational publications irreligious. We use religious press in a technical sense. For our purposes in this chapter we confine our consideration to publications in any form which set forward the religious education enterprise.

Products.—Rather loosely we may classify the products of the religious press as follows: church school or Sunday school periodicals, books, publications for young people's societies and related groups, denominational weekly journals, general religious journals and magazines, professional ministerial magazines, professional religious education journals, missionary and service magazines, publications of Christian colleges, seminaries, and training schools, religious bulletins, pamphlets, leaflets, tracts. In addition a very large page-output is in the space of thousands of daily and weekly newspapers, given over to religious matters. In the above classification there is some overlapping. This would be true of any grouping of the products of the religious press.

Measured by the total number of pages the Sunday school periodicals issued by the several denominational and other publishing houses far outdistance the entire output of all other kinds of religious publications. The total page-output in one single year for any one of half a dozen large denominations would run into the billions. The

[1] Bower, W. C., Editor, *The Church at Work in the Modern World*, pp. 236-237, University of Chicago Press, Chicago, 1935.

entire production of Sunday school periodicals is enormous. The vastness of the contribution may be partially realized, at least when it is known that one single periodical may have a million readers a week.

There would be no particular advantage in comparing religious and educational values in the several types of publications. Each apparently fills a need. Each makes its own valuable impact upon the religious thinking of its constituency. Each, let us hope, is true to the spirit and idealism in Christ.

Nine hundred and ninety-nine out of a thousand Christians have very little to do with the actual making of these press-products, certainly with their educational content. However, even if ten out of every thousand church members, able and aggressive, set themselves resolutely to make regnant the printed pages of religious education publications, the teaching ministry of the church would make triumphant the kingdom of Christ in a single generation.

Religious Journalism

Brief History.—Journalism, religious and secular, has had a remarkable development in America since the Revolutionary War. Perhaps the first newspaper in the American colonies was the *Boston News-Letter*, founded in 1704. But it is estimated that there were about two hundred newspapers in the United States by 1800, and one thousand by 1830. Religious liberty and freedom of the press have been two cardinal principles in this country; and consequently we have had a multiplicity of denominations, and these denominations almost from the beginning have made use of journalism for the promotion of their various doctrines and programs. It is said that perhaps the first religious journal in America was started after 1800. These papers were promoted as a part of early missionary work, and for the dissemination of religious knowledge and for the promotion of various sects and movements. The influence of these various papers has been immense during the last century and a half.

Present Situation.—It is said that it is more difficult to maintain denominational papers today than in former years, but still there are many of these religious papers, and they have immense influence in spreading Christian truth and promoting various denominational programs. There has been a tendency toward consolidation of many papers, and in the direction of the inter- or nondenominational paper like *The Christian Century*, published in Chicago. However, there are still many denominational papers, especially in the South. Southern Baptists, for instance, maintain a denominational paper in practically every state in its territory. Most of these papers are prospering, and are making a rather vigorous contribution toward the promotion of the various causes of the denomination. However, they have a tendency to become merely theological and professional in emphasis and are read mainly by the preachers.

Needed Improvements.—For the last year or two (1937-38) there has been a special committee appointed by the Southern Baptist Convention to make a study of the various state papers and make recommendations for improvements. Among the suggestions made were that the papers give more space to laymen and their work; that the papers have a more attractive make-up, and that the material in them be of such a nature as to appeal to the whole family circle. Articles should be briefer, of more vital human interest, and with more light and inspiration for the average member of the family circle. There should be a south-wide news agency, the editors should follow the best newspaper technique in making up the paper, and the paper should be put in the local church budget and sent to the homes of the people; for, "to double the subscriptions to all our papers would mean to double all our work."

Religion and the Secular Press

Most important daily papers have "religious editors," who are often ministers or retired ministers. The amount of religious news which they publish, in the aggregate, is very large; and, considering their immense circulation, the value of the publicity which they give to religious ideas and enterprises is inestimable. We should appreciate the services rendered, and do what we can to learn how to coöperate with the newspapers for the mutual advantage of all concerned. It is unfortunate that much which passes for religious news is mere sensationalism and gives a distorted view of true religion. We need to help furnish legitimate news to the papers, and also to educate our people so that they can discriminate between sensational rubbish and important religious news and movements. We should furnish interesting and important religious news to the newspapers in attractive form, prepared so that it will require but little editing or rewriting; and we should avoid mere propoganda under the guise of furnishing news. Usually newspaper men will gladly coöperate with sincere people who are honestly trying to do the right thing.

CHURCH PAPERS, TRACTS

Church Papers.—It is well at this point to make special mention of the matter of church papers, for in recent years there has been quite a trend in the direction of local church papers or bulletins as means for educational activities and publicity purposes. Apparently this development is on the increase and will so continue at least for a while.

There are at least two *types* of them. One is confined almost entirely to the local church, stressing the order of services or the organizations or both. In such cases it is almost entirely local in coloring. The other deals very little or not at all with the above but contains quite a bit of the editor's views and general denominational and other matters and becomes a medium for more general information.

There are three *ways of fostering them*. One is for the church to publish them or have it done. Sometimes the mimeograph or multigraph is used for this purpose. Another plan is to buy forms already largely printed and finish them, or a small space in a general church paper such as the *All Church Press*. The third is for the state denominational paper to furnish an extra cover page, devoted to the local church, and usually have the subscription provided through the church budget.

These local papers have tremendous educational value. More significant still, however, are the state, national or sectional papers, which can go much further not only in creating religious ideals but also in interpreting current events from a moral standpoint.

Religious Tracts.—Various religious tracts are published by denominational boards, by Christian schools and organizations of various kinds, and by independent religious groups. These tracts deal with denominational programs and work; with doctrines and beliefs, with the message and methods of evangelism, and so forth. Religious tracts have been widely used for the purposes of religious propaganda of almost all kinds. Pastors, directors of religious education, and Christian workers generally should keep informed as to how and where good tracts can be secured, and should study how to make the best use of them. They should not be distributed wholesale. This would be but to cheapen the matter and would result in great waste. Giving out tracts to individuals, with an oral or written suggestion as to use, will be found most effective, and this after careful and prayerful study of the real needs of the individual. Some special individual in the church might be elected or appointed to supervise the use of tracts in the work of the church, and working with him would be those workers responsible for the distribution of the curriculum material in the various organizations and departments.

CHURCH PUBLICITY

Between the religious groups that do not have so much as a "name board" on their church buildings and those who sensationally keep before the public eye, are the church people who make known their church, its minister, the regular and special activities of the church and the whole round of religious education by legitimate, common-sense methods of publicity.

The Problem.—Do we believe that Christian truth should permeate all life, reaching down and out into every area of human experience? And if so, do we believe it is the educational duty of the church to make this truth known in all possible, desirable ways? Should the church organize through a director of publicity to make known the business of the church as the divine enterprise? If so, who should such a director be? What should be his duties and how can he best function in honoring the church and setting forward the Kingdom of Christ?

The Director.—The ideal director of religious education publicity for a church may not be found but certainly some of the qualifications mentioned below are essential if he would make good. The reader can make his own sequence.

He should be one who knows and loves the truth, who recognizes his duty and privilege to propagate that truth, and one who is continually on the alert for new truth which should be made known.

He should be punctual, scrupulous in keeping promises, discriminating, cautious, tactful, correct in speech, devoted in spirit, courteous in manner, a good mixer, poised, genial, original, sane, unselfish in his motives, sincere, impartial, dependable, reverent, one whose character is unimpeachable, who puts his work to one final test, viz.: will this piece of publicity honor Christ?

The Duties.—The following will probably suggest some of the duties of the director of publicity in the ordinary churches and communities:

It is well for him to have a desk in the church making it convenient for him to gather material which should be given publicity. He should by proper means keep in touch with the movements of the board of religious education in the church, helping to further its projects. He should put himself in a position to give such publicity as will further the plans of the pastor, recognizing the pastor as the head of the church in all such matters. He should keep in touch with the director of reading or religious education, giving his full coöperation in that work.

He should be familiar with publications of the Sunday school or other denominational boards, basing all publicity on certified facts; he should know his own denominational journals and continually boost the same; he should also know the interdenominational periodicals and be able intelligently to give publicity concerning same.

During religious education week, usually observed toward the end of September, in coöperation with other such leaders in the community, he may give special publicity in the local papers and otherwise. In communities largely Protestant it will be well for him to seek opportunity to make brief, pointed announcements concerning such work in clubs and other such gatherings. He is the logical person through whom community matters in religious education should be introduced to his church; and he will be on the alert to contact all persons and institutions in his community where religious education publicity values may be found. He should contact local parent-teacher associations with religious education materials having special value in character education in the school and home.

He will seek to assist the pastor and director of reading in posting lists of new books and other material of value available. He will be on the lookout for ways and means of making his publicity fruitful, suggesting mechanical devices such as duplicating and mailing machines, etc., for office use in the church. He will perhaps lead in having on the outside of the church building attractive, substantial service boards, supplying same with items for day and night presentation. He will make use of the young people in the preparation of posters for publicity purposes, stimulating their interest in such work through contests and so forth.

He should prepare terse, timely religious education items for the church weekly calendar or bulletin; occasionally for the local newspapers he should prepare human interest stories, reports of religious education conventions, local, state or national, especially when "home-town" people participate. He may also maintain a regular paid-for space in the local daily and weekly newspapers.

RELIGIOUS BOOKS

Statistics compiled annually by the *Publishers' Weekly*, showing the number of books in each general field published during the preceding year, reveal a surprising number of titles classified under religion. As would be expected, fiction is always the most numerous class, but religion generally comes either second or third. The number of books actually read would perhaps not show as large a rating as the above figures might suggest, nevertheless religious books are published and read in great numbers. Besides many books not listed as religious actually carry a helpful religious emphasis or message.

Nearly all the leading publishers have religious book departments, and denominational publishing houses send out an immense volume of religious books. Every church should have a library, and a good librarian to supervise the distribution of books. Also there is an important place for guiding the people in the finding and selection of good books for purchase for the home and in borrowing from public libraries. There is no greater service which can be rendered to our people, and especially to our young people, than to help get into their hands good books on all kinds of subjects.

Church or Sunday School Libraries

Former Kinds.—The old-fashioned Sunday school library of goody-goody books for dear little boys and girls has gone, or should go. Instead today we have libraries made up of the most up-to-date books and of the choicest literary quality, as well as books dealing with all phases of religious living and service both of a practical and inspirational nature. Our books should be of the highest literary quality, of compelling human interest, and dealing with the various interests and needs involved in moral and spiritual living. This calls for a wide variety in the selection of the books.

Present-day Scope.—*Leadership training.* Books for the training of Sunday school officers and teachers, church officers, leaders in young people's societies, in men's and women's church organizations, this is the kind of a library which any church should have, even if it must start with only a few books. Ordinarily they will not be found in a public library. Dr. W. E. Raffety says that he was once president of a community board of religious education which secured the use of an alcove in the local public library and put in it a most excellent collection of about a hundred of the best books for Sunday school leaders. Lists were prepared carefully and divided among the churches. Unitedly the entire cost was thus cared for. The books were made available to all officers and teachers of all the churches in the little city of about fifteen thousand population. In such a library will be books on psychology, principles and method in teaching religion, evangelism, music, worship, missions, recreation and social service, content courses in Bible study and doctrines, and all aspects of the modern program of religious education.

Parent Training.—Any church might well establish a small but very valuable library of books for the training of younger parents. Fortunately now most helpful books in this field are available. One church has about a dozen of the best of these neatly boxed, and circulates this library for a month at a time in the homes of young married folks in the church. These may cover many phases of child life and training but particularly those which relate to morals and religion. There is a tremendous need here if the home is to be the ally of the church that it should be.

Personal Culture.—In addition to the books useful in leadership and parent training there are many that are valuable in enriching the lives of the members of the church personally. Among these are the ones that deal with personal soul-winning, the devotional life, missionary lands, and achievements, church history and doctrines, and present-day social and moral problems. Religious fiction also has a certain place.

General Reading.—There are rural communities not readily accessible to a public library and even sections of cities not any too convenient, where good wholesome literature of a general nature may be valuable. Some churches have found it helpful to have on hand some of the best books used as parallel reading in the public schools. These are not only character-building themselves, but also the securing of them may lead the pupils to take an interest in other books in the church library more distinctively religious in nature.

The director. No group in any church has any right to use good church money to purchase books and then put them under lock and key where nobody gets the potential benefits from them. It is one thing to get a workers' library, quite another to keep it working. All of which leads us to the thought of the church director of reading. In suggesting such an officer for the church or church school we are having in mind mainly the religious education needs of children and young people, although there are many adults who would appreciate kindly, sensible guidance. Especially is this true of parents who are concerned about the best reading for their children.

Qualifications. In this instance the "man" more often is a woman. Manifestly there are qualifications for this office, distinctive and highly desirable in view of the far-reaching significance of it. In no one person can we expect to find all of the things mentioned below.

Wise choosers, however, will look for as many of these traits as possible.

(1) What the director should be. Such officer should be one of genuine Christian character, whose personality radiates the spirit of Christ for, after all, the life back of the book suggestions means much. His judgment should be such as to command confidence when he suggests a book for reading. Most of all he should be one who is blessed with common sense and the ability to approach all ages tactfully and with an understanding of their likes and dislikes. A patronizing type of character is not the kind to guide people inspirationally in their reading.

(2) What he should know. He should be a person of broad culture, knowing not only the best of American and English classics, but also able to choose and recommend the best in the present-day books and magazines. Often a former public school teacher will best possess this trait. He should know the inestimable value of the printed page in the matter of character-building, believing with Browning in "the companionship of good books" and the danger of bad ones. He should know people, both as to the psychology of the age-group, the fancies of the individuals of the group, and their nature and needs as related to their reading, being able to suggest the books and other reading material best suited to any particular age and need and tell them where to find it whether in the church library, the public library or the book store. It is quite necessary that he be acquainted with the program of reading in the public schools and know how to accommodate the reading activities of the church library to the development of similar programs in the schools, especially the extra-curricular activities. He should also be familiar with the Boy Scouts, Camp Fire Girls and other organizations. He should have both the time and the disposition to keep in touch with the newer books and magazines and tie the pupils on to these.

(3) What he should accomplish. The director in this work should make it his business to keep informed as to the best of the current books and magazines. This will take time, to be sure, but its rewards are more than equal to the effort expended, for his influence may be next to that of the minister himself. He must make it his business to study to serve all ages and make this his main or sole church duty. He must be willing to begin most often as a pioneer in his field and must persistently work against odds. He must not allow himself to specialize on any one phase to the hurt of a well-rounded, comprehensive program of reading. He must be one of vision, seeing the end from

the beginning and counting no effort too dear to attain the end desired. He must have more than a self-starter. Rather he must have the spirit of the pioneer who keeps at it week by week. He must ride no hobbies and be no partisan propagandist. Rather he must see the main task of the church school and of reading and strive faithfully to fulfill his mission.

Assistants. Whenever the church or church school is a large one, the director of reading will have assistants. There may be three, viz.: one who specializes in children's reading, one who gives special attention to best books and periodicals for young people, and a third who keeps in mind the reading interests and needs of adults.

Duties. Such workers will find the following suggestive and helpful.

Have desirable books classified in a card index or loose-leaf notebook. Post on bulletin boards in convenient places lists of the best available books for the different ages, urging that such books be used.

Be continually on the lookout for new books, scanning current book reviews, stationers' shelves, periodic publications sent out on request by publishers, by reading regularly such publications as the *Bulletin of the American Library Association*, the *Publishers' Weekly*, the annual catalogue of one's own denominational publishing house, and so on, keeping in touch with the public library in search for new books and old, offering suggestions for improvement for the church reading program, studying constantly lists of books given in the handbooks of Boy Scouts, Camp Fire Girls, Pioneers and Comrades, getting from time to time personal reaction through visits to such organizations of the boys and girls.

Seek the viewpoint of the public school teachers and leaders of parent-teachers organizations concerning the needs of the children and the books best suited to the different ages.

Visit women's missionary groups, men's botherhood organizations and young people's societies, seeking to learn and fill the needs of their various activities. Offer to help parents in the selection of gift books. Offer to serve the needs of hospitals and other public institutions in this field. Assist in helping public librarians to put on their shelves books of religious value. Create and operate a helpful library of training books for officers and teachers in the church school. Make an effort to enlist as many of the church members as possible in the reading of the state and national religious publications, or certain articles therein.

Plan for the formation of small circulating libraries for the aged, invalids or other shut-ins, and a library especially suited to the needs of young married folks.

Make occasional short, pointed announcements concerning the church reading program in the regular church services and in monthly and annual gatherings of the denominational forces.

Keep in touch with the local news stands and know the books and magazines that are being purchased and read by the children and others; and where necessary to clear these news stands of undesirable literature, seek the coöperation of leaders of a similar work in other churches.

CONTACTING PEOPLE WITH RELIGIOUS LITERATURE

One of the biggest practical problems that faces all leaders in the field of religious education is not the making of more religious books and journals, but the bringing of these into vital, everyday, character-making relationship with Christian and non-Christian individuals and groups in every community. It is important in religious education to secure able, acceptable writers. It is necessary to put the thoughts of these writers on attractive printed pages, bound in beautiful book or magazine form. But all of this comes to nothing or nearly so unless the people are contacted, unless those press-products are put in the hands and heads of available readers.

Advertising and Promotion.—Practically all religious publishers, as others, employ some or all of the following ways of contacting the public with their books and other forms of literature: sales and promotion stores or repositories sometimes scattered throughout the nation and even with foreign distribution centers, field agents traveling part or full time making sales and winning patrons, advertising through the publishers' own channels or through the purchased space in magazines and periodicals of others, the issuance of descriptive leaflets or bulletins broadcast through regular or special mailing outlets, the usual catalog listing and statements, free copies of books or journals to be used for the book-review columns of certain magazines, likewise gratis copies put into the hands of leaders in the religious world who may in turn speak or write the favorable word, special displays or exhibits at conventions through posters, book flaps, and actual copies. We can here offer only a few hints, for advertising has become a real science, or should we say, art, recognized and professionally rated, with ample remuneration for industry and cleverness.

Religious Press Representative and the Local Church.—In every church, no matter how large or how small, there should be a wide-awake man or woman appointed by the church as its official contacter with denominational journals, missionary magazines, and other literature. The same person might very well also introduce general religious journals. His (her) chief responsibility, however, should be the securing of subscriptions to the regularly endorsed and much needed denominational weeklies and monthlies. Samples will be kept on hand to be seen in the church vestibule or other convenient places. In many churches a table is provided and the contacter is there at stated times not only with journals and subscription blanks but often with books especially of the devotional type. During a leadership training school or institute, a school of missions, or special evangelistic campaign, such a helper proves very valuable in setting forward that particular Christian enterprise by making readily accessible the best in books, pamphlets and journals. Publishers and supply houses generally are delighted to coöperate, furnishing samples of periodicals, price lists, and other needed information. Managers of denominational journals often make satisfactory financial arrangements where capable, energetic representatives are appointed. One such person is all any church needs. Let that person, carefully chosen, be the only religious press representative of the church. Quietly by word or bulletin board notice, such a servant will be welcomed and fully rewarded.

Leading Our People in the Use of Curriculum Material.— We have an immense volume of religious literature distributed to our people monthly and quarterly for use in the various organizations and programs of the church. Much of this material is largely wasted because it is used by the individuals in a very limited way or not at all. It is the duty and the privilege of every teacher, worker and leader to do his best to get our people to make proper use of this material. Every educational agency in the church is vitally interested in this matter. At many places throughout this book one will find helpful suggestions in the direction of getting the proper reading and study of our curriculum materials and programs.

Constant Emphasis on Good Literature.—Pastors, directors of religious education, officers, teachers, and leaders in all phases of the work of the church will find occasions constantly to emphasize good religious literature and the best possible use of it. The library staff will give special attention to the reading of good books. This is a reading age. People will be reading something, but what shall it be? John Ruskin used to say very earnestly to the young people in his day, in trying to get them to read good literature rather than trash: "Don't you know that if you read this you cannot read that?" Our time is limited. We should not waste it in reading worthless or harmful literature but use it well in reading and studying the best that has been thought and written by the great writers of the world.

CHAPTER XXIV

UNIFICATION AND PROMOTION

Unifying the Program

In a church which maintains all the organizations required for the promotion of a complete program of religious education there is overlapping of organization and duplication of effort with much lost motion. So much energy is used in maintaining the efficiency of the various organizations and meeting the requirements of the various standards that frequently the development of individual character is neglected. One wonders whether the people are in the church for the purpose of making standard organizations or the church is organized for the purpose of making better individual Christians.

Present System of Organization

Multiplicity and Overlapping.—There is much duplication in the *church*. Often there are friction and petty jealousies between conflicting organizations. Instead of loyalty to the church we often find loyalty to some organization superseding church loyalty. In the majority of churches we find at least three organizations competing with each other for the time, interest, activity and sometimes the money of the same group of church members. They are the Sunday school, the young people's society and the woman's missionary union. Many churches also promote a recreational organization for the boys and girls such as the Boy Scouts and Camp Fire Girls. The daily vacation Bible school is rapidly making a place for itself in the church's program. And in an increasing number of communities we find various schemes for enlisting the boys and girls of the public school in some form of week-day religious education.

In addition to these agencies which have a place in the regular program of the church there are other educational agencies with paid promotional secretaries whose aim is to give moral training to the youth of America *independent of the church*. The Young Men's Christian Association, the Young Women's Christian Association with their Christian citizenship training program, the Hi Y clubs and the Girl Reserves also make their bid for the time and energy of our young people. In rural communities the Four-H clubs are enlisting the activities of many young people. Fraternal bodies also promote organizations which train the sons and daughters of members of the lodges. These, together with various propaganda organizations such as Junior Woman's Christian Temperance Union, the Allied Youth Movement, Anti-cigarette League and societies for the promotion of world peace make inroads on the time and interest of the church's young people with the stated purpose of character development and moral training.

Functional Origin.—All of these organizations originated and have been promoted not as integral parts of the church's program, but by movements from without the church. Each has created its own program for its own purpose and has insisted on the coöperation of the churches when they have not demanded a place within the program of the churches. The particular educational function of each is necessary in the development of well-balanced Christian character, and since the churches were not giving proper emphasis to each function in their program it became necessary for some outside agency to promote a program which would accomplish the purpose.

When *Sunday schools* were first advocated only a century and a half ago for the purpose of teaching the children the Bible they were vigorously opposed by the churches and even denied the use of the buildings.

One hundred years later leaders of young people, realizing that the Sunday schools were not emphasizing the principle of expressional activity, organized *young people's societies* to provide for this function. The general *missionary* organizations, believing that the hope of the future lay in the missionary education of children and youth of the present generation, also constructed their program of missionary education. And so it goes. Whenever a new function of religious education has been determined a new organization has been erected.

Each of these organizations is doing great good and this writer would not for a moment advocate removing from the educational program of the church any of the functions for which each was originally organized. The denomination is indebted to those leaders who so faithfully have promoted them.

SOME DEFECTS IN THE SYSTEM

There are some defects in our present church program. If the aim of the church is to develop mere machines, people who rely upon organization and mechanical efficiency as the expression of Christian life and character, then our present system cannot be surpassed. For whether it intends to do so or not, it places the emphasis on organization. It must do this in order to promote all the organizations which it fosters. There must be provided a set of administrative officers for each and these must be trained for their duties according to the "manual" of each organization, so the church can report all its organizations A-1 to the various state headquarters.

Overlapping of Function.—Is not the true aim of religious education the development of Christian character in the individual? In order to reach this objective it is necessary that the program consist of the elements of instruction, worship, expression and social activity. At present each of our organizations—the Sunday school, the young people's society, the woman's missionary organization, and the men's brotherhood—includes all of these elements in its program in varying degrees.

Now we have the *daily vacation Bible school* and the *week-day church school* which would add other courses of study and other organizations. In these the emphasis is upon instruction, but the elements of worship and expression are also included. In each of these we find the elements of instruction, expression and worship all so crowded that none is given sufficient emphasis.

Duplication in Curriculum.—Each has a distinct course of study with no relation to the others, except that they are all in the field of religious education. There is much overlapping in subject matter. Two of them provide special mission lessons which are not related to either of the other two. Each has its own special study courses, and each its own social life.

It is practically a physical impossibility for our people to do all the study required for each, if they should be so inclined, but when they see so much overlapping in subject matter they either neglect all but one or else divide their study over so much material that they get only a smattering of it.

Overlapping of Administrative Duties.—As undesirable as is overlapping of subject matter the present program would not be so objectionable if it stopped with that. But each has a distinct plan of organization and administration. Each must have its own president and full quota of officers and committees who are responsible for the promotion of all the elements of religious education in their respective organizations.

This administrative work usually falls upon a few choice workers, remarkable for their patience and endurance, so that in the Sunday school class one person will be responsible for one form of activity, in the young people's society for another, and the same person doing still a third kind of work in the missionary organization. Instead of concentrating his best energy and thought upon one thing at a time and becoming efficient in that, it is scattered out over so many varied activities that he cannot become efficient in any one of them. This overlapping in organization is one of the most serious defects in our present system. It discourages many of our finest young people who really are anxious to serve in the best way they can.

Not Church-centered.—But probably the most serious defect is that the agencies are not centralized in the local church. They might be so organized theoretically but in reality they are not centered in the church. Instead of feeling responsible to the local church for its work each organization looks to the office of its state secretary for orders. The church is to blame in that it has been willing for the various state headquarters to direct its programs. As a result loyalty is divided. Instead of being loyal to the whole church the member usually manifests his loyalty to the particular organization in which he is most interested. Sometimes the state secretary of his organization speaks to him with more authority than does his own church. Happily, this is not always the case, but it might be avoided in a unified program centered in the local church.

Such conditions of overlapping as exist in the present plan of organization in our churches should cause us to seek a remedy. Most denominations are facing such problems. Some have worked out a plan of correlation, and experiments are being made by the merging of promotional agencies in general denominational life.[1] Also the interdenominational forces are beginning to unify their programs through the International Council of Religious Education with Dr. W. C. Bower as chairman of the Committee on Curriculum. The Southern Baptist Convention in its annual meeting in 1937 appointed a committee on Co-ordination and Correlation of church agencies and activities which has made some much needed studies and recommendations. Among the recommendations made to the Convention were the following: (1) "We recommend to pastors and churches, the formation of a church council, representing the several agencies of the church, to meet as often as may be found necessary, in order to formulate an integrated and comprehensive church program to devise a calendar of activities; to co-ordinate the work of all the church

[1] Plan was adopted first by General Convention of Christian Church, November, 1922.

agencies; and to discover and develop the needed workers and leaders." (2) That the Boards and Auxiliaries of the Convention work together, and with the local churches, to the ends of better coördination and correlation.

A Suggested Program

Plan of Organization.—There are three. They are a separate organization for each functional activity, correlation and integration. The first of these plans, *separate organization for each functional activity,* is the plan which is now used by most churches and is the cause of the present over-organization.

The plan of correlation, which a few churches are trying to work out is simply an effort at compromise between the different organizations in the church. A council is formed of representatives of the various organizations for the purpose of working out a program of education for the church which correlates all the activities. This theory sounds very plausible, but it has not remedied the situation in actual practice.

The third plan, *integration,* seems to be the best solution. It is being tried to some extent by the Northern Baptists, Disciples of Christ, Methodist Episcopal, Presbyterian and Congregational Churches on a denominational basis. Its distinguishing feature is the merging of the plans and programs of all the educational agencies at work in the denomination into one program with one organization for each age group. This necessitates the merging of the educational departments of all the boards of the denomination into a board of religious education, which prepares one integrated program of education for the churches, to be administered by one organization, the church school, or the department of religious education of the church. This program is not a combination of all the programs as they now exist, but is a new program into which all the elements and activities of the present conflicting organizations are built as integral parts.

Guiding Principles.—There are certain fundamental principles which should underlie and guide in the promotion of such a program for the church: (1) the program should be pupil-centered; (2) it should be church-centered; (3) it should be based on sound educational theory and practice; and (4) it should be integrated. It should include all of the elements necessary to the complete religious education of the individual. Worship, both public worship and private devotions; instruction, Biblical, social and missionary; expressional activity in the form of young people's societies, missionary service and evangelistic activities; together with social and recreational activities should be built into the program, not as separate elements but as integral parts of one unified educational program administered by one organization for each age group.

The Integrated Organization.—The plan of organization is to have one set of officers and committees to function in the administration of the whole religious educational program of the church for each department. Instead of selecting a separate set of officers and committees for each type of activity one set of officers should plan and lead in all the necessary activities of the department. One from each department above the elementary division should be elected by the group as president. He should preside or be responsible for leadership of every meeting of the group as a department, whether for worship, study, expressional activity or social life. His cabinet should consist of as many additional officers as are necessary for the promotion of every activity of the department. Local conditions should determine the size of the cabinet.

The average department would need officers responsible for at least the following activities: enlargement, social and recreational life, worship and devotion, missions and stewardship, evangelism and church relationship. Instead of standing committees it would be better to have one member of the cabinet to be responsible for each particular kind of activity required by the program of the department. These officers might be designated as vice-presidents or leaders. There should be an adult advisory superintendent for the department and adult teachers for the classes, which should meet on Sunday morning and also on a week-day for study. In the case of large departments there should also be adult advisers or supervisors for each special kind of activity. Whenever the church can afford it a departmental director should be employed at a salary to devote full time to the work of each department.

Meetings of the Department.—The department as such should have at least three meetings a week, a week-day session and two Sunday sessions. At the week-day meeting plans should be made for the Sunday sessions, a preview of the lesson should be given by the teacher and assignments made for the Sunday sessions. The pupils should be assisted in looking up assignments and instructed in matters of Biblical investigation. This week-day session might be held during public school hours at the regular time allowed for religious instruction. If this is not possible the week-day session should be held at the church on some afternoon or night. All business matters pertaining to the department should be disposed of and all plans for departmental activities should be made at this week-day session.

The Sunday morning session should be given to worship and Bible study. The entire department should engage in the worship service together. The Bible study should be by small groups. Each group should be led by an adult teacher. The Sunday evening session should be devoted to expressional activity. It should usually be a program given by the pupils similar to our present B. Y. P. U. program, but the topics for discussion should be related to the subject studied at the morning session and the speeches should be an expression of ideas received at the instructional meetings of the department and an application of the truths learned to the problems and needs of the pupils. The expressional activity for the older members might take the form of evangelistic services in jails, mission stations, churchless communities, or the organization of mission Sunday schools in needy places.

An Integrated Curriculum Needed.—The greatest difficulty in undertaking to carry out an integrated program of religious education is the lack of a unified curriculum. Curriculum has been defined by Dr. W. A. Harper as the "sum total of the educational influences that enter into the direction and formation of Christian character."[2] As indicated above we have three or more independent organizations each with a separate program consisting of worship, instruction, expression and social activities in varying degrees. Each has different topics for study, a different plan of daily devotions and Bible reading and each has a definitely outlined study course or reading course as well as a distinct plan of missionary instruction. Each also considers some form of expressional activity necessary.

What we need most of all is to build from the cradle roll up through the adult department an integrated curriculum graded to meet the needs of each department, but in the absence of such material, the workers in each department will be compelled to make their own curriculum if the church feels the need of such a program.

Correlaton of Home, Church and School

The home was the first institution of religious instruction, and the church school was established to supplement the training of the home rather than to supplant it. Their coöperation is necessary for the religious education of the child. The influence of the home is more

[2] Harper, W. A., *An Integrated Program of Religious Education*, p. 64 (The Macmillan Company, New York, 1926).

potent than that of the church school in habit formation and character building. Daily activities in the home offer the greatest opportunity for the expression of religious truths, and should be used as a laboratory for such, as well as for helping prepare Sunday lessons.

In order to secure coöperation between the *home and church each must understand the work of the other* and know what the other is doing for the child. There are three ways to accomplish this. One is for parents to visit the church school so as to know better how to coöperate with the teacher. Another is for the teacher to visit the home so as better to understand its life and teach in the light of it. And the other is for both to come together in parent-teacher meetings for mutual counsel and aid. Perhaps, also, the home or extension departments could do more at this task.

There is need, also, that the church school teacher as well as the parent shall understand what goes on in the public school and teach in the light of it. To that end both should keep in close touch with the public school teachers and curricula and understand the problems the pupil is facing. Also the church school curricula should be planned more with this situation in mind. If such things are done we shall be able to save in the future, better than in the past, from religious doubts and moral delinquency.

Our churches should also keep a closer touch with their youth as they go away to college, guiding them into the right institutions, keeping in touch with them while away, recognizing them when at home during holidays, using them during the vacation season and helping to keep a guiding hand on their spiritual nurture. This, also, will save from doubts and delinquencies, bind closer to the church and develop Christian character.

THE TASK OF PROMOTION

Thus far we have seen the place of religious education in the Bible, Christian history and modern life, some of the principles underlying it, and the agencies involved in carrying it on. It remains to give a general idea of the promotional phase, though the more extensive task of administration has been left largely to another volume.[3]

ITS IMPORTANCE

It is very evident that the program of religious education must have some sort of plan for its promotion. No matter how beautiful our ideal, how noble our purpose, or how splendid our program, we will fail without an adequate plan for promotion. For no plan, ideal, or program has ever fostered itself. There must be some person, organization or activity back of it to give it push and power. Tracks and coaches alone will not run a train.

This is true in every phase of life. In the political world a candidate for office does not get very far if he waits for the people to seek him out and get interested in him. Rather he must sell himself and his cause to the people. In the business world an invention or new commodity does not go far without publicity and backing. The large industrial concerns spend tremendous sums in setting forth the merits of their products and creating an appetite for them. The most effective psychology is utilized to this end.

What is true in these and other realms is especially true in the field of religion. Those who have the best doctrines or programs are not always the ones who have succeeded best with them. Rather it is the agency that has been most efficient in promotion. In fact one cannot judge the truthfulness of a cause by its seeming success, for sometimes the worst heresies are the best promoted, as for example Mormonism and Russellism. In reality it is just this which keeps the issue of intemperance forever to the fore, and also that of war. If the forces of righteousness were as aggressive in promotional activities as those of unrighteousness things would be very different.

In the realm of religious education there are two definite handicaps that have to be overcome which are not so evident in other realms of endeavor. One is the fact that church school activity is not compulsory. People are not required to attend as in the public schools. In other words we have no ready-made constituency for our work.

[3] *A Program of Religious Education*, Price, Carpenter and Tibbs, Fleming H. Revell Co., New York, 1937.

It is up to us to get them. Not only is there no law or custom requiring attendance but often there is not even compulsion or example in the home. In many situations it is left entirely to the child as to what he shall do. So promotion is necessary.

Along with this is the fact of the *natural inertia of life*. People do about what they have to do either from inner constraint or outward pressure. And it is naturally just a little easier to lie in bed on Sunday morning than to get out, and if one is away from home at school he is free from the constraint of home influence and custom. Furthermore there is the natural tendency of the human being toward evil—the disposition of the soil to grow weeds—which requires that influence and cultivation be exercised. In other words the natural conditions of life call for promotional activities in religious work.

These facts are further accentuated and the importance of this phase of the task is seen in the large *number unenlisted*. Some time back Dr. W. S. Athearn showed that there were 42,891,850 Protestant or nominal Protestant youth under twenty-five years of age in the United States; 14,361,900 of them were enrolled in Sunday school; leaving 28,529,950 or about two-thirds not enrolled at all.[4] A survey in Chicago showed only one-fifth of the public school children in Sunday school. A prominent religious denomination shows only two-thirds as many enrolled in Sunday school as are members of the churches, when a large number of those enrolled are not church members! In the light of these facts it would seem that promotion is both one of the most important and at the same time one of the most neglected tasks.

CHANNELS OF PROMOTION

There are three possible channels or means of promoting education in religion and morals which may be mentioned, and which are in one place or another and to some degree or other being used or have been used in the recent past.

Secular.—One of these is the state educational system. The time was when the Bible and other religious material were a part of the public school curriculum, and the teachers definitely fostered religion. But the separation of church and state and the multiplicity of denominations have gradually changed all of this. We would have it otherwise, for it makes the state the promoter of religion through controlling the teaching of it, and we do not accept that principle.

There has been in recent days, however, some tendency to go

[4] *World Survey*, Vol. I, p. 210 (Interchurch Press, New York, 1920).

back to an educational emphasis on religion through public education, due to the inadequate activity of the churches. In Oklahoma, Mississippi, and other places the reading of the Bible in the public schools is required by law. In the University of South Carolina, some teachers' colleges in Texas, and elsewhere, the Bible is an integral part of the curriculum. The University of Iowa has established a character-research station and gives graduate degrees to those who major in this field. And the American Association of Universities has urged that Bible study be included. But there are too many dangers in formalism and liberalism for most Christian people to back such plans very far. We believe that religious education must be promoted by religious organizations and not by those of a secular nature, if it is to have the freshness and vitality needed.

Interdenominational.—Much also has been done through non-denominational and interdenominational agencies. *Special movements* such as the Sunday school started that way, through the activities of Robert Raikes and others. The Christian Endeavor, which led to the various young people's societies, also got its start on that basis, through Dr. Francis E. Clark's leadership. The daily vacation Bible school movement has a similar beginning, under Dr. Robert G. Boville, as did the week-day church school in Gary, Indiana, and elsewhere. And organized Bible class work had its greatest impetus through Marshall A. Hudson and the Baraca and Philathea organizations. We must not forget this fact. In fact most forward movements have started outside of denominational channels and often with disinterest or opposition from denominational leaders. Even yet many of the ideals and new developments come that way. So out of fairness we must recognize the facts as they are, give credit where credit is due, and utilize the experiments and developments made by independent leaders.

Promotional organizations as well as individual movements have likewise had such beginnings in this country as well as in others. The American Bible Society has for more than a century furnished Bibles for Sunday school work and rendered a tremendous service. The American Sunday School Union for nearly as long has sent out Sunday school missionaries throughout the length and breadth of the nation establishing schools, building church libraries and doing other work. The International Sunday School Association and its successor, the International Council of Religious Education, have through their conventions, regularly employed staff, and publication done much to shape Sunday school life. The World Sunday School Convention has likewise done a great deal to promote new schools in the mission fields of the world, develop ideals and bring about a better world fellowship. These organizations along with the community movements fostered by Dr. W. S. Athearn and others, and the Christian Endeavor Society, International Daily Vacation Bible School Association previously mentioned, and others have done much to bring religious-educational development to the point where it is. And most of them are yet powerful factors in its promotion. While we may or may not join organically in these movements there is no good reason why we should not learn all that we can from them, incorporate their development into our work and profit by their achievements.

Denominational.—The fact still remains that the best promotional work is carried on through denominational channels. In fact practically all of the organizations which have started outside of denominational channels have finally been taken over by the denominations and found their most effective promotion after such had been true. This is no argument for a selfish, unchristian attitude between denominational groups. Happily we have come to the day when the feeling between denominations is much better than in earlier days, and on matters of common interest they are working together as never before.

But as long as *churches* are denominational the things that relate vitally to their lives will be such too. This accounts for much of the failure of Dr. Athearn's community organizations for religious education. It practically ignored the churches and sought to build on a foundation which did not exist.

There is a conviction which attaches to denominational life which gives it a warmth and a fervor not found elsewhere. In fact he who has definite convictions is always more aggressive in his activities then he who does not. And along with this the element of competition enters in, which is not without its value in religious as well as in business life.

Also the organization and integration in denominational life is in its favor in carrying on promotional work. They are in position to train and provide the leaders for it and to get access to the people to be taught. The denominations are equipped for this. They have their local churches with good church buildings and pastoral and educational leadership, schools and colleges, their publishing houses with a well developed literature and stores for its distribution, and their field forces for counties, state and larger units.

Then too, promotion calls for a considerable amount of *financial* *resources.* It cannot be done on charity. Money must be provided and this is not easy. The safest, sanest and surest way to secure the necessary funds for this work is through the denomination, as experience has shown. The people who give most are members of churches, have a conscience on the matter, and budgets and lines of support are already set up. Also the profits that are made on the books and literature used often go back to denominational headquarters and are available for promotional work.

REALMS OF ACTIVITY IN THE DENOMINATION

This work of promotion within the denomination falls in the main upon three agencies, namely, the Christian schools, the field force, and the local church leadership. In previous chapters these various realms of activity have been dealt with, and so it is not necessary to say much about them in this last chapter.

The School.—There are at least three directions in which the Christian school has functioned in promoting religious education: in providing a vocational leadership; in training lay workers for the local churches; and in evaluating and improving the quality of the work. There is no greater nor more important function of the Christian college than to lead and inspire in this vastly important work. We need vision, an aroused public conscience, and a trained leadership. How can we think of the function of the denominational school without including this for main emphasis and development?

The Field.—Perhaps the oldest phase of promotional activity is that which is carried on by the field workers. Much of the credit for what we have today must be given to these faithful men and women, who have left their homes behind and literally gone into the "highways and hedges" throughout the length and breadth of the land, instructing and inspiring the people and organizing the work. They have truly been pioneers and missionaries.

Every phase of the educational work of the church has been promoted by these field workers—the work of the Sunday school, the young people's society, the missionary societies, and so forth. Conferences have been held, training schools, enlargement campaigns, and every type of individual and group work has been emphasized. How poor and inadequate our programs of religious education would be without the inspiration and leadership of this great body of field workers!

The Church.—After all, the final phase of promotion rests with the local church. What the school man and field man do will largely come to nought unless backed by and carried on by the local church forces. The school man studies in a wider and deeper way and the field man covers a wider territory, but the local church workers are at the finger tips of responsibility for a longer period—three hundred and sixty-five days out of the year; consequently these workers have the opportunity of seeing and doing some things the other two groups cannot have, and have perhaps the most difficult phase of promotion. They are the ones who really know whether or not a thing will work, and especially the vocational leaders in the local church are usually in the vanguard in making improvements. Both the school and the field men will give major emphasis in their work to the training of an adequate leadership in the local church for the promotion of religious education. All of these types of workers will pull together to reach all the people and to provide vital Christian education for all of them.

An Adequate Dynamic

As we have looked at the whole field with all of the agencies and activities involved we have seen that it is a tremendous task. It is a worthy program but a hard one. It calls for infinite patience and effort. The question naturally arises, Why go to all of this trouble in time, money and labor? Who is equal to the task?

It is evident that a strong dynamic is necessary to carry us through. Several things are involved in it. For one thing one must *realize keenly the need.* Nothing will do much more to spur us on than a realization that civilization and the salvation of mankind are at stake. The let-down in personal morals, the crime wave, the dissolution of the home, the struggle between capital and labor, the menace of race relations and war will overwhelm us if something is not done. We must recognize that we face a real crisis in civilization. As President Wilson has said "Our civilization cannot survive materially unless it be redeemed spiritually." This realization is basal to the whole enterprise.

We must come to *believe fully that Christian education is the way out.* We have used force and it has failed. We have tried legislation and found it inadequate. We have turned to secular education and seen that it is insufficient. These do not furnish the dynamic necessary. Only religion can supply this, and it cannot be wielded most effectively through inspirational addresses, drives and crowd pressure, or in later life. We must begin with youth and carry on a continuous process of teaching and training. As Roger Babson has indicated, we do not need more battleships and material goods but more religious education. A realization of this fact is absolutely fundamental.

And we must *have a consciousness of being in league with God.* Nothing so stimulates an individual or people as the feeling of a divine mission. It stood out prominently in the ministry of Christ. It was outstanding in the activity of Luther. Every great leader and reformer has had this feeling. Both sides during the World War emphasized this fact. The drab routine of continuous effort in good weather and bad, during success and failure, day in and day out, calls for such a sense of divine compulsion. And indeed we have it, for the great command of the Master Teacher is "Go ye therefore and make disciples of all the nations, baptizing them into the name of the Father and of the Son and of the Holy Spirit; teaching them to observe all things whatsoever I have commanded you; and lo, I am with you always even unto the end of the world" (Matt. 28:19-20). In this consciousness we shall not fail.

A SELECTED BIBLIOGRAPHY FOR CLASS USE

Athearn, W. S., *Religious Education and American Democracy,* Pilgrim Press, Boston, 1917.

Beaven, Albert W., *Fireside Talks for the Family Circle,* The Judson Press, Philadelphia, 1928.

Bower, W. C., Editor, *The Church at Work in the Modern World,* The University of Chicago Press, Chicago, 1935.

Case, F. H., *Handbook of Church Advertising,* Abingdon Press, New York, 1921.

Cope, H. F., *Religious Education in the Family,* University of Chicago Press, Chicago, 1915.

Dobbins, G. S., *Baptist Churches in Action,* Baptist Sunday School Board, Nashville, Tenn., 1929.

Fiske, G. W., *The Changing Family,* Harper and Brothers, New York, 1928.

Flake, Arthur, *Building a Standard Sunday School,* Baptist Sunday School Board, Nashville, Tenn., 1922.

Germane and Germane, *Character Education,* Silver, Burdett and Company, New York, 1929.

Gulick, L. H., *A Philosophy of Play,* Charles Scribner's Sons, New York, 1920.

Harper, W. A., *An Integrated Program of Religious Education,* The Macmillan Company, New York, 1926.

Hart, Hornell, *Personality and the Family,* D. C. Heath and Company, Boston, 1935.

Hartshorne, Hugh, *Character in Human Relations,* Charles Scribner's Sons, New York, 1932.

Hayward and Hayward, *The Home and Christian Living,* Westminster Press, Philadelphia, 1931.

Heaton, K. L., *Character Building Through Recreation,* University of Chicago Press, Chicago, 1929.

Heaton, K. L., *The Character Emphasis in Education,* The University of Chicago Press, Chicago, 1933.

Hites, Laird T., *The Effective Christian College,* The Macmillan Company, New York, 1929.

Jackson and Malmberg, *Religious Education and the State,* Doubleday, Doran and Company, New York, 1928.

Kelly, Robert L., *The Effective College,* Association of American Colleges, New York, 1928.

Lavender, Leona, *The Church Library,* Baptist Sunday School Board, Nashville, Tenn.

Leach, W. H., *Church Publicity,* Cokesbury Press, Nashville, 1930.

Leavell, F. H., *Baptist Student Union,* Baptist Sunday School Board, Nashville, 1927.

Leavell, Martha Boone, *Building a Christian Home,* Baptist Sunday School Board, Nashville, Tenn., 1936.

Lotz and Crawford, *Studies in Religious Education,* Cokesbury Press, Nashville, 1931.

McKown, Harry C., *Character Education,* McGraw-Hill Book Company, New York, 1935.

Maston, T. B., *A Handbook for Church Recreation Leaders,* Baptist Sunday School Board, Nashville, Tenn., 1937.

Palmer, Archie M., *The Liberal Arts College Movement,* Association of American Colleges, New York, 1930.

Price, Carpenter and Tibbs, *A Program of Religious Education,* Fleming H. Revell Company, New York, 1937.

Squires, W. A., *A Parish Program of Religious Education,* Westminster Press, Philadelphia, 1923.

Threlkeld, A. L., Chairman, *Character Education,* The Department of Superintendence, N. E. A., Washington, 1932.

Wegner, A. B., *Church and Community Recreation,* The Macmillan Company, New York, 1924.

Weigle, Luther A., *The Training of Children in the Christian Family,* Pilgrim Press, Boston, 1922.